The Boy Scout Handbook
and Other Observations

Other Books by Paul Fussell

Theory of Prosody in Eighteenth-Century England

Poetic Meter and Poetic Form

The Rhetorical World of Augustan Humanism:
Ethics and Imagery from Swift to Burke

Samuel Johnson and the Life of Writing

The Great War and Modern Memory

Abroad: British Literary Traveling Between the Wars

Editor

English Augustan Poetry

The Ordeal of Alfred M. Hale

A Long Journey: The World of an English Officer
and Gentleman during World War I

Co-Editor

Eighteenth-Century English Literature

The Boy Scout Handbook
and Other Observations

PAUL FUSSELL

New York   Oxford
OXFORD UNIVERSITY PRESS
1982

Library of Congress Cataloging in Publication Data

Fussell, Paul.
The boy scout handbook and other observations.

Includes index.
I. Title.
AC8.F93   081   81–18730
ISBN 0–19–503102–4   AACR2

Grateful acknowledgment is made to the following for permission to quote material in copyright:

Jonathan Cape Ltd., for "Where Are the War Poets?" from *Collected Poems* by C. Day Lewis, copyright 1943, 1954 by C. Day Lewis.

Chatto & Windus Ltd., for excerpt from "The Fury of Aerial Bombardment," from *Collected Poems 1930–1976* by Richard Eberhart, copyright © 1960, 1976 by Richard Eberhart.

Gavin Ewart for "When a Beau Goes In," copyright 1948 by Gavin Ewart.

Harper & Row, Publishers, Inc., for "Where Are the War Poets?" from *Selected Poems* by C. Day Lewis, copyright 1943 by C. Day Lewis. Reprinted by permission of Harper & Row, Publishers, Inc.

Lincoln Kirstein, for excerpts from "Basic Training," "Rank," and "Hymn," copyright © 1966 by Lincoln Kirstein.

Oxford University Press, Inc., for excerpt from "The Fury of Aerial Bombardment," from *Collected Poems 1930–1976* by Richard Eberhart, copyright © 1960, 1976 by Richard Eberhart, reprinted by permission of Oxford University Press, Inc.; for excerpts from "The Songs I Had," "Time To Come," "To God," and "To His Love," from *Collected Poems of Ivor Gurney*, ed., P. J. Kavanaugh, copyright © 1982 by Oxford University Press, Inc. Reprinted by permission of Oxford University Press, Inc.

Random House, Inc., for excerpts from "In Memory of W. B. Yeats," from *The English Auden: Poems, Essays, and Dramatic Writings, 1927–1939*, ed., Edward Mendelson, copyright © 1977 by Random House, Inc.

Vogue Music, Inc., for excerpt from lyric of "Pistol-Packin' Mama" by Al Dexter, copyright 1943 by Vogue Music, Inc.

Printing (last digit): 9 8 7 6 5 4 3 2 1

Printed in the United States of America

To
Florence and Norman Lind

Preface

Please note that this is not *The Official Boy Scout Handbook*. It is a collection of my essays and reviews and bagatelles on appearances, institutions, and society, writers, travel, and war written over the past fifteen years or so, and written on very different occasions and for different purposes. If it's consistency of tone you want, you'd better get *The Official Boy Scout Handbook*. Consistency of view is another thing, and taken together these pieces will be found to project one large single view. Some of the reasons for it are disclosed in the final essay, "My War."

I am persuaded by the performance of George Orwell that literary, cultural, social, ethical, and political commentary can be virtually the same thing, and I am persuaded that the audience for each one is in the nature of things the audience for the others. I have rejected the notion that readers of literary criticism must be learned in mathematics, linguistics, computer science, and analytic philosophy: I have expected them to be interested only in human nature as revealed in human behavior. I have rejected likewise the notion that criticism demands the masquerade of solemnity. In the literary pieces I have tried to understand *literature* very broadly, assuming that regardless of its social status or intellectual pretensions a thing is literature if it's worth reading more than a couple of times for illumination or pleasure.

My debt to the Orwell of "Boys' Weeklies" is obvious. Perhaps less obvious is what I owe to the Herbert Read who says: "I stand by the English empirical school. I feel their spirit in my very bones and anything new will for me be a development of that great tradition."

I want to thank the editors of periodicals who have been kind enough to welcome some of these pieces originally: Peter Ackroyd,

Martin Amis, Staige D. Blackford, Digby Diehl, Joseph Epstein, Howard Goldberg, John Gross, Susan Heath, Michael E. Kinsley, Lewis H. Lapham, Melvin J. Lasky, Rima Drell Reck, Harvey Shapiro, Lewis P. Simpson, Donald Sinclair, Donald E. Stanford, Matthew Stevenson, and Mary-Kay Wilmers. I owe a special debt to the encouragement and resourcefulness of Jack Beatty of *The New Republic*, who with notable tact, delicacy, and patience winkled many of these pieces out of me. I'm grateful too to readers who have offered corrections and comments, especially Alfred Appel, Alfred Bush, Harold Leoy, and Arthur Shay. My friend C. F. Main has kindly read the proofs. The difference between the two cookie-tin lids was first noticed by my wife Betty, who has my thanks and love as always.

Princeton, New Jersey   P. F.
Summer, 1982

Contents

Illustrations

I
AMERICANA

The Boy Scout Handbook

It's amazing how many interesting books humanistic criticism manages not to notice. Staring fixedly at its handful of teachable masterpieces, it seems content not to recognize that a vigorous literary-moral life constantly takes place just below (sometimes above) its vision. What a pity Lionel Trilling or Kenneth Burke never paused to examine the intersection of rhetoric and social motive among, say, the Knights of Columbus or the Elks. That these are their fellow citizens is less important than that the desires and rituals of these groups are desires and rituals, and thus of permanent social and psychological consequence. The culture of the Boy Scouts deserves this sort of look-in, especially since the right sort of people don't know much about it.

The right sort consists, of course, of liberal intellectuals. They have often gazed uneasily at the Boy Scout movement. After all, a general, the scourge of the Boers, invented it; Kipling admired it; the Hitlerjugend (and the Soviet Pioneers) aped it. If its insistence that there is a God has not sufficed to alienate the enlightened, its khaki uniforms, lanyards, salutes, badges, and flag-worship have seemed to argue incipient militarism, if not outright fascism. The movement has often seemed its own worst enemy. Its appropriation of Norman Rockwell as its official Apelles has not endeared it to those of exquisite taste. Nor has its cause been promoted by events like the TV appearance a couple of years ago of the Chief Pardoner, Gerald Ford, rigged out in scout neckerchief, assuring us from the teleprompter that a Scout is Reverent. Then there are the leers and giggles triggered by the very word "scoutmaster," which in knowing circles is alone sufficient to promise comic pederastic narrative. "*All* scoutmasters are homosexuals," asserted George Orwell, who also insisted that "*All* tobacconists are Fascists."

But anyone who imagines that the scouting movement is either sinister or stupid or funny should spend a few hours with the latest edition of *The Official Boy Scout Handbook* (1979). Social, cultural, and literary historians could attend to it profitably as well, for after *The Red Cross First Aid Manual, The World Almanac,* and the Gideon Bible, it is probably the best-known book in this country. Since the first edition in 1910, twenty-nine million copies have been read in bed by flashlight. The first printing of this ninth edition is 600,000. We needn't take too seriously the ascription of authorship to William ("Green Bar Bill") Hillcourt, depicted on the title page as an elderly gentleman bare-kneed in scout uniform and identified as Author, Naturalist, and World Scouter. He is clearly the Ann Page or Reddy Kilowatt of the movement, and although he's doubtless contributed to this handbook (by the same author is *Baden-Powell: The Two Lives of a Hero* [1965]), it bears all the marks of composition by committee, or "task force," as it's called here. But for all that, it's admirably written. And although a complex sentence is as rare as a reference to girls, the rhetoric of this new edition has made no compromise with what we are told is the new illiteracy of the young. The book assumes an audience prepared by a very good high-school education, undaunted by terms like *biosphere, ideology,* and *ecosystem.*

The pliability and adaptability of the scout movement explains its remarkable longevity, its capacity to flourish in a world dramatically different from its founder's. Like the Roman Catholic Church, the scout movement knows the difference between cosmetic and real change, and it happily embraces the one to avoid any truck with the other. Witness the new American flag patch, now worn at the top of the right sleeve. It betokens no access of jingoism or threat to a civilized internationalism. It simply conduces to dignity by imitating a similar affectation of police and fire departments in anarchic towns like New York City. The message of the flag patch is not "I am a fascist, straining to become old enough to purchase and wield guns." It is, rather, "I can be put to quasi-official use, and like a fireman or policeman I am trained in first aid and ready to help."

There are other innovations, none of them essential. The breeches of thirty years ago have yielded to trousers, although shorts are still in. The wide-brimmed army field hat of the First World War is a fixture still occasionally seen, but it is now augmented by headwear deriving from succeeding mass patriotic exercises: overseas caps and berets from World War II, and visor caps of the sort worn by General Westmoreland and sunbelt retirees. The scout handclasp has been changed, perhaps because it was discovered in the context of the new internationalism that the former one, in which the little finger was separated from the other three on the right hand, transmitted inappropriate suggestions in the Third World. The handclasp is now the normal civilian one, but given with the left hand. There's now much less emphasis on knots than formerly; as if to signal this change, the neckerchief is no longer religiously knotted at the tips. What used to be known as artificial respiration ("Out goes the bad air, in comes the good") has given way to "rescue breathing." The young are now being familiarized with the metric system. Some bright empiric has discovered that a paste made of meat tenderizer is the best remedy for painful insect stings. Constipation is not the bugbear it was a generation ago. And throughout there is a striking new lyricism. "Feel the wind blowing through your hair," the scout is adjured, just as he is exhorted to perceive that Being Prepared for life means learning "to live happy" and—equally important—"to die happy." There's more emphasis now on fun and less on duty; or rather, duty is validated because, properly viewed, it is a pleasure. (If that sounds like advice useful to grown-ups as well as to sprouts, you're beginning to get the point.)

There are only two possible causes of complaint. The term "free world" surfaces too often, although the phrase is mercifully uncapitalized. And the Deism is a bit insistent. The United States is defined as a country "whose people believe in a supreme being." The words "In God We Trust" on the coinage and currency are taken almost as a constitutional injunction. The camper is told to carry along the "Bible, Testament, or prayer book of your faith," even though, for light backpacking, he is advised to leave behind air mattress, knife and fork, and pancake turner. When the scout finds himself lost in the woods, he is to "stay put and have faith that someone will find you." In aid of this end, "Prayer will help." But the religiosity is so broad that it's harmless. The words "your church" are followed always by the phrase "or synagogue." The writers have done as well as they can considering that they're saddled with the immutable twelve points of Baden-Powell's Scout

Law, stating unambiguously that "A Scout is Reverent" and "faithful to his religious duties." But if "You have the right to worship God in your own way," you must see to it that "others retain their right to worship God in their way." Likewise, if "you have the right to speak your mind without fear of prison or punishment," you must "ensure that right for others, even when you do not agree with them." If the book adheres to any politics, they can hardly be described as conservative; they are better described as slightly archaic liberal. It is broadly hinted that industrial corporations are prime threats to clean air and conservation. In every illustration depicting more than three boys, one is black. The section introducing the reader to some Great Americans pays respects not only to Franklin and Edison and John D. Rockefeller and Einstein; it also makes much of Walter Reuther and Samuel Gompers, as well as Harriet Tubman, Martin Luther King, and Whitney Young. There is a post-Watergate awareness that public officials must be watched closely. One's civic duties include the obligation to "keep up on what is going on around you" in order to "get involved" and "help change things that are not good."

Few books these days could be called compendia of good sense. This is one such, and its good sense is not merely about swimming safely and putting campfires "cold out." The good sense is psychological and ethical as well. Indeed, this handbook is among the the very few remaining popular repositories of something like classical ethics, deriving from Aristotle and Cicero. Except for the handbook's adhesions to the motif of scenic beauty, it reads as if the Romantic movement had never taken place. The constant moral theme is the inestimable benefits of looking objectively outward and losing consciousness of self in the work to be done. To its young audience vulnerable to invitations to "trips" and trances and anxious self-absorption, the book calmly says: "Forget yourself." What a shame the psychobabblers of Marin County will never read it.

There is other invaluable advice, applicable to adults as well as to scouts. Some is practical, like "Never use flammable fluids to start a charcoal fire. They burn off fast, lighting only a little of the charcoal." Some is civic-moral: "Take a 2-hour walk where you live. Make a list of things that please you, another of things that should be improved." And then the kicker: "Set out to improve them." Some advice is even intellectual, and pleasantly un-compromising: "Reading trash all the time makes it impossible for anyone to be anything but a second-rate person." But the best advice is ethical: "Learn to think." "Gather knowledge." "Have initiative." "Respect the rights of others." Actually, there's hardly a better gauge for measuring the gross official misbehavior of the seventies than the ethics enshrined in this handbook. From its explicit ethics you can infer such propositions as "A scout does not tap his acquaintances' telephones," or "A scout does not bomb and invade a neutral country, and then lie about it," or "A scout does not prosecute war unless, as the Constitution provides, it has been declared by the Congress." Not to mention that because a scout is clean in thought, word, and deed, he does not, like Richard Nixon, designate his fellow citizens "shits" and then both record his filth and lie about the recordings ("A scout tells the truth").

Responding to Orwell's satiric analysis of "Boys' Weeklies" forty years ago, the boys' author Frank Richards, stigmatized by Orwell as a manufacturer of excessively optimistic and falsely wholesome stories, observed that "The writer for young people should . . . endeavor to give his young readers a sense of stability and solid security, because it is good for them, and makes for happiness and peace of mind." Even if it is true, as Orwell objects, that the hap-piness of youth is a cruel delusion, then, says Richards, "Let youth be happy, or as happy as possible. Happiness is the best prepara-tion for misery, if misery must come. At least the poor kid will have had something." In the current world of Making It and Getting Away with It, there are not many books devoted to asso-ciating happiness with virtue. The shelves of the CIA and the State Department must be bare of them. "Horror swells around us like an oil spill," Terrence Des Pres said recently. "Not a day passes without more savagery and harm." He was commenting on Philip Hallie's *Lest Innocent Blood Be Shed,* an account of a whole French village's trustworthiness, loyalty, helpfulness, friend-liness, courtesy, kindness, cheerfulness, and bravery in hiding scores of Jews during the Occupation. Des Pres concludes: "*Goodness.* When was the last time anyone used that word in earnest, without irony, as anything more than a doubtful cliché?" *The Official Boy Scout Handbook,* for all its focus on Axmanship, Backpacking, Cooking, First Aid, Flowers, Hiking, Map and Compass, Semaphore, Trees, and Weather, is another book about goodness. No home, and certainly no government office, should be without a copy. The generously low price of $3.50 is enticing, and so is the place on the back cover where you're invited to inscribe your name.

The Persistent Itchings
of Poe and Whitman

My words itch at your ears till you understand them.
Song of Myself

"Poetry ought to be as well written as prose." Pound's dictum applies to editions too, which we can say ought to exhibit as much tact, art, and intelligence as we demand of original books. Whether an editor knows it or not, an edition is necessarily an act of criticism. The providing or withholding of explanatory comment, the kinds and quality of recommendation implicit in introductions and headnotes—these are rhetorical actions as subtle and risky as any acts of thought or art. It is a sad thing that editorial tasks are so often undertaken by the rhetorically inept.

These melancholy reflections are prompted by two big books standing before me, two editions of classic American poets: *The Poems of Edgar Allan Poe*, edited by Floyd Stovall, and *Whitman's Leaves of Grass: Comprehensive Reader's Edition,* edited by Harold W. Blodgett and Sculley Bradley. In one sense, both these items are beautifully edited: they print, and they print legibly and even prettily, accurate texts of the poets—the Poe edition even gives us the poems in two colors; and their apparatus offers the reader what he needs to trace the bibliographical history of the texts. But critically and rhetorically both volumes are notably inadequate, registering the chasm between accomplished American literary "scholarship" and subtle American cultural and social understanding. Although none of these editors hesitates to utter critical judgments, nowhere do they perform criticism half sophisticated enough to come to grips with these two most persistent Americans or to recommend them persuasively to a new, ungenteel generation scornful of pretension, vagueness, good intentions, and euphemism, readers who will come to Poe and Whitman in the same spirit in which they encounter Camus and Pynchon and Sontag. Failing to sense who their readers are and what sorts of illumination they will demand, not to mention the way, at every point, they will be reacting, the performance of these editors suggests that the ghost of Professor Stuart Pratt Sherman (1881–1926) still presides over the academic presentation of American writing. No wonder the intelligent young more and more eschew literary history for physics.

Some years ago the late W. K. Wimsatt sent abroad his indispensable essay "The Intentional Fallacy," whose sharp distinctions and careful admonitions should have worked wonders in directing contemporary editorial criticism away from vagueness and sentimentality. But his warnings have fallen upon Floyd Stovall's deaf ear, and throughout Stovall's introduction to Poe's poems intention is confused with accomplishment, good will with achievement, poetic theory with poetic realization. A poem will be taken to be artistically valuable because it illustrates a theory of Poe's, and, as we are told, "Poe's poems can be said to lack substance only if the theory which they exemplify is wrong." Thus a clearly bad poem is to be redeemed because the (presumed) intentions of the poet are interesting. We get observations like the following, a classical example of critical irrelevance and of confusion between the demonstrable and the unknowable: "The poet's sole purpose in these unreal scenes was to produce an effect corresponding to the mood in which he conceived them." *What?* But that is Stovall criticism at its best. At its worst, it sounds like this: "Of these [poems addressed to women], the sonnet ["To My Mother"] is the best, as it is the most sincere." To entangle oneself in propositions like that is not merely to ignore the wisdom of Wimsatt: it is to behave as if nothing had been done during the past half-century to discipline the premises and terms of literary discourse.

Blodgett and Bradley's "Comprehensive Reader's Edition" of *Leaves of Grass,* one of the many volumes of *The Collected Writings of Walt Whitman* issued by the New York University Press, is a much more satisfying artifact than Stovall's. Like his book, this one is heavy, expensive, and elegantly produced. It presupposes a "general reader" of Whitman—the variorum edition will be addressed to scholars—who is at once devoted, literary, and rich. That such a reader today seems largely a fictive thing does nothing to spoil the physical handsomeness of this edition, although we assume that Whitman's great audience of poor students will continue to brood over him in cheap editions.

Blodgett and Bradley indicate their editorial design with some wit. Whitman, they point out, "firmly insisted on his [1891–1892] title leaf that all future printings should be a copy and facsimile of this text. The present editors have honored his injunction, reprinting the 1891–1892 text precisely as he left it, with its occasional typographical errors corrected in the footnotes. Then they have proceeded, as the work of a major poet deserves, to collect and edit what he left out from previous editions." The strength of Blodgett and Bradley's edition lies largely in their resuscitation of poems and passages excluded from *Leaves of Grass* and their accumulation of uncollected poems. It is delightful to have in print again, for example, these lines dating from Whitman's fertile, impudent 1850's:

Priests! . . .
Until your creeds can do as much as apples and hen's eggs, let
    down your eyebrows a little. . . .

And it is useful to have readily available the numerous homo- and autoerotic passages excluded, finally, from *Leaves of Grass*. Their presence here may encourage the continuing reinterpretation of Whitman as a poet whose intense and once-dangerous lyric center wraps itself up in an all-but-obligatory cover of "epic" ambitions. The editors' provision of "An Album of Whitman Portraits"— eleven likenesses, running from the 1850's to 1891—is also a happy idea: no oversimplified conception of Whitman as a consistent and coherent artist could survive this pictorial evidence of his artful moment-to-moment shape-changing, from dandy to woodsman to "author" to queen to sage and blind prophet. And we must be grateful too for the appearance here of first editions of the prose connected with the poems, prose on which the editors justly set a high value.

Blodgett and Bradley have performed their bibliographical duties superbly, and in their introduction we are guided through the wilderness of Whitman's successive revisions and rearrangements with grace and skill. In their bibliographical part, likewise, the footnotes are impeccable. But alas—in their explanatory and critical function, the notes return us to the naïve psychological and critical world of Stovall. They are intellectually so primitive that it is hard to see how they can do anything but retard the understanding of Whitman, and indeed the understanding of literature.

Sometimes the editors let pass obscurities without noting them at all, and the suspicious reader may feel that they have done so because they don't know what to say. Thus the general reader gets no help in clarifying the syntax of the first line here:

> I do not snivel that snivel the world over,
> That mouths are vacuums and the ground but wallow and filth.

In the note on "A Font of Type" the reader is informed that nonpareil and long primer are type-sizes, but unless he's also told about the type-case, he will puzzle over "the pallid slivers" between which the types are "slumbering." To this line of *Song of Myself,*

> I know I shall not pass like a child's carlacue cut with a burnt
> 　　stick at night,

the editors affix this note: "Carlacue] A variant of 'curlique,' something fancifully curled, as a flourish in writing." The reader is not assisted by this sort of obviousness to perceive Whitman's image, when a mention of contemporary children whirling sparklers outdoors in the darkness would clarify things immediately. One suspects here and elsewhere that the editors simply don't get it. But if sometimes the reader is assumed to be able to figure out images like this on his own, at other times the editors take him to be positively cretinous. Thus of this line in *Song of Myself,*

> I project my hat, sit shame-faced, and beg,

the editors say: "I project my hat] The beggar then commonly extended his hat to receive alms." The implications of *then* are too rich for comment, and even satire must retire abashed: can the editors be that innocent of real life, not just in Turkey, India, Spain, and southern Italy, but in New York?

But if the notes are feeble as explanation, as criticism they are disastrous. Sometimes they tell the reader directly what to think about the poems, and tell him in the most retrograde and jejune ways: "This distinguished little poem ["Beginners"] . . . shows WW's power to withhold and challenge." Sometimes they are comical in their vulgarity and irrelevance: "These lines are echoed by Thomas Wolfe in his story 'The Four Lost Men.' " And some-time they are too silly for words: "["To Think of Time"] poses the question of death, which absorbed such nineteenth century poets as Poe, Tennyson, Bryant, Wordsworth, and Dickinson." The authority of Havelock Ellis is invoked to recommend Section 11 ("Twenty-eight young men bathe by the shore") of *Song of Myself;* and Swinburne rather than Richard Chase is quoted to illuminate "When Lilacs Last in the Dooryard Bloom'd." Except for his influence on such as Thomas Wolfe, the notes present Whitman as writing largely in a vacuum, as little determined by the literary past as fecund for the literary future. To comment on "Prayer of Columbus" without mentioning Tennyson's "Ulysses," on the one hand, or Eliot's "Gerontion," on the other—while carefully citing Washington Irving—is a real achievement in literary innocence and provincialism. The reader of these lines from *Song of Myself,*

> Of the turbid pool that lies in the autumn forest,
> Of the moon that descends the steeps of the soughing twilight,
> Toss, sparkles of day and dusk—toss on the black stems that
>   decay in the muck,
> Toss to the moaning gibberish of the dry limbs,

who suspects that in those brilliant images and rhythms he may perceive a prolegomenon to Eliot receives no encouragement from these editors. The reader of this line,

> I heard you solemn-sweet pipes of the organ as last Sunday
>   morn I pass'd the church,

who hears—not least in the unexpected, ironic *pass'd*—a tonality made fully accessible by William Carlos Williams in "The Cath-olic Bells" is given no note to gratify and educate him. The reader who suspects that the lines

> The second First-day morning they were brought out in
>   squads and massacred, it was beautiful early summer,
> The work commenced about five o'clock and was over by
>   eight

may be feeding something useful to the interchapters of Hemingway's *In Our Time* is left quite darkling.

But sensitivity to idiom (as in *work commenced,* above) is not
what we can expect from editors who say of Lincoln's final return
to Springfield that "interment took place." Our loss of confidence
in the face of such language is like our sinking feeling when Stovall
tells us that "If [Poe] had been content to be merely a popular
writer, catering to the literary taste of the time, he could probably
have earned far greater pecuniary rewards than he did earn in the
course he followed." Euphemisms and awkward genteelisms like
this conspicuously mar Blodgett and Bradley's notes on Whitman's
Calamus poems. It would be hard indeed for a reader of their
edition to gather that Whitman was a homosexual whose program
for national reform, including his projection of a new "democratic"
poetry, was an infinitely careful and delicate extension of his most
passionate internal longings for affection.

All in all, the emphasis in the commentary is on the tiresome
old gas-bag of the all-too-familiar cosmic and "mystical" pretensions, the Whitman delineated in Gay Wilson Allen's *Walt Whitman Handbook,* fleshed out in James E. Miller's *Critical Guide to
Leaves of Grass,* and embraced by those who insist that poetry be
at once vague, portentous, solemn, and puritan. It is the Whitman
who has been successfully boring high-school students and their
hapless teachers for fifty years. Blodgett and Bradley never unwind
the mummy wrappings, ignoring the contemporary critical inquiry
which has uncovered a more risky, witty, ironic, literary, and
hence more interesting Whitman. Their scrupulous inattention to
the most penetrating criticism is as odd as it is sad, for they know
a vast amount about Whitman and Whitman commentary of the
duller sort, and in their technical work they are able editors.
The news about Whitman—that he is not a bore, that he is not the
kind of respectable national monument they are willing to take
him for—just never seems to have reached them. Whatever the
cause of their backwardness, it is deplorable that they have chosen
to present, in such definitive, permanent, and costly wrappings, the

same old dull, garrulous, witless Whitman of Mrs. Gilchrist and Swinburne. If Whitman is really the kind of poet their critical view implies, God help the Republic.

But no matter how they are dealt with by academic editors, Poe and Whitman have staying power, serving as fixed poles of two kinds of American imaginative behavior. The classical distinction between the opposite directions pursued by Poe and Whitman ("Most of our later poets could be described as descendants of Whitman or as descendants of Poe"—F. O. Matthiessen) was made first by Whitman himself, speaking out of his "inner" identity as a lyric empiricist. "Poe's verses," Whitman wrote in *The Critic* in 1882, "illustrate an intense faculty for technical and abstract beauty, with the rhyming art to excess, an incorrigible propensity toward nocturnal themes, a demonaic undertone behind every page." Poe's poems, he concluded, "probably belong among the electric lights of imaginative literature, brilliant and dazzling, but with no heat." And Poe's urge toward the outré and eccentric, his "abnegation of the perennial and democratic concretes at first hand," left Whitman genuinely puzzled and also perhaps a bit fearful that it was his own kind of poem that, for all its insistent grounding in universal fact and observable data, was destined in the long run to occupy the mere border of literature: "The lush and the weird that have taken such extraordinary possession of Nineteenth century verse-lovers—what mean they?"

Whitman's perception of 1882 was as acute as usual. We do have "a Poe tradition" in American poetry, and we do have "a Whitman tradition," although ultimately the two define themselves more as styles now, as learned habits of idiom, than as initial ways of perception. These two stylistic conventions have persisted more or less in opposition for over a century. The antithetic idioms of Poe and Whitman do still itch at the American ear, and each continues to produce a very different feel and to generate in poets responding to each a very different sort of poetry.

The Poe tradition is our Alexandrian one: it constitutes a flight from the colloquial toward décor; toward ostentatious rhyme (Poe's *valley-musically* is definitive: compare Wallace Stevens's *tambourines-Byzantines,* or Theodore Roethke's *dizzy-easy*); and toward closed form and tight prosody. The drift is in the direction of a self-sufficient artistic abstraction in which pattern itself becomes meaning. Poe's spookiness, his compulsive melancholy and terror, are less central than the urge toward the hypnotisms and distancings of music and pattern and refrain: both Poe and Whitman grew up on Edward Young's eighteenth-century *Night Thoughts,* and Whitman wants to make your flesh creep almost as often as Poe: "What is removed drops horribly in a pail."

The Whitman tradition, on the contrary, is our demotic one, instinct always with a sense of local detail, embracing the givens and the undeniable particulars, ugly or insignificant as they may be. Nothing is more characteristic of Poe than the ease with which, in his fictions, he escapes Baltimore to occupy imaginatively and plausibly such scenes as Eton, Oxford, or the back streets of Paris; and nothing is more pathetic than Whitman's occasional ill-advised attempts ("*Allons,*" "I am a habitan of Vienna") to do something similar. Whitman and his successors return always to the roots of the local and colloquial (it is impossible to imagine Poe, the dandy of American style, even thinking Whitman's "I reckon"). The tendency in the Whitman tradition is an ever more insistent empiricism. The pressure of sense data is too overwhelming to be evaded, and open forms and loose prosody are conceived to be the fittest vehicles for registering the infinitely plural realities of the unimpeachably local.

If Stevens can be regarded as the most conspicuous major modern legatee of Poe, then William Carlos Williams is the most visible modern descendant of Whitman. Stevens's triumphant roosters, cockatoos, and toucans derive from the same exotic aviary as Poe's ravens, condors, and parakeets; while Williams's pathetic, defeated weeds and wild-carrot leaves struggle up from the same daily earth as Whitman's mullein and pokeweed.

These imply the two poles between which an American poet sensitive to the pressure of the literary past will locate his style, although sometimes he will seem to enact in his career a movement from the one to the other. This is what Robert Lowell did. *Lord Weary's Castle,* with its graveyard gestures and incantatory tone, on stilts all the way, takes up where Poe leaves off; but by the time of *Life Studies,* which risks an open prosody and a more colloquial idiom, we are directed, if not to, at least toward Whitman.

The excesses of adornment, of color and music, which we meet in Poe and his successors are the sort which issue almost syllogistically from such a conception of poetry as set forth in Poe's "The Rationale of Verse": "Verse . . . cannot be better designated than as inferior or less capable music." Thus "The Raven" and "Annabel Lee." Thus textual "improvements" like one recorded by Stovall: in the first edition of "The City in the Sea" we hear of the "Babylon-like walls"

> Whose entablatures intertwine
> The mask—the viol—and the vine.

But for Poe music must take precedence over even symbolism and semantic meaning, and he revises the passage until it stands as the very locus classicus of sweetness overtaking sense:

> Whose wreathèd friezes intertwine
> The viol, the violet, and the vine.

If Poe's ultimate poetic analogue is musical harmony, Whitman's analogues are the sea-surge and the organic dynamics of "savage and luxuriant man" himself. Art and nature: the two conceptions seem irreconcilable.

Another important difference between Poe's instincts and Whitman's is found in their conception of poetic dynamics. Both Poe's theory and practice insist that the poem must project one intense mood only: the poem is not to shift and double back on itself once the mood has got fairly established. And indeed, one thing the matter with Poe is that the "one intense mood" proves to be the same old one, over and over: thus the ease with which we can interchange his titles without really altering his poems—"Romance" is "Dream-Land" is "Fairy-Land" is "Dreams." A poet who really believes that, as Poe says in "The Philosophy of Composition," "Melancholy is . . . the most legitimate of all the poetical tones" is destined to find himself in the hell of writing the same humorless, unironic poem repeatedly. A poet who really believes that, as Poe says in the same place, "The death . . . of a beautiful woman is unquestionably the most poetical topic in the world" is destined to a career in verbal theater but not to a successful life of poetry. Whitman, on the other hand, never displays more power than when, as in *Song of Myself,* he shifts abruptly and bravely from one mood to its sharp antithesis, from the comic to the mock-solemn to the farcical to the serious, and yet manages to sustain the atmosphere of unity by the energy, curiosity, and oddity of his performance in all these tones. Poe is notorious as the enemy of "the long poem," which necessarily, intensity being attainable for only brief periods, includes a variety of tones and moods. Whitman, although he wrote only one successful long poem, reveals by his obsession with the "unity" of *Leaves of Grass* that he conceives poetry is to be recovered in an iron time partly by its recovery of amplitude.

Yet for all their differences, differences whch define opposite fields of force for two kinds of subsequent American writing, Poe and Whitman exhibit some curious similarities which would prevent either being confused with a British poet of his time. One sign of their kinship is their common possession of that kinky mid-nineteenth-century diction derived by literary autodidacts from pseudo-science and pseudo-philosophy for the purpose of astonishing an illiterate but self-satisfied audience, the audience once of Chatauqua, now, perhaps, of Broadway. Each poet has his weakness for "Eidolons" and "Ideality," his delight in wingèd words from phrenology and show business. There's a bit of P. T. Barnum in both.

In both too we find a dissolution of syntax—is there not something "American" about it?—betokening some disaffection with older, more logical, more respectably grammatical methods of organizing poetic materials. In Poe, exotic diction and ostentatious overriding meter tend to displace syntax; in Whitman, the unlimited accumulation of empirical images becomes its substitute. The grammatical ambiguities and suspensions of Hart Crane, on the one hand, and of Williams, on the other, are modern reflections of these two mid-nineteenth-century American ways of avoiding the commitments of unambiguous predication. The phrase replaces the clause, and syntactical incompletion stands as an enactment of a metaphysical principle. The Republic's not finished yet, and no one knows what it's going to be.

But the most striking thing Poe and Whitman possess in common is their loneliness, their sense of separateness and exclusion. "The Raven" and the *Sea Drift* poems (not to mention *Calamus*) register alike a common unhappy solitude. One of Poe's favorite images is that of inaccessible women, the counterparts of Whitman's inaccessible boys. Poe's dead girls, like Lenore or Ulalume, are more closely related than we might think to the dead boys of Whitman's *Drum Taps*. W. C. Williams has written: "Had he lived in a world where love throve, his poems might have grown differently. But living where he did, surrounded as he was by that world of unreality, a formless 'population'—drifting and feeding —a huge terror possessed him." He is speaking of Poe, of the Poe whose head swings from the swollen strap in the nightmare sub- way of Crane's *The Bridge*. But if we change Williams's *terror* to *loneliness,* the observation applies with equal force to Whitman. The same "formless 'population'—drifting and feeding" is the cause of Whitman's eloquent despair in *Democratic Vistas*. Poe's escapist gothicism, his adolescent obsession with destruction and disaster, is his response to the grindings and boredom of his philis- tine newspaper environment. Whitman's response to the national dullness is to rationalize his forbidden affections into exciting versions of democratic pastoral. Gavin Ewart's impertinent desig- nation of Whitman as "the faggot who burst into flame" brings us closer to his achievement than anything the well-mannered Blodgett and Bradley have to tell us. For both Poe and Whitman, America is too big, too terrible, too threatening for acceptance except through bold defensive transformations. It is in the simi- lar transformations of Stevens and Williams that we perceive the persistence of Poe and Whitman, whose words will itch at the American ear just as long as there are poets and readers who can hear them.

Sincerity Abroad

The scene at the Hoboken pier on December 4, 1915, was "so grotesque," the *New York Sun* reported, "as to be almost beyond belief." Henry Ford was sailing to Europe on the Danish vessel *Oscar II* to persuade the Allies and the Central Powers to stop fighting the First World War, and in his party were 163 hurriedly assembled pacifists, divines, "lecturers," cranks, "educators," woman's suffragists, Single-Taxers, Sunday-school zealots, prohibitionists, ribald journalists, and student observers. "A group of very eccentric people," commented Jane Addams, who had been invited but decided not to go.

My father, a twenty-year-old debater and "student leader" at the University of California, was invited and decided to go, both because the proceedings might do some good and—an important motive for all participants—the trip was unexpected and thoroughly paid for and looked like an adventure. My father wrote: "I think . . . that there is not one chance in a thousand that the plan will succeed, but it can certainly do no harm, and if, as Ford says, our efforts should result in one hour's less fighting, our work would have been worth while." "At any rate," he adds, "we are having a wonderful trip."

Amidst the bedlam at the dock bands played "I Didn't Raise My Boy To Be a Soldier." Former Secretary of State William Jennings Bryan, the naturalist John Burroughs, and Thomas A. Edison went on board to bless the enterprise and then dashed off again to dissociate themselves from it. So many nuts seemed to be gathered together that someone dispatched a cage of squirrels to the pier.

Ford perceived that "war is murder." The Battle of Loos had recently proved him right, and by the end of 1915 over two million sons, husbands, and fathers had been killed or mutilated. He had come afire with enthusiasm about getting the boys of all countries out of the trenches by Christmas. Undaunted by ridicule, he stood on the bridge of the *Oscar II* and threw roses to the crowd on the pier, many of whom were laughing rudely and shouting contemptuous witticisms. As the ship left the harbor to mingled cheers and satiric howls, one enthusiast for peace threw himself off the dock and swam after it. In one way, it was one of the great comic moments in American history, but it was more than comic. Nothing connected with modern war, including *Catch-22* and *Slaughterhouse-Five,* is ever really funny, and the Ford Peace Expedition, as Barbara Kraft's *The Peace Ship: Henry Ford's Pacifist Adventure in the First World War* admirably indicates, was at bottom a winningly humane venture aborted by naïveté, administrative ineptitude, and profound—and at the time thoroughly American—ignorance of European history and politics. The idea of Ford's peace effort is inherently no funnier than that of the peace movement that helped close down the Vietnam War. The missing element in Ford's try was stomach-turning news photography and television coverage. Their effect in ending the Vietnam War makes one wonder whether World War One could have lasted two months if there had been any anti-patriotic impulse to evade the censorship.

Despite his merits as an engineer, Ford was virtually unschooled. His learning was all *McGuffey Reader* maxims like—as he wrote down himself—"Money, the Root of all Eval unless used for good purpus." He thought 1812 the date of the American Revolution and, having heard that Matthew Arnold was a writer, imagined that Benedict Arnold was one too. The enemies he set himself against were drink and tobacco; idleness; Eastern sophistication; Wall Street; and "Jewish bankers." By paying a munificent five-dollar-a-day wage at his auto plants, he had become "an instant folk-hero," as Barbara Kraft says, "a St. Francis caring for his followers." Appalled both by the well-known wickedness of Europe and the bizarre slaughters of the first six months of the war, in April, 1915, he had begun to speak out, arguing that the war was against reason, that it had been caused by money lenders and munitions makers, and that the United States, the most powerful of all the neutrals, must stop it. Because President Wilson felt no official mediation possible until the belligerents asked for it, Ford decided to try what a private effort could do.

He was set on this course by the most fascinating character of the whole charade, Mme. Rosika Schwimmer, a husky, resolute Hungarian pacifist, feminist, and self-publicist. She had, she said, been conferring in Europe with both belligerents and neutrals. She carried in her capacious black handbag, she said, written agreements from many of the countries affected stating that they would welcome an end to the war if only someone would mediate. Finding Ford in a moment of sadness, outrage, and frustration, she persuaded him to lead, publicize, and pay for the expedition, but she herself gradually wormed her way into total command, and before Ford could bring himself to fire her a year later she had brought his venture to ruin by such autocratic techniques as spying on colleagues, opening other people's mail, and insisting on everyone's absolute "loyalty." She also expended Ford's funds extravagantly, not least on comforts for herself. "It now seems almost incredible," wrote the pacifist Louis Lochner to Ford when it was all over, "that Mme. Schwimmer should so long have tyrannized all of us."

It was she more than anyone who devised the scenario, and it was she, not Ford, who dominated events from the outset. But if she was behind the flats, it was Ford, as the figurehead of the enterprise and its Croesus, who had to take the ridicule, especially of the New York press, long annoyed by Ford's "Western" attacks on the East as the core of corruption and eager to stigmatize him not just as a moron but as an enemy of culture, humor, wit, and drink.

The campaign against Ford's pacifistic venture was so virulent that one could almost imagine that editors, journalists, and publicists treasured the war and resented any attempt to stop it. An editorial in *The New Republic* was headed "A Little Child Shall Lead Them." Bud Fisher's cartoon characters Mutt and Jeff were depicted (naturally) as members of the expedition, and their life aboard the *Oscar II* was rendered in a context of stowaway squirrels and on-board squabbles. Judge Alton Parker called Ford "a mountebank and a clown." And a nightclub comic asserted that the Ford factories were closing down because "Henry is sending all the nuts to Europe." *Punch,* in a satirical cartoon, registered Britain's contempt for peace initiatives as if the war were a national asset too precious ever to be forgone.

The voyage of the *Oscar II* to Christiania (now Oslo) took fifteen days. So many distinguished invitees had declined that, next to Ford, Schwimmer, and Lochner, about the most impressive people aboard were the mocking journalists, including Elmer Davis, William C. Bullitt, and Ben Huebsch. Drinks at the bar cost them only fourteen cents, and they were happy. So at first were the pacifists as they organized themselves and began contriving position papers and issuing manifestos. But almost at once deep disagreements arose between the two main factions, one favoring some degree of U.S. "preparedness," the other espousing total pacifism. Before long, debate turned acrimonious and fists were shaken in faces, all to the delight of the reporters, one of whom cabled home, "War has broken out aboard Henry Ford's peace argosy." Another cabled news of a "mutiny," and a British cruiser captained by a literalist stopped and boarded Ford's vessel to put down the trouble. The reporters—"the snakes in our Eden," one clergyman called them—loved it.

The British, suspicious that the whole thing was some sort of crazed German plot, confined the ship at Kirkwall for three days and treated its passengers as virtual prisoners, and not very nice ones at that. Arriving finally in Norway, the expedition found a reception cold in all respects. Most people in the neutral Scandinavian countries thought Ford's venture either a pro-German ploy or a shrewd ad for the products of the Ford Motor Co. Nevertheless, Ford's cash fueled dinners and receptions and mass meetings as the group travelled on to Stockholm and Copenhagen and finally arrived in The Hague after being allowed to cross Germany in a sealed train. But sick and bored, Ford had already deserted—in Christiania, from where he sneaked back to the U.S.A. early one morning amid fantastic scenes of passion and recrimination. Six weeks after leaving Hoboken the expedition fell apart, and everyone found his way home except Schwimmer and Lochner and their staff of typists and duplicating-machine crankers. They settled comfortably into the Grand Hotel, Stockholm, on Ford's money and quarreled over which five Americans they would send to the Neutral Conference for Continuous Mediation. After weeks of extravagant intrigue and dissension, Schwimmer was finally forced out. A few months later Ford, who had spent more than a half million on the expedition and related peace agitation, found himself making munitions for the newly belligerent U.S.A. Ironically, while the Ford peacemakers were abroad trying to find a foothold for mediating between the Allies and the Central Powers, they had failed to notice that, behind their backs, their own country, whose destiny most critics thought their proper, if not their only, business, was drifting into the war that would spectacularly terminate their efforts. After the American declaration of war in April, 1917, the whole country set out to "end the war" in the only way now possible—by winning it.

Once the United States was involved, the reputation of the Ford pacifists who had tried in their futile, highminded, amateur way to end the war sank precipitately. Professors on tenure found themselves fired, and divines were hounded from their pulpits. Joining "that absurd and disgusting expedition," said the Rev. Charles Aked of Los Angeles, was "the greatest mistake of my life." But some of the press finally made amends. In 1940, on the anniversary of the great comic embarkation at Hoboken, the *Detroit Free Press* wrote: "We do not laugh anymore, or joke, when that unique argosy is mentioned. We mourn, rather, the disappearance of times when we could still believe in progress in human enlightenment." Considered now, after the Holocaust and related revelations about human nature, Ford's adventure does look silly, defining a moment in American history when it seemed possible to believe anything so long as it was optimistic. But on Ford's behalf it should be said that he was not the only one in 1915 not to understand not merely how much of human motive is irrational, but, worse, how awful human motive could be if it ever turned wholly rational.

"We know we are ridiculous," wrote the pacifist Emily C. Balch, winner of the Nobel Peace Prize, "but even being ridiculous is useful sometimes." Wilson's Fourteen Points, the basis, finally, for the Armistice, bore an uncanny resemblance to the Appeal to the Belligerents issued in April, 1916, by Schwimmer and Lochner and others like them led abroad by Henry Ford in the innocence of his poor, uneducated heart.

And what happened to the *Oscar II*? In 1930 it was sold as scrap to the Japanese.

The Life of Art

In the twenties, some people, especially his wife Caresse, thought Harry Crosby a poet, but now the *Oxford Companion to American Literature* knows as little of him as *A Literary History of the United States*. What fame he has achieved he earned largely through his final act. Keats once deposed that he was half in love with easeful death. Harry Crosby was wholly in love with it, and he consummated his affair with it in 1929 when at the age of thirty-one he calmly shot his married girlfriend and then himself in a ninth-floor apartment of the Hotel des Artistes on West 67th Street in New York. For once the tabloid headlines got it right: "Tragedy and Disgrace." What brought this rich, brave, drunken, self-centered neurotic to this pass is the burden of Geoffrey Wolff's instructive biography, *Black Sun: The Brief Transit and Violent Eclipse of Harry Crosby*.

Keeping watch over Crosby's corpse, trying to avoid looking at the hole in his head, Archibald MacLeish "kept saying to him: you poor, damned, dumb bastard." "He was the most literary man I ever met," says MacLeish, "despite the fact that he'd not yet become what you'd call a writer. I never met anyone who was so imbued with literature; he was drowned in it." But there was one fatal problem: "Harry took it literally." For Harry, what was "said" by Baudelaire and Rimbaud, Blake and the Wilde of *The Picture of Dorian Gray*, was *true*, and you had to act on it. Harry's squalid end is a tragedy of American high-minded literalism. His satanic last act was grounded way back in a philistine, moralistic education. It was, terribly, the fruit of innocence.

His origins were classy: Back Bay Boston, St. Mark's School, Harvard. His mother was a Van Renssalaer, and J. Pierpont Morgan, Jr., was his uncle. "Too much money," was D. H. Lawrence's comment after Harry's end. In 1916, when he was nineteen, he exchanged the dropping of water-bombs for the real thing. Like E. E. Cummings, he went to France as an ambulance driver attached to the French army. Full of piety and pep, he was in all respects a good boy, and he prayed and read his Bible as avidly as he lusted for the Croix de Guerre. He was changed from boy to man on November 22, 1917, when a shell atomized his ambulance but left him miraculously alive. Henceforth to the end of his brief life, writes Wolff, "mutilation, vermin, cowardice, relentlessness, insanity, hysteria and cruelty played in the theater of his imagination." And henceforth his ambition was to shock "Boston," to scandalize and punish that world which had acquiesced in the rape of his innocence.

He began with flagrant drunkenness, violence, willfulness. He proceeded to a public affair with Mrs. Richard R. Peabody, recently married to a Harvard drunk. What Harry wanted he took. He finally married her, and with a stunning want of taste they agreed that her name should be changed from Polly to "Caresse." (That will give you some idea of his literary abilities.) Harry was nominally in banking, but couldn't work up any interest in it— too much like Boston. Together with practically everyone else, the Crosbys fled to Paris, and Harry concluded that he should become a writer. But it was hard for him to concentrate, what with the hashish, the absinthe, the baccarat and horse-racing, the opium, and always the alcohol and the public adulteries.

The social life of the Crosbys took place among a horde of well-born illiterates, strident about art but effectively unacquainted with any. Remittances arrived regularly from Boston, and Harry's Beacon Street father was shaken often by a command to "sell stock" so that Harry could keep up his showy Paris establishment. Harry began to grow nutty. He chose to present himself as one of Death's familiars, wearing only dark suits with black ties and a black cloth carnation in his buttonhole. He looked, as Wolff says, "half bank president, half hangman." He painted his fingernails black and furnished his flat with bones and skulls. "I ponder death more frequently than I do any other subject," he wrote in a notebook, and he became pedantic about suicide, involving all the girls he slept with in melodramatic death pacts.

At the same time, imagining that a "writer" needs some "system," preferably self-devised, he contrived a pretentious, ramshackle scheme of sun-worship, complete with homemade rites and accouterments, like the sun tattoos on his back and right foot, a cloak to wear while intoning his daily prayers to the sun, obsessive nude sunbathing and solar masturbation, a "thing" about gold coins. Like all else, "his sun-stroke," as Wolff says, "was extreme." He bought a little Belgian automatic for his ultimate self-murder with a girl, and on it he had engraved an image of the sun. What attracted him to the sun was its appearing to be the only thing "pure" in a naughty world. He was a type of American idealist, and in our literature examples are not far to seek. In the midst of his gravest excesses he remained a puritan, deeply offended, like a sort of violent Margaret Fuller, that the universe was so imperfect. He elected himself the prophet of the Way. As he wrote in one poem,

> I am a bridge to the sun
> bridge leading away from a world of pain
> bridge leading from a night of sin.

The sun was best worshipped, he conceived, at Le Moulin du Soleil, a restored mill on the ample estate of the Comte de la Rochefoucauld, where people like Mary Pickford and Douglas Fairbanks and various nonentities of title joined the Aldous Huxleys, the Lawrences, and Hart Crane to swim, drink, flirt, smoke opium, and play comic polo on donkeys. After one riotous house party Robert McAlmon observed: "They're wraiths, all of them. They aren't people. God knows what they've done with their realities."

But life was not all parties. Harry's poems and "dreams" were beginning to appear in Eugene Jolas's magazine *Transition,* now that Harry had begun sending it money, and his copious writings, and Caresse's, appeared under the imprint of their own publishing enterprise, the Black Sun Press, which now and then also brought out important work by Joyce and Lawrence. Through all this Harry, like Jay Gatsby, applied himself wistfully to intellectual self-improvement. "Once he had begun a [reading] project like the fifty-volume set of *The Sacred Books of the East* he would invariably see it through to its end." He was a great keeper of lists and writer of resolutions, among which appears the injunction, "Read a book every week." Gatsby, but with "advantages."

He never assuaged the itch to affront what he imagined to be Boston. On the Lido he met a girl named Josephine Rotch, late of Bryn Mawr, but known now to Harry as the Fire Princess. She was just one of the reasons why "Caresse increasingly passed her time in tears," although her self-pity did not impede her own pursuit of a string of lovers. Josephine later married Albert Bigelow of Harvard. Harry chose her as his terminal girl, and he put a bullet through her head while Uncle J. P. fretted over Harry's tardiness at a tea party. Despite his bohemianism Harry was never able to shake off the Boston axiom of his time that there is an afterlife, and he and Josephine went happily into it together. "If anything of Harry Crosby commands respect, perhaps even awe," says Wolff, "it was the unswerving character of his intention. He killed himself not from weariness or despair, but from conviction." He would be pleased to know that Boston never got over it.

Just as the policeman requires the criminal, the confessor the sinner, the shockable the shocking, George F. Babbitt requires Harry Crosby. As McAlmon noticed, by 1926 it was "passionately the fashion to be an artist or a genius," largely because such postures could give so much offense to hometown complacency, mercantilism, and boosterism, but also because France was the main theater of artistry and genius, and France had not only no Prohibition but offered a juicy exchange-rate. Crosby became one of the swarm of twenties poetasters more excited by the crude melodrama of art colliding with bourgeois philistinism (as they would express it) than by any imperatives of art and its traditions. For Crosby the poet was a flaming magus rather than a deliberate maker. Ponderously literary, he never managed to become really literate, or even very "modern." He made lists of decadent words to be worked into poems: *lurid, macabre, orchid, pagan, seer*— all redolent of the musk of the nineties. His poems overflow with retrograde stuff about "My Soul," and one of his anti-war sonnets flutes prettily of "barbèd wire." His terrible book titles, like *Aphrodite in Flight: Being Some Observations on the Aerodynamics of Love,* tell the whole story of his literary capacity. If he had studied and thought and practiced all his life he might—just might—have become a fourth-rate Hart Crane. As it was, he became only one of the numberless casualties of the prestige accorded to "art" in his own iron time.

Edith Wharton thought him "a sort of half-crazy cad," but for all his willfulness he was generous, charming even when obsessed, honest for all his violence. His "virtue and vice," Wolff perceives, was a "fanatical purity of intention." It was not only money that allowed him to proceed directly toward objects of desire: it was an amazing energy and singlemindedness. In the way St. Mark's had demanded, he developed "character"; but the objects of his rigorous will were those of a Bostonian reversed.

Geoffrey Wolff sympathizes with his man while remaining deeply critical, not just of Harry but of his childish conception of literature and art as mechanisms of personal rebellion and Making It. Wolff writes:

> After the final holocaust, should some new race mutate from the ruins and come to examine our culture and its artifacts, it may well conclude that our literature—like a hockey puck or a squash ball—was merely the device by which contests were decided.

Like Harry's with Boston.

Wolff is hard on Caresse for the relentlessly self-serving inaccuracy of her memoir, *The Passionate Years* (what a vulgar title!); and he's hard on Malcolm Cowley for making this untalented rich amateur an emblem of the twenties "exiles"—and here there may be room for honest disagreement. But I'd like to think there can be none over Wolff's unstylish refusal to euphemize or sentimentalize Crosby's murderousness. Wolff resolutely declines to romanticize The Savage God, designating the final event in Crosby's life as "the Crosby-Bigelow slaughter," just as he refers to Hart Crane's last performance in no kinder terms than "self-slaughter." Such clarity of moral perception—I'm tempted to add "these days"—does Wolff as much credit as his sympathy for Harry's stuffy, limited father, who, he says, "never wholly recovered from the crime his son had committed against them all." If Harry likewise could have learned to eschew euphemism and call things by their right names he might have grown into something like a writer.

William Carlos Williams
and His Problems

We are now far enough past the "modernist" movement in American poetry and art to observe its social motives and contours in relation to other phenomena. Instructed by Hugh Kenner's *The Pound Era* and his *Homemade World,* we can appreciate now as seldom before the desperate autodidacticism of those who ended babbling of Social Credit or mooning about the Variable Foot. What the lapse of time and the calming of the polemic atmosphere have allowed us to perceive about William Carlos Williams is that he was psychologically more complex than we may have suspected, but intellectually more simple.

A fact crucial to Williams's psychological and social career is that he never went to college at all, at a moment when college was thought to be a great thing, proceeding directly from the Horace Mann School in New York to the Medical School of the University of Pennsylvania. Of "liberal education"—including intellectual history—he had a minimum, although he had a lot of technical learning. And it's not really that he didn't "know anything": what's important is that he thought he didn't know anything. As "Evans," the naïve American abroad in *A Voyage to Pagany* (1928), he designates himself "a great zero," and in his *Autobiography* (1951) he registers his dismay when *The Waste Land* appeared and showed what a learned poet could do with a historical past fully possessed. Of himself and his native modernist colleagues he says, "Literary allusions, save in very attenuated form, were unknown to us. Few had the necessary reading." The Williams who quit Latin after one term in high school was not likely to be illuminated by the *Waste Land* footnote directing him to consult "*Aeneid,* I, 726."

As a self-made American artist consciously isolated from Europe and from history, Williams is an archtype, and it is both the pathos and the bravery of his predicament that Reed Whittemore delineates in his touching and quietly funny biography *William Carlos Williams: Poet from Jersey*. The book is touching because Whittemore the poet has entered Williams's troubled soul sympathetically, but it is funny because Whittemore the critic has applied the scalpel of irony to Williams's occasionally grandiose formulas and theories, to his fancied "enormous America-saving obligations," and to his instinct for martyrdom at the hands of the philistines. Whittemore reveals a Williams closer to the "culture-"drunk Sinclair Lewis than we may have perceived. And closer to F. Scott Fitzgerald as well. As Whittemore writes, "Underneath the common man, the kindly tough-guy doctor, he was one of the most determined of that American species, the self-made man, knowing that he had begun as nothing, as an outsider with his nose pressed against the window, but believing in his inexhaustible Americanness that he could *be* something, in fact anything he wanted if he just kept at it." Like the 138-pound Fitzgerald breaking his heart on the practice football-field at Princeton, or the over-age Zelda pursuing her hopeless ballet career in Paris. Williams did doggedly keep at it during the long lonely nights, typing up in the attic of the respectable house in Rutherford, N.J., expressing himself in the improvisations of "automatic writing" or, as the village sage, instructing his townspeople in the rudiments of what he imagined to be the new perception.

Whittemore reveals Williams as a divided soul, "a Puritan on odd days, a libertine on even." He liked to think of himself as a dissenter, a loner, a "solo sensibility"; but at the same time he desperately wanted his theories validated by society, and he was inordinately cast down when the outside world ignored or disagreed with him. He was capable of rude belligerence and seemed to require, like Pound, the threat of a fantasy "enemy"—conceived variously as a defender of the iambic pentameter line or a partisan (usually at a university) of European forms of literary culture. Yet he was shy, mild, sensitive. In the twenties and thirties he split himself between Rutherford (medical practice, family life) and Manhattan ("art," little magazines, bohemianism). He was the first of his line to be born in America, and as Whittemore sensitively understands, his Americanness was really as frail as his desire to "locate" was intense. Regarded by the Rutherford philistines, boosters, and businessmen as the author of "those shitty verses," to New York artistic circles he sometimes seemed a mere envious outsider, an angry "doctor-hick." Sensing that he had no real home, he struggled to achieve an environment for himself by passionately embracing the local particulars, even if they were only the weeds along the borders of "the sick society of Northern New Jersey." The two terms of Whittemore's subtitle—*Poet* and *Jersey*—seem designed as a sardonic oxymoron, laconically implying the problems encountered by the romantic sensibility set down in a *hortus siccus*. While yet an intern in both medicine and writing, trying to get his bearings in both, "he commuted daily," as Whittemore says, "from tough guy to Keats."

In 1912 the *Titanic* sank. Harriet Monroe founded *Poetry*. Williams married Flossie. The Imagist Manifesto appeared, and "the word 'modern' was in the wind." That year Williams broke away from his early Georgian efforts and published one of the first poems identifiable as his own, the one about "the coroner's merry little children": they are in clover because "Kind heaven fills their little paunches!" Williams had made the discovery that anything could enter a "poem," just the way Van Gogh had discovered in the 1880's that anything—old shoes, for example—could enter a painting. Williams was now on his way, propelled by hot enthusiasms—for Cubism, for Duchamp and Kandinsky, for Stieglitz and Man Ray. The modern style was to be "the broken style": the imagination was to be put back to work making new unities from new fragmentations. It was to be, indeed, nothing short of a revolution in consciousness. But as Whittemore observes, "WCW was having trouble locating the revolution and coming to grips with it as a public event. He didn't even know where it was. Sometimes he put it on one side of the Hudson, sometimes on the other. But though he was confused . . . he had the solace that the confusion was built into the revolution as a whole. It was a revolution in seclusion, an anomaly." The enemy was puritanism—we must never underestimate the impact of Prohibition on artistic theorizing of this period—and puritans were bad because they harbored cautiously within forms and boundaries: they were "bad because they were not lonely wanderer souls like WCW in his attic," writing "spontaneously." Up in that attic Williams indulged "the persecution thoughts so common to American writerdom," persuading himself that "good writing wouldn't sell, ever—wouldn't sell because *they* didn't want it to." But at least his prickly individualism secured him from the grosser perversions associated with the literary collectivism of the thirties, and as his passions began to calm he meditated *Paterson,* his conspicuously American lyric-epic adding the modern technique of "collage" to the tradition received from Whitman and Hart Crane.

Late in life came invitations to read and explain at the hated universities—he accepted them all—and honors from a bemused but respectful public. (They embraced Williams in part because he *looked* right—benign, thoughtful, tame.) Disciples gathered: Allen Ginsberg, Charles Olson, Denise Levertov, Cid Corman, Robert Creeley. Whittemore is perhaps a bit too satiric in his treatment of their messianic obscurantism, their absurd theories of Projective Verse, their zeal over the Variable Foot. "What WCW, Olson, and Creeley . . . had in common," Whittemore says, "was a conviction that the intuited forms and cadences of verse that they reached for could be talked about most learnedly, elevated to a science. If the three of them had been born in the Middle Ages they would all have been astrologers, and if in the modern world they had not been in poetry but over where science was supposed to be, they would have been the inventors of per-petual-motion machines or devices to extract soy-beans from sea water." For Williams the problem remained: how to reconcile two irreconcilables, spontaneity and art. Perhaps he came close to a reconciliation in the triadic stanza of "Asphodel, That Greeny Flower," his late lyric celebration of a lifetime's stormy love with Flossie.

Despite Whittemore's sometimes too facile irony, his book suc-ceeds in conveying a lifelike—here, a touching—portrait of the artist as American. But it is more than a biography: it is an im-plicit critical inquiry into the theoretical shakiness of modernist aesthetics, and indeed of all a priori theoretical prescriptions for artistic effectiveness.

The disjunctions in Williams's psyche perceived by Whittemore are common in late-romantic careers committed to an ideal of "authenticity" or entirely honest self-expression. Inevitably in conflict are the ideal of perfect sincerity, on the one hand, and, on the other, the rhetorical (or even the social) imperative, the requirement that original correlatives of idea and emotion be so devised and arranged that the reader is bound to react the way the artist wants him to. A telling example of Williams's confusion between artistic wish and artistic accomplishment is the end of *Paterson IV,* where the man, after playing with a dog on a beach, resumes his clothes, picks

> some beach plums from a low bush and
> sampled one of them, spitting the seed out,
> then headed inland, followed by the dog.

That is the snapshot Williams provides in the poem. That is what he gives us. But what he thinks he has given us he tries to make clear in the *Autobiography:* "In the end the man rises from the sea where the river appears to have lost its identity and accompanied by his faithful bitch . . . turns inland toward Camden where Walt Whitman, much traduced, lived the latter years of his life and died." But the reader of the poem gets no Camden, no Whitman—the details he needs are not vouchsafed. To the reader, the "inland" embraces everything between Cape May and Port Newark, and the man might as well be heading for Lakewood as for Camden. But Williams has no doubts that he has transmitted what he "has in mind." The trouble is that it's still "in mind." An old-fashioned way of diagnosing what has gone wrong is to say that he has neglected rhetoric, and that neglect haunts much later poetry inspired by Williams's example. Poetry, say, like Charles Olson's, where the subject very seldom attains the form of the publicly available.

Self-division is also at the center of the uncertain young Williams whose "wrongly directed apprenticeship" to Keats and the Georgian understanding of Beauty is brightly explored by Rod Townley in *The Early Poetry of William Carlos Williams.* Townley has done valuable research in Williams's papers, and his critical study is informed everywhere by the sensitivity of a poet and the psychological accuracy and tact of a thoughtful scholar who understands human motives. Scrutinizing early Williams sympathetically but analytically too, Townley observes that "it is not always easy to tell when Williams is being ingenuous and when he is being devious." He was capable of being both almost simultaneously. Innocence belonged to "poetry"; experience, to the medical career. Held between these "conflicting vectors," as Townley calls them, Williams struggled to educe beauty from the squalors of "the great industrial desert" (i.e., Northern New Jersey), finally bursting through to his own kind of lyric notating of freshly observed "situational perversities"—the gaiety of the coroner's children, for example, or the avidity of the sparrows (WCW has learned by painful experience to abjure nightingales) pecking amidst scattered horse turds. Like Whittemore, Townley positions Williams within a context, though a context perhaps intellectually more prepossessing than the one Whittemore is willing to allow. Townley says: "The implicit advice in these poems [in *Spring and All*] is to be one of those on whom, in James' phrase, 'nothing is lost.' Williams' work suggests a variant of the American obsession to possess the environment, to wrest from it its secrets and powers." Throughout, Townley is more respectful than Whittemore of Williams the aesthetic theorist, but he is equally acute at discerning the pitiful uncertainties faced by the American who aspires to proceed as if history, especially literary and mythic history, can be repealed by strength of will or intensity of desire.

It is an irony worth noting that Williams seems to succeed better in prose fiction than in the long poem: in such fictions as the stories in *Life along the Passaic River* (1938) and the trio of novels, *White Mule* (1937), *In the Money* (1940), and *The Build-Up* (1952), he has no literary theory to argue or demonstrate, nor are his artistic means self-consciously struggling with the past. A monitory, finger-wagging T. S. Eliot is not hovering about, nor an Ezra Pound ready to patronize. The result is narrative that responds at every point to the vivid particulars of daily life as experienced by bright "ordinary" people. Williams was a gifted overhearer, and his dialogue is at once true and delightful. The unpretentious narrative prose is transparent: with delight the reader passes right through to touch the flesh and blood of down-and-out patients and their wry physician, and to live with the immigrant Stecher family, advancing in one generation from poverty to affluence and finally to fake culture. It is these brilliant stories and novels that Robert Coles has set himself to recommend in the three public lectures he has gathered in *William Carlos Williams: The Knack of Sur-*

vival in America. It is a little book and not a very good one: it tends to confuse people with literary constructs and too often summarizes plots instead of analyzing. Coles seems to be trying to show that fiction can "study" people more accurately than "social science," but that's hardly news, and his immersion in the assumptions of the therapeutic and welfare culture tends to fog his vision and emasculate his prose. But the book has the merit of recalling the reader constantly to Williams's successful encounters with the American local concrete. Shown a cast of Cocteau's hands in Paris, Williams remembers in his *Autobiography* the way he responded: "His hands are narrow through the palm, with fingers of extreme slenderness such as I can recall seeing elsewhere only upon the wrists of a tall Negress, captain of one of our local high-school basketball teams." That—especially "upon the wrists of"—is quintessential Williams, triumphantly if only for a moment free of his problems, and writing like an angel.

What We Look Like

"There is something here to delight, amaze, and inform each of us." Thus James B. Rhoads, archivist of the United States, in his foreword to *The American Image: Photographs from the National Archives, 1860–1960,* a stunning selection of some two hundred photographs from the National Archives's five million. If you want to be delighted, look at the late-nineteenth-century formal portraits of the incredibly good-looking Idaho Indians, proudly posing as Noble Savages in full regalia. If they've not read *Hiawatha,* the photographer has. If you want to be amazed, study the picture of a 1910 biplane taking off tipsily from the street between the White House and the Executive Office Building, watched by thousands in three-piece suits and hats. If you want to be informed, linger over the adolescent coal-mine boys posing zombie-like in front of their place of work in South Pittston, Pennsylvania, in 1911. Near the beginning of this collection the Washington Monument is being built in the 1870's, and at the end, in 1963, that monument operates as a broadly ironic exclamation point behind Martin Luther King's March on Washington for Jobs and Freedom. Those two moments enclose a vast amount of American actuality, and a close student of these photographs, "official" though they may be, can infer volumes about the unique texture of life in this country.

For one thing, it is notably ad hoc and temporary. Because there's little agreement about what it is and what it ought to look like, the Republic never appears quite finished. It is being constantly built and rebuilt. In a curious way Henry Van Dyke's once-popular bad poem "America for Me" locates the psychological essence:

We love our land for what she is *and what she is to be.*

Indians from Southeastern Idaho (National Archives)

In these photographs there is a special emphasis on construction with a glance toward a grander future, because the object often is to document governmental works. But still, the place has the general look of an immense mining camp, with hardly a building proposing to last fifty years. The current tearing down and re-building of New York and other large cities are entirely in the American grain. The United States is the only country I know where the number of "housing starts" per month constitutes a standard, official index of prosperity and even virtue, usually held to be identical here. From the beginning, as these photographs suggest, it's been one of the Republic's main functions to provide jobs for the construction industry, and for that reason nothing must last too long. One photograph shows citizens of Charleston, South Carolina, camping out in a city park after an earthquake in 1898: their tents make the scene look normal rather than outré —they make it look like a town in the West, prepared to fold and move on at any moment. In these photographs litter and lumber and construction equipment are commonly strewn about, and it's hard to distinguish the ruins occasioned by the Civil War and the San Francisco earthquake from buildings haphazardly "going up."

Another thing these images tell us is that in America everyone's selling something all the time, largely by means of signs (compare the contemporary "Garage Sale"). In 1893, a settlement in Oklahoma has a flourishing sign shop although it has virtually nothing else, one shack proclaiming itself the "Hotel Moran," another indicating that "Attorneys" are to be found within. Besides being delightful and instructive in their own right ("Segars Tobacco & Snuff"; "No Goods Sold on Sunday"; "Colored Only. Police Order"; "Jax Ale Beer Stout"; "Buy More Liberty Bonds"), the signs indicate that it has always been part of the American character to play fast and loose with the apostrophe. Thus a sign on a section of

Claude Grahame-White Taking Off (National Archives)

Breaker Boys (Lewis Hine; National Archives)

an indoor swimming pool in San Francisco, *circa* 1900: "For Ladies' Only." ("Dad, what's an only?")

The well-known stubborn American resistance to uniformity,
the snotty pride and individualism and scorn for rigid discipline,
surface repeatedly. A nice example is a formal group portrait by
Brady of Civil War General Martin McMahon attended by his
staff. All are captains or field-grade officers but one, who is a lieutenant and clearly much put upon. He is not at all happy about
being only a lieutenant in this crowd, and as if to underline the
displeasure on his face he has insolently opened his jacket eight
buttons' worth to exhibit his flagrant checked shirt underneath.
Screw you all, he is saying, and although only the photographer
can see his gesture at the moment, when the picture's ready and
shown around, he's going to be in big trouble. Pure Huck Finn.
The very American message he's transmitting resembles General
Sherman's, who, although posing for Brady in full uniform, has
declined to brush his hair. There's a telling continuity between

these images and the photograph of the soldier in the South Pacific in 1943 posing at an anti-aircraft machine-gun while wearing a kimono and holding up a parasol.

In fact, the selection of photographs here has been so sensitive and the design (by Robert Aulicino) so subtly unifying that despite the whirligigs of styles (no one smiles in photographs until 1902, and no one laughs until around 1937), the often anomalous continuity of American life is what this collection argues. We half expect the Walt Whitman of page 58 to move forward, eyes troubled, to comfort the boy terribly wounded on Okinawa of page 163, smoothing his hair and pressing upon him a little paper bag of sweets and tobacco. The main street of Guthrie, Oklahoma, in 1893, with its alternating drugstores and shoe emporiums, is, except for the horses and the absence of paving, identical with the main street of Welch, West Virginia, in 1946 ("Florsheim Shoes," "Cut-Rate Drugs").

Contemporary critics who think "self-reflexiveness" in works of art or virtu a special property of post-modern expression could

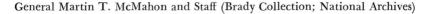

General Martin T. McMahon and Staff (Brady Collection; National Archives)

Walt Whitman (Brady Collection; National Archives)

profit from at least two photographs here. One is a typical 1940's
depression documentary showing a sad pea-pickers' settlement in
the San Joaquin Valley—unpainted shacks, tents, beat-up Okie cars
and trailers. And adjacent to them an outsized billboard advertising the current film feature at the Princess Theater, *The Grapes
of Wrath*. A more striking self-reflexive performance dates from
1918. It is a photograph by some unknown, infinitely patient, and
doubtless slightly deranged genius (he has taken it either from a
tall water-tower or, more likely, a balloon) depicting a whole
army brigade formed up on a vast field into a Brobdingnagian
one-starred service flag, pedantically complete with rod, cords, and
tassels. It's not until the realization gradually dawns that each of
these thousands of men is represented at home by such an actual
flag hanging in his mother's window that we fully get it, and then
we may gasp with admiration. It's the paradox of the one and the
many, and the photograph is a native, unlikely, and bizarre illus-

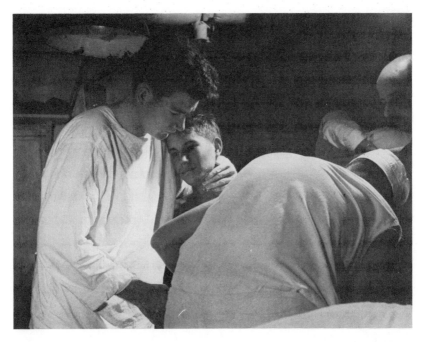

Private J. B. Slagle Aboard the USS *Solace* (Victor Jorgenson; National Archives)

tration of Coleridge's understanding of "beauty" as the spectacle of multëity in unity.

Since America is "about" abundance and multiplicity and replication and mass-production and high numbers, a photographer seems to catch something like its spirit when he emphasizes its repetitions and its numerousness. These official photographers are fond of rendering things lined up in rows, especially individual items (as in the service flag picture) not normally found in rows. Thus here the rows—of plucked chickens, bunches of bananas, plexiglass bomber noses, dead bodies, war wounded, crosses "row on row," Hawaiian cowboys, telephone operators, dynamos, moulds for doll legs. If mass-production is boring and deadly, maybe refracting it in artful images can redeem it.

Near the end of this book there's a photograph suggesting the comic-touching anomalies Americans will recognize as uniquely

164th Depot Brigade, Camp Funston, Kansas (National Archives)

President Eisenhower, Helen Keller, Polly Thompson (Abbie Rowe; National Archives)

their own. Dwight D. Eisenhower is submitting to having his face palpated by an ecstatic Helen Keller. Both stand in front of a very bad painting of the Kremlin, no doubt an official gift of the Soviet Union. The photograph is odd, alarming, charming, and thoroughly native, as we realize when we compare its values with the dead painting behind or try to imagine such a photograph emerging from the country the painting came from.

Notes on Class

If the dirty little secret used to be sex, now it is the facts about social class. No subject today is more likely to offend. Over thirty years ago Dr. Kinsey generated considerable alarm by disclosing that despite appearances one-quarter of the male population had enjoyed at least one homosexual orgasm. A similar alarm can be occasioned today by asserting that despite the much-discussed mechanism of "social mobility" and the constant redistribution of income in this country, it is virtually impossible to break out of the social class in which one has been nurtured. Bad news for the ambitious as well as the bogus, but there it is.

Defining class is difficult, as sociologists and anthropologists have learned. The more data we feed into the machines, the less likely it is that significant formulations will emerge. What follows here is based not on interviews, questionnaires, or any kind of quantitative technique but on perhaps a more trustworthy method —perception. Theory may inform us that there are three classes in America, high, middle, and low. Perception will tell us that there are at least nine, which I would designate and arrange like this:

> Top Out-of-Sight
> Upper
> Upper Middle
>
> ---
>
> Middle
> High-Proletarian
> Mid-Proletarian
> Low-Proletarian
>
> ---
>
> Destitute
> Bottom Out-of-Sight

46

In addition, there is a floating class with no permanent location in this hierarchy. We can call it Class X. It consists of well-to-do hippies, "artists," "writers" (who write nothing), floating bohemians, politicians out of office, disgraced athletic coaches, residers abroad, rock stars, "celebrities," and the shrewder sort of spies.

The quasi-official division of the population into three economic classes called high-, middle-, and low-income groups rather misses the point, because as a class indicator the amount of money is not as important as the source. Important distinctions at both the top and bottom of the class scale arise less from degree of affluence than from the people or institutions to whom one is beholden for support. For example, the main thing distinguishing the top three classes from each other is the amount of money inherited in relation to the amount currently earned. The Top Out-of-Sight Class (Rockefellers, du Ponts, Mellons, Fords, Whitneys) lives on inherited capital entirely. Its money is like the hats of the Boston ladies who, asked where they got them, answer, "Oh, we *have* our hats." No one whose money, no matter how ample, comes from his own work, like film stars, can be a member of the Top Out-of-Sights, even if the size of his income and the extravagance of his expenditure permit him temporary social access to it.

Since we expect extremes to meet, we are not surprised to find the very lowest class, Bottom Out-of-Sight, similiar to the highest in one crucial respect: it is given its money and kept sort of afloat not by its own efforts but by the welfare machinery or the prison system. Members of the Top Out-of-Sight Class sometimes earn some money, as directors or board members of philanthropic or even profitable enterprises, but the amount earned is laughable in relation to the amount already possessed. Membership in the Top Out-of-Sight Class depends on the ability to flourish without working at all, and it is this that suggests a curious brotherhood between those at the top and the bottom of the scale.

It is this also that distinguishes the Upper Class from its betters. It lives on both inherited money and a salary from attractive, if usually slight, work, without which, even if it could survive and even flourish, it would feel bored and a little ashamed. The next class down, the Upper Middle, may possess virtually as much as the two above it. The difference is that it has earned most of it, in law, medicine, oil, real-estate, or even the more honorific forms of trade. The Upper Middles are afflicted with a bourgeois sense of shame, a conviction that to live on the earnings of others, even forebears, is not entirely nice.

The Out-of-Sight Classes at top and bottom have something else in common: they are literally all but invisible (hence their name). The façades of Top Out-of-Sight houses are never seen from the street, and such residences (like Rockefeller's upstate New York premises) are often hidden away deep in the hills, safe from envy and its ultimate attendants, confiscatory taxation and finally expropriation. The Bottom Out-of-Sight Class is equally invisible. When not hidden away in institutions or claustrated in monasteries, lamaseries, or communes, it is hiding from creditors, deceived bail-bondsmen, and merchants intent on repossessing cars and furniture. (This class is visible briefly in one place, in the spring on the streets of New York City, but after this ritual yearly show of itself it disappears again.) When you pass a house with a would-be impressive façade addressing the street, you know it is occupied by a mere member of the Upper or Upper Middle Class. The White House in an example. Its residents, even on those occasions when they are Kennedys, can never be classified as Top Out-of-Sight but only Upper Class. The house is simply too conspicuous, and temporary residence there usually constitutes a come-down for most of its occupants. It is a hopelessly Upper- or Upper-Middle-Class place.

Another feature of both Top and Bottom Out-of-Sight Classes is their anxiety to keep their names out of the papers, and this too suggests that socially the President is always rather vulgar. All the classes in between Top and Bottom Out-of-Sight slaver for personal publicity (monograms on shirts, inscribing one's name on lawn-mowers and power tools, etc.), and it is this lust to be known almost as much as income that distinguishes them from their Top and Bottom neighbors. The High- and Mid-Prole Classes can be recognized immediately by their pride in advertising their physical presence, a way of saying, "Look! We pay our bills and have a known place in the community, and you can find us there any time." Thus hypertrophied house-numbers on the front, or house numbers written "Two Hundred Five" ("Two Hundred and Five" is worse) instead of 205, or flamboyant house or family names blazoned on façades, like "The Willows" or "The Polnickis."

(If you go behind the façade into the house itself, you will find a fairly trustworthy class indicator in the kind of wood visible there. The top three classes invariably go in for hardwoods for doors and panelling; the Middle and High-Prole Classes, pine, either plain or "knotty." The knotty-pine "den" is an absolute stigma of the Middle Class, one never to be overcome or disguised by temporarily affected higher usages. Below knotty pine there is plywood.)

Façade study is a badly neglected anthropological field. As we work down from the (largely white-painted) bank-like façades of the Upper and Upper Middle Classes, we encounter such Middle and Prole conventions as these, which I rank in order of social status:

Middle	1.	A potted tree on either side of the front door, and the more pointy and symmetrical the better.
	2.	A large rectangular picture-window in a split-level "ranch" house, displaying a table-lamp between two side curtains. The cellophane on the lampshade must be visibly inviolate.
	3.	Two chairs, usually metal with pipe arms, disposed on the front porch as a "conversation group," in stubborn defiance of the traffic thundering past.
High-Prole	4.	Religious shrines in the garden, which if small and understated, are slightly higher class than
Mid-Prole	5.	Plaster gnomes and flamingos, and blue or lavender shiny spheres supported by fluted cast-concrete pedestals.
Low-Prole	6.	Defunct truck tires painted white and enclosing flower beds. (Auto tires are a grade higher.)
	7.	Flower-bed designs worked in dead light bulbs or the butts of disused beer bottles.

The Destitute have no façades to decorate, and of course the Bottom Out-of-Sights, being invisible, have none either, although both these classes can occasionally help others decorate theirs—painting tires white on an hourly basis, for example, or even watering and fertilizing the potted trees of the Middle Class.

Class X also does not decorate its façades, hoping to stay loose and unidentifiable, ready to re-locate and shape-change the moment it sees that its cover has been penetrated.

In this list of façade conventions an important principle emerges. Organic materials have higher status than metal or plastic. We should take warning from Sophie Portnoy's aluminum venetian blinds, which are also lower than wood because the slats are curved, as if "improved," instead of classically flat. The same principle applies, as *The Preppy Handbook* has shown so effectively, to clothing fabrics, which must be cotton or wool, never Dacron or anything of that prole kind. In the same way, yachts with wood hulls, because they must be repaired or replaced (at high cost) more often, are classier than yachts with fiberglass hulls, no matter how shrewdly merchandised. Plastic hulls are cheaper and more practical, which is precisely why they lack class.

As we move down the scale, income of course decreases, but income is less important to class than other seldom-invoked measurements: for example, the degree to which one's work is supervised by an omnipresent immediate superior. The more free from supervision, the higher the class, which is why a dentist ranks higher than a mechanic working under a foreman in a large auto shop, even if he makes considerably more money than the dentist. The two trades may be thought equally dirty: it is the dentist's freedom from supervision that helps confer class upon him. Likewise, a high-school teacher obliged to file weekly "lesson plans" with a principal or "curriculum co-ordinator" thereby occupies a class position lower than a tenured professor, who reports to no one, even though the high-school teacher may be richer, smarter, and nicer. (Supervisors and Inspectors are titles that go with public schools, post offices, and police departments: the student of class will need to know no more.) It is largely because they must report that even the highest members of the naval and military services lack social status: they all have designated supervisors—even the Chairman of the Joint Chiefs of Staff has to report to the President.

Class is thus defined less by bare income than by constraints and insecurities. It is defined also by habits and attitudes. Take television watching. The Top Out-of-Sight Class doesn't watch at all. It owns the companies and pays others to monitor the thing. It is also entirely devoid of intellectual or even emotional curiosity: it *has* its ideas the way it has its money. The Upper Class does look at television but it prefers Camp offerings, like the films of Jean Harlow or Jon Hall. The Upper Middle Class regards TV as vulgar except for the highminded emissions of National Educational Television, which it watches avidly, especially when, like the Shakespeare series, they are the most incompetently directed and boring. Upper Middles make a point of forbidding children to watch more than an hour a day and worry a lot about violence in society and sugar in cereal. The Middle Class watches, preferring the more "beautiful" kinds of non-body-contact sports like tennis or gymnastics or figure-skating (the music is a redeeming feature here). With High-, Mid-, and Low-Proles we find heavy viewing of the soaps in the daytime and rugged body-contact sports (football, hockey, boxing) in the evening. The lower one is located in the Prole classes the more likely one is to watch "Bowling for Dollars" and "Wonder Woman" and "The Hulk" and when choosing a game show to prefer "Joker's Wild" to "The Family Feud," whose jokes are sometimes incomprehensible. Destitutes and Bottom Out-of-Sights have in common a problem involving choice. Destitutes usually "own" about three color sets, and the problem is which three programs to run at once. Bottom Out-of-Sights exercise no choice at all, the decisions being made for them by correctional or institutional personnel.

The time when the evening meal is consumed defines class better than, say, the presence or absence on the table of ketchup bottles and ashtrays shaped like little toilets enjoining the diners to "Put Your Butts Here." Destitutes and Bottom Out-of-Sights eat dinner at 5:30, for the Prole staff on which they depend must clean up and be out roller-skating or bowling early in the evening. Thus Proles eat at 6:00 or 6:30. The Middles eat at 7:00, the Upper Middles at 7:30 or, if very ambitious, at 8:00. The Uppers and Top Out-of-Sights dine at 8:30 or 9:00 or even later, after nightly protracted "cocktail" sessions lasting usually around two hours. Sometimes they forget to eat at all.

Similarly, the physical appearance of the various classes defines them fairly accurately. Among the top four classes thin is good, and the bottom two classes appear to ape this usage, although down there thin is seldom a matter of choice. It is the three Prole classes that tend to fat, partly as a result of their use of convenience foods and plenty of beer. These are the classes too where anxiety about slipping down a rung causes nervous over-eating, resulting in fat that can be rationalized as advertising the security of steady wages and the ability to "eat out" often. Even "Going Out for Breakfast" is not unthinkable for Proles, if we are to believe that they respond to the McDonald's TV ads as they're supposed to. A recent magazine ad for a diet book aimed at Proles stigmatizes a number of erroneous assumptions about body weight, proclaiming with some inelegance that "They're all a crock." Among such vulgar errors is the proposition that "All Social Classes Are Equally Overweight." This the ad rejects by noting quite accurately:

> Your weight is an advertisement of your social standing. A century ago, corpulence was a sign of success. But no more. Today it is the badge of the lower-middle-class, where obesity is *four times* more prevalent than it is among the upper-middle and middle classes.

It is not just four times more prevalent. It is at least four times more visible, as any observer can testify who has witnessed Prole women perambulating shopping malls in their bright, very tight jersey trousers. Not just obesity but the flaunting of obesity is the Prole sign, as if the object were to give maximum aesthetic offense to the higher classes and thus achieve a form of revenge.

Another physical feature with powerful class meaning is the wearing of plaster casts on legs and ankles by members of the top three classes. These casts, a sort of white badge of honor, betoken stylish mishaps with frivolous but costly toys like horses, skis, snowmobiles, and mopeds. They signify a high level of conspicu-ous waste in a social world where questions of unpayable medical bills or missed working days do not apply. But in the matter of clothes, the Top Out-of-Sight is different from both Upper and Upper Middle Classes. It prefers to appear in new clothes, whereas the class just below it prefers old clothes. Likewise, all three Prole classes make much of new garments, with the highest possible polyester content. The question does not arise in the same form with Destitutes and Bottom Out-of-Sights. They wear used clothes, the thrift shop and prison supply room serving as their Bonwit's and Korvette's.

This American class system is very hard for foreigners to master, partly because most foreigners imagine that since America was founded by the British it must retain something of British institutions. But our class system is more subtle than the British, more a matter of gradations than of blunt divisions, like the binary distinction between a gentleman and a cad. This seems to lack plausibility here. One seldom encounters in the United States the sort of absolute prohibitions which (half-comically, to be sure) one is asked to believe define the gentleman in England. Like these:

> A gentleman never wears brown shoes in the city, or
> A gentleman never wears a green suit, or
> A gentleman never has soup at lunch, or
> A gentleman never uses a comb, or
> A gentleman never smells of anything but tar, or
> "No gentleman can fail to admire Bellini"—W. H. Auden.

In America it seems to matter much less the way you present yourself—green, brown, neat, sloppy, scented—than what your backing is—that is, where your money comes from. What the upper orders display here is no special uniform but the kind of psychological security they derive from knowing that others recognize their freedom from petty anxieties and trivial prohibitions.

"Language most shows a man," Ben Jonson used to say. "Speak, that I may see thee." As all acute conservatives like Jonson know, dictional behavior is a powerful signal of a firm class line. Nancy Mitford so indicated in her hilarious essay of 1955, "The English Aristocracy," based in part on Professor Alan S. C. Ross's more sober study "Linguistic Class-Indicators in Present-Day English." Both Mitford and Ross were interested in only one class demarcation, the one dividing the English Upper Class ("U," in their shorthand) from all below it ("non-U"). Their main finding was that euphemism and genteelism are vulgar. People who are socially secure risk nothing by calling a spade a spade, and indicate their top-dog status by doing so as frequently as possible. Thus the U-word is *rich,* the non-U *wealthy.* What U-speakers call *false teeth* non-U's call *dentures.* The same with *wigs* and *hairpieces, dying* and *passing away* (or *over*).

For Mitford, linguistic assaults from below are sometimes so shocking that the only kind reaction of a U-person is silence. It is "the only possible U-response," she notes, "to many embarrassing modern situations: the ejaculation of 'cheers' before drinking, for example, or 'It was so nice seeing you' after saying goodbye. In silence, too, one must endure the use of the Christian name by comparative strangers. . . ." In America, although there are more classes distinguishable here, a linguistic polarity is as visible as in England. Here U-speech (or our equivalent of it) characterizes some Top Out-of-Sights, Uppers, Upper Middles, and Class X's. All below is a waste land of genteelism and jargon and pretentious mispronunciation, pathetic evidence of the upward social scramble and its hazards. Down below, the ear is bad and no one has been trained to listen. Culture words especially are the downfall of the aspiring. Sometimes it is diphthongs that invite disgrace, as in *be-yóu-ti-ful.* Sometimes the aspirant rushes full-face into disaster by flourishing those secret class indicators, the words *exquisite* and *despicable,* which, like another secret sign, *patina,* he (and of course she as often) stresses on the middle syllable instead of the first. High-class names from cultural history are a frequent cause of betrayal, especially if they are British, like Henry Purcell. In America non-U speakers are fond of usages like "Between he and I." Recalling vaguely that mentioning oneself last, as in "He and I were there," is thought gentlemanly, they apply that principle uniformly, to the entire destruction of the objective case. There's also a problem with *like.* They remember something about the dangers of illiteracy its use invites, and hope to stay out of trouble by always using *as* instead, finally saying things like "He looks as his father." These contortions are common among young (usually insurance or computer) trainees, raised on Leon Uris and *Playboy,* most of them Mid- or High-Proles pounding on the firmly shut door of the Middle Class. They are the careful, dark-suited first-generation aspirants to American respectability and (hopefully, as they would put it) power. Together with their deployment of the anomalous nominative case on all occasions goes their preference for jargon (you can hear them going at it on airplanes) like *parameters* and *guidelines* and *bottom lines* and *funding, dialogue, interface,* and *lifestyles.* Their world of language is one containing little more than smokescreens and knowing innovations. "Do we gift the Johnsons, dear?" the corporate wife will ask the corporate husband at Christmas time.

Just below these people, down among the Mid- and Low-Proles, the complex sentence gives trouble. It is here that we get sentences beginning with elaborate pseudo-genteel participles like "Being that it was a cold day, the furnace was on." All classes below those peopled by U-speakers find the gerund out of reach and are thus forced to multiply words and say, "The people in front of him at the theater got mad due to the fact that he talked so much" instead of "His talking at the theater annoyed the people in front." (But *people* is not really right: *individuals* is the preferred term with non-U speakers. Grander, somehow.) It is also in the domain of the Mid- and Low-Prole that the double negative comes into its own as well as the superstitious avoidance of *lying* because it may be taken to imply telling untruths. People are thus depicted as always *laying* on the beach, the bed, the grass, the sidewalk, and without the slightest suggestion of their performing sexual exhibitions. A similar unconscious inhibition determines that *set* replace *sit* on all occasions, lest low excremental implications be inferred. The ease with which *sit* can be interchanged with the impolite word is suggested in a Second World War anecdote told by General Matthew Ridgway. Coming upon an unidentifiable head and shoulders peeping out of a ditch near the German border, he shouted, "Put up your hands, you son of a bitch!", to be answered, so he reports, "Aaah, go sit in your hat."

All this is evidence of a sad fact. A deep class gulf opens between two current generations: the older one that had some Latin at school or college and was taught rigorous skeptical "English," complete with the diagramming of sentences; and the younger one taught to read by the optimistic look-say method and encouraged to express itself—as the saying goes—so that its sincerity and well of ideas suffer no violation. This new generation is unable to perceive the number of syllables in a word and cannot spell and is baffled by all questions of etymology (it thinks *chauvinism* has something to do with gender aggressions). It cannot write either, for it has never been subjected to tuition in the sort of English sentence structure which resembles the sonata in being not natural but artificial, not innate but mastered. Because of its misspent, victimized youth, this generation is already destined to fill permanently the middle-to-low slots in the corporate society without ever quite understanding what devilish mechanism has prevented it from ascending. The disappearance of Latin as an adjunct to the mastery of English can be measured by the rapid replacement of words like *continuing* by solecisms like *ongoing*. A serious moment in cultural history occurred a few years ago when gasoline trucks changed the warning word on the rear from *Inflammable* to *Flammable*. Public education had apparently produced a population which no longer knew *In-* as an intensifier. That this happened at about the moment when every city was rapidly running up a "Cultural Center" might make us laugh, if we don't cry first. In another few generations Latinate words will be found only in learned writing, and the spoken language will have returned to the state it was in before the revival of learning. Words like *intellect* and *curiosity* and *devotion* and *study* will have withered away together with the things they denote.

There's another linguistic class-line, dividing those who persist in honoring the nineteenth-century convention that advertising, if not commerce itself, is reprehensible and not at all to be co-operated with, and those proud to think of themselves not as skeptics but as happy consumers, fulfilled when they can image themselves as functioning members of a system by responding to advertisements. For U-persons a word's succeeding in an ad is a compelling reason never to use it. But possessing no other source of idiom and no extra-local means of criticizing it, the subordinate classes are pleased to appropriate the language of advertising for personal use, dropping brand names all the time and saying things like "They have some lovely fashions in that store." In the same way they embrace all sub-professional euphemisms gladly and employ them proudly, adverting without irony to hair stylists, sanitary engineers, and funeral directors in complicity with the consumer world which cynically casts them as its main victims. They see nothing funny in paying a high price for an article and then, after a solemn pause, receiving part of it back in the form of a "rebate." Trapped in a world wholly defined by the language of consumption and the hype, they harbor restively, defending themselves against actuality by calling habitual drunkards *people with alcohol problems,* madness *mental illness,* drug use *drug abuse,* building lots *homesites,* houses *homes* ("They live in a lovely $250,000 home"), and drinks *beverages.*

Those delighted to employ the vacuous commercial "Have a nice day" and those who wouldn't think of saying it belong manifestly to different classes, no matter how we define them, and

---

EXERCISE

To what class would you assign each of the following?

1. A fifty-five-year-old pilot for a feeder airline who cuts his own grass, watches wrestling on TV, and has a knotty-pine den?

2. A small-town podiatrist who says "Have a nice day" and whose wife is getting very fat?

3. A young woman trust officer in a large New York bank who loves to watch Channel 13, WNET, and likes to be taken out to restaurants said to serve "gourmet" food?

4. A periodontist in a rich suburb? Is his class higher than that of an exodontist in a large midwestern city who earns more?

5. A man in a rich Northeastern suburb who, invited to a dinner party on Tuesday night, appears in a quiet suit with a white shirt but at a similar, apparently more formal dinner party on Saturday night shows up in a bright green linen jacket, red trousers, no tie, and no socks?

6. Students of all kinds?

ANSWERS

1. Pilots have roughly the same class as field-grade Army
officers, that is, High Prole. Feeder airline pilots have
less status than national airline pilots, and those who
work for the longest established international airlines
like Pan Am and TWA have the highest status of all.
The Middle-Class den and the Mid-Prole TV wrestling
addiction cancel each other out.

2. At the moment, High Prole. If his wife gets much fatter,
he will sink to Mid-Prole.

3. Middle, with hopeless fantasies about being Upper-
Middle.

4. The periodontist is Middle. Because he is not a "professional specialist," the exodontist is slightly lower, regardless of where he lives or what he earns.

5. He is from the Upper-Middle Class, but he'd like to be
taken for a member of the Upper. The suit on Tuesday
night is to give the impression that he's just returned
from the city, where he "works." The weekend get-up
validates his identity as a suburbanite, devoting his
weekend to much-needed unbuttoning and frivolity.
The difference between Tuesday and Saturday is supposed to be significant. But I don't trust this man. He
pays too much attention to his clothes to be really
Upper Class.

6. All students, regardless of age or institution attended,
are Mid-Proles, as their large consumption of beer and
convenience foods suggests. Sometimes they affect the
used clothing of the Destitute, but we should not be
fooled.

it is unthinkable that those classes will ever melt. Calvin Coolidge said that the business of America is business. Now apparently the business of America is having a nice day. Tragedy? Don't need it. Irony? Take it away. Have a nice day. Have a nice day. A visiting Englishman of my acquaintance, a U-speaker if there ever was one, has devised the perfect U-response to "Have a nice day": "Thank you," he says, "but I have other plans." The same ultimate divide separates the two classes who say respectively when introduced, "How do you do?" and "Pleased to meet you." There may be comity between those who think *prestigious* a classy word and those who don't, but it won't survive much strain, like relations between those who think *momentarily* means in a moment (airline captain over loudspeaker: "We'll be taking off momentarily, folks") and those who know it means for a moment. Members of these two classes can sit in adjoining seats on the plane and get along fine (although there's a further division between those who talk to their neighbors in planes and elevators and those who don't), but once the plane has emptied, they will proceed toward different destinations. It's the same with those who conceive that *type* is an adjective ("He's a very classy type person") and those who know it's only a noun or verb.

The pretence that either person can feel at ease in the presence of the other is an essential element of the presiding American fiction. Despite the lowness of the metaphor, the idea of the melting pot is high-minded and noble enough, but empirically it will be found increasingly unconvincing. It is our different language habits as much as anything that make us, as the title of Richard Polenberg's book puts it, *One Nation Divisible*.

Some people invite constant class trouble because they believe the official American publicity about these matters. The official theory, which experience is constantly disproving, is that one can earn one's way out of his original class. Richard Nixon's behavior indicates dramatically that this is not so. The sign of the Upper Class to which he aspired is total psychological security, expressed in loose carriage, saying what one likes, and imperviousness to what others think. Nixon's vast income from law and politics—his San Clemente property aped the style of the Upper but not the Top Out-of-Sight Class, for everyone knew where it was, and he wanted them to know—could not alleviate his original awkwardness and meanness of soul or his nervousness about the impression he was making, an affliction allied to his instinct for cunning and duplicity. Hammacher Schlemmer might have had him specifically in mind as the consumer of their recently advertised "Champagne Recork": "This unusual stopper keeps 'bubbly' sprightly, sparkling after uncorking ceremony is over. Gold electro-plated." I suspect that it is some of these same characteristics that make Edward Kennedy often seem so inauthentic a member of the Upper Class. (He's not Top Out-of-Sight because he chooses to augment his inheritance by attractive work.)

What, then, marks the higher classes? Primarily a desire for privacy, if not invisibility, and a powerful if eccentric desire for freedom. It is this instinct for freedom that may persuade us that inquiring into the American class system this way is an enterprise not entirely facetious. Perhaps after all the whole thing has something, just something, to do with ethics and aesthetics. Perhaps a term like *gentleman* still retains some meanings which are not just sartorial and mannerly. Freedom and grace and independence: it would be nice to believe those words still mean something, and it would be interesting if the reality of the class system—and everyone, after all, hopes to rise—should turn out to be a way we pay those notions a due if unwitting respect.

II
HAZARDS OF LITERATURE

The Purging of *Penrod*

In "Black Culture and White America" (*Encounter,* January, 1970), Marcus Cunliffe depicts the intellectual and moral nightmare occasioned by the scramble of American universities to equip themselves with plausible programs in Black Studies. It is all going forward, Cunliffe perceives, according to a "lurid scenario," one entailing "frantic reversals, rewriting of textbooks, revisions on a scale worthy of the Soviet *Encyclopedia.*" That the ends of Black Studies may be achieved it is not merely black culture and history that have had to be fiddled with: white culture and history have had to be managed as well. Consider what has been done to the text of Booth Tarkington's *Penrod,* first published in 1914.

No one would want to argue that *Penrod,* Tarkington's celebration of pastoral Indiana boyhood just before the First World War, is a manifestation of a very high culture. It belongs rather to the world of center culture, where as Orwell has noticed the persisting "good bad books" reside, things like Ernest William Hornung's Raffles adventures, the Sherlock Holmes stories, the writings of Rider Haggard, *Uncle Tom's Cabin.* These represent, as Orwell says,

> a type of book which we hardly seem to produce in these days, but which flowered with great richness in the late-nineteenth and early twentieth centuries . . . , that is, the kind of book that has no literary pretensions but which remains readable when more serious productions have perished.

What honest man, condemned to solitary for his crimes, wouldn't rather read *Penrod* (or *The Education of Hyman Kaplan,* or *Bella, Bella Kissed a Fella,* or the early works of Benchley and Thurber, or the waggeries of Stephen Potter) than the highest performances of, say, George Moore or Robert Bridges, James Branch Cabell or Christopher Fry?

Not that even a reader *in extremis* would find *Penrod* everywhere satisfactory. Its small-town snobbery and complacency are sometimes oppressive. In places it's badly over-written, and occasionally the philistine mock-literary and arch pseudo-Biblical style betrays uneasiness about "literature" and what the better sort of people will think. But these are small blemishes. While not comparable with *Huckleberry Finn*, *Penrod* does radiate something like its electric humanity and clear-sightedness.

Believing it a book that should be placed in the hands of every young person, I was pleased a while ago when my adolescent daughter showed me her own paperback copy (Grosset & Dunlap Tempo Books, 1965). I turned to one of my favorite chapters, nicely titled "Coloured Troops in Action." But right away I saw that something was wrong: the chapter was now titled "Troops in Action." And it wasn't an error, for the emended chapter title was repeated in three running-heads and in the table of contents. This alteration seemed odd in view of what the flyleaf asserted:

> This Tempo Books edition contains the complete text of the original hard-cover edition.

Clearly a serious collation was in order.

What this revealed was that the paperback text had been slyly manipulated throughout to purge the evidence of Tarkington's characteristic affectionate condescension toward Negroes. And as the evidence had been secretly destroyed, so had Tarkington's wit. This purge had reduced the text to inspidity: we have now, as William Carlos Williams might have put it, a *Penrod* consonant with our day.

For example: at one point Penrod, confined to the tedium of the classroom, is moved by exotic sounds from outside. (My square brackets indicate materials excised from the paperback edition.)

> . . . the sound was the spring song of a mouth-organ, coming down the sidewalk. The windows were intentionally above the level of the eyes of the seated pupils; but the picture of the musician was plain to Penrod, painted for him by a quality in the runs and trills partaking of the oboe, of the calliope,

and of cats in anguish, [an excrutiating sweetness obtained only by the walloping, walloping yellow-pink palm of a hand whose back was Congo black and shiny].

The "picture of the musician" is no longer "plain to Penrod," nor is it at all plain to us. Indeed, the effect is now that of an author who doesn't know what he is doing. The whole point is that Penrod *wants* to be Black so that he can (1) eschew school, and (2) participate in that delicious music. But the prissy emender carefully prevents Penrod's daydream from fulfilling the shape it obviously aspires to:

> Emotion stirred in Penrod a great and poignant desire, but (perhaps fortunately) no fairy godmother made her appearance. Otherwise Penrod would have gone down the street [in a black skin], playing the mouth-organ, and an unprepared [coloured] youth would have found himself enjoying educational advantages for which he had no ambition whatever.

After this, we may be surprised to find that in the next paragraph *blackboard* has not been emended to *chalkboard*.

Again: in Chapter 26 we find a group of boys lounging bored in a stable on a hot August afternoon. Present are Penrod, Sam Williams, Georgie Bassett, and their Negro friend Herman. Also present is Maurice Levy, who appears throughout the revised text wholly unaltered, remaining conspicuously the stereotyped "Jewboy" of the Midwestern bourgeois imagination: he is a shrewd, ambitious child animated only by images of his prospective "deportment store: ladies' clothes, gentlemen's clothes, neckties, china goods, leather goods, nice lines in woollings and lace goods." Languidly the conversation of this little group turns to the theme "when I'm a man":

> "When I'm a man," said Sam Williams, "I'm goin' to hire me a couple of fellas [*original:* a couple of coloured waiters] to swing me in a hammock and keep pourin' ice-water on me all day out o' those waterin'-cans they sprinkle flowers from. . . ."

Herman interrupts:

> "Ain' nobody goin' to hire me [*original:* nobody goin' hiah me] when[s] *I'm* a man. Goin' to be [Goin' be] my own boss. I'm goin' to be [goin' be] a rai'road man."

And now these ten lines of the original are entirely suppressed:

> "You mean like a superintendent, or sumpthing like that, and sell tickets?" asked Penrod.
>
> "Sup'in—nev' min' nat! Sell ticket? *No* suh! Go be a *po*'tuh! My uncle a po'tuh right now. Solid gole buttons—oh, oh!"
>
> "Generals get a lot more buttons than porters," said Penrod. "Generals————"
>
> "Po'tuhs make the bes' livin'," Herman interrupted. "My uncle spen' mo' money 'n any white man n'is town."

This pleasant, visually realized, and hence instructive exchange safely past, the reviser allows Penrod to utter his last line, which appears now as if in answer to Herman's "I'm goin' to be a rai'road man":

> "Well, I rather be a general," said Penrod.

A final example: the episode of Rupe Collins, a bully who wanders into Penrod's orbit from a rougher neighborhood. He tyrannizes Penrod, who instantly adopts Rupe's sadistic mannerisms and turns to victimize his friends: "He twisted the fingers and squeezed the necks of all the boys of the neighborhood, meeting their indignation with a hoarse and rasping laugh" modelled precisely after Rupe's. Penrod tyrannizes even Herman, who responds only by laughing. In the presence of the contemptuous Rupe himself, Penrod, anxious for Rupe's approval, turns on his closest friend Sam Williams and humiliates him. Rupe responds by obliging both boys to "lick dirt." At this the Negroes Herman and Verman remonstrate with Rupe—they're the only ones who do. In Tarkington's text he answers with:

> "Chase them nigs out o' here!"

This highly appropriate viciousness the righteous expurgator emends to:

> "Chase them out o' here!"

In the original, Tarkington has Herman answer:

> "Don' call me nig. I mine my own biznuss. You let 'em boys alone."

In the revision:

> "I mine my own biznuss. You let 'em boys alone."

What of course animates the scene is precisely the loathsomeness of Rupe's racial sadism, now carefully expunged. That sadism is what motivates Penrod's belated reaction: "A sudden dislike of Rupe and Rupe's ways rose within him, as he looked at the big boy overwhelming the little one [*original:* darky] with that ferocious scowl." Penrod's altered vision and his subsequent shame are like Huck's, and he cures himself of imitating Rupe by witnessing a specific act of sadism which Tarkington has depicted in racial terms precisely to make it seem the more hateful. Rupe continues his assault on Herman:

> "You ol' black nigger," the fat-faced boy said venomously to Herman.

Here the paperback text reads:

> "You ole ——," the fat-faced boy said venomously to Herman.

Herman and Verman, once "Coloured Troops," now—meaning-lessly—"Troops," go into action, one with a scythe, the other with a lawn-mower (a nice Midwestern touch). Their vigorous retalia-tion against Rupe Collins is rendered by Tarkington in a context of village Darwinism and Herbert Spencerism. Rupe, we are told, "had not learned that an habitually aggressive person runs the danger of colliding with beings [in one of those lower stages of evolution] wherein theories about 'hitting below the belt' have not yet made their appearance." Indeed, "Primal forces operated here, and [the two blanched, slightly higher products of evolution] Sam and Penrod no more thought of interfering than they would have thought of interfering with an earthquake." Tarkington's point, here as elsewhere, is Twain's: dogs, Negroes, and white boys occupy essentially the same universe, one happily distant from that peopled by adult Whites like policemen, dancing and music masters, school teachers, parents, barbers, the clergy, and other Establishment personnel. This point is effectively blunted by the expurgator, programmatically unable to make the necessary distinction between two uses of racial diction, the affectionate and

Cookies from Georgia. Before.

the abusive. Or even the patronizing and the abusive. Rupe Collins is punished—the lawnmower makes a terrible mess of his shins—for the aggressive use of language. At least he is in Tarkington's version. What he's punished for in the revision is anybody's guess.

(And lest we get the idea that it's only in literary or artistic revisionism that we meet this sort of pusillanimous transformation of the innocent into the cautious, knowing, calculating, and offensive, let's study these two cookie-tin lids. The moment of furtive metamorphosis there is roughly coincident with the moment *Penrod* was meddled with.)

My point requires, I hope, little elaboration. The past is not the present: pretending it is corrupts art and thus both rots the mind and shrivels the imagination and conscience. Twain's Jim *was* called Nigger Jim. Conrad's novel *is* titled *The Nigger of the Narcissus*. H. L. Mencken *did* amuse his correspondents by using

Cookies from Georgia. After.

stationery headed "The American Institute of Arts and Letters (Colored)."

Are Grosset & Dunlap's disingenuous revisions "on a scale worthy of the Soviet *Encyclopedia*"? Not quite, perhaps. But what's worth noting is the way both sorts of "revisions" imply the same rhetorical scenario, one in which a knavish manipulator exploits an ingenuous audience. As the addressees, we are not supposed to know or—more important—care about these revisions, for we are assumed to be insecure, half-educated folk mesmerized by a compound of sentimentality and fear, sensing nothing so much as the obligation to exhibit on all occasions the prescribed quantity of public shame.

A recent resolution of the American Historical Association sums it up: "The past may be manipulated in an authoritarian state, but this can never be permitted in a free society."

Smut-Hunting in Pretoria

"Hairdressers: Unisex and Ladies," reads a sign in Cape Town. Odd dualistic distinctions like that are endemic in the Republic of South Africa, a venue devoted largely, it would seem, to conceiving and enforcing divisions designed to simplify an actuality irredeemably complex and ambiguous. If the melting-pot was the industrial image once thought suggestive of American social possibilities, the South African image would have to be the cream-separator, or the industrial seives in the Johannesburg mines that separate diamond from rock. In the same way, Afrikaner is divided from British, Asian and "colored" from white, and black from all. Apartheid applies not just to blacks but to everybody and everything. It expresses the essential action of the ascendant South African sensibility, which can be described as late-nineteenth-century rural Dutch, aggressively provincial— humorless, unimaginative, philistine. Just as synthesis is, or used to be, the American ideal, analysis is the South African one. "Non-White Only," say the signs on the buses. "Asians and Coloreds Only."

This eagerness to classify and separate allies itself with another Afrikaner speciality, prudery, to produce the local institution of censorship. This divides all expression into two categories: the acceptable and the "undesirable" (the official term). "Are you carrying any undesirable books or magazines?" asks the customs officer at the Johannesburg airport. He means *Portnoy's Complaint* and *Playboy*. The censorship derives from two acts of Parliament: the Internal Security Act of 1950, designed to repress utterance that might encourage communism, and the Publications Act of 1974, designed primarily to dampen erotic imagining. The Publications Act forbids not just indecency. It also prohibits expression found to be "blasphemous, or . . . offensive to the religious convictions or feelings of any section of the inhabitants of the Republic." Furthermore, it prohibits utterance which brings any section of the populace (no matter how high and powerful) into ridicule or contempt. Thus, satire of Afrikaner sexual anxiety, as registered in the Publications Act, is prohibited as undesirable. Which means that the Act cannot be much commented on locally, since to comment is to satirize. And to judge from the behavior of the censors, lust poses a more powerful threat to the Republic than Liberalism: only about 10 percent of publications are banned for political reasons. All the rest are prohibited for sexual provocativeness.

The Publications Act is administered by committees arranged in three echelons. At the bottom (forgive the expression), local committees (club ladies, etc.) receive, and sometimes solicit, complaints from scandalized readers and make recommendations to the Directorate of Publications, a division of the Department of the Interior located at Pretoria. The Directorate rules on each case and promulgates its list of forbidden books and artifacts weekly in the *South African Government Gazette*. Above the Directorate, the Publications Appeal Board hears appeals from the Directorate's rulings and sometimes reverses them, as it did, say, with Nadine Gordimer's *Burger's Daughter*. All three echelons in the censorship process are enjoined by the Act to remember in their deliberations "the constant endeavor of the population of the Republic to uphold a Christian view of life." The importation, production, or distribution of proscribed works is a criminal offense. With certain particularly flagrant items, mere possession is criminal.

The local guide through this bizarre situation is *Jacobsen's Index of Objectionable Literature . . . Containing a Complete List of All Publications . . . Prohibited from Importation into the Republic of South Africa*. The compiler of this indispensable work, to be found in all bookstores and public libraries, is the indefatigable K. J. K. Jacobsen, whose assiduity in solemnly recording the rulings of the Directorate of Publications might be thought to veer close to satire. He keeps his *Index* up to date weekly with loose-leaf pages registering the ukases of that week's *Gazette*. At the moment the Index contains more than three hundred pages of tiny print listing more than thirteen thousand no-no's, not all of them books. Some are phono discs (or their jackets) like *Hair* and the performances of Pete Seeger. Some are rude postcards, of the old-fashioned Donald McGill seaside sort, displaying comic hypertrophied breasts and behinds. Some are waggish novelty stickers ("Tennis players have hairy balls"; "Candy is dandy, but sex won't rot your teeth"). A number of printed T-shirts are forbidden, including such classics as the one showing two pigs copulating (broad smiles), labeled "Makin' Bacon," and the ones with the legends "Only You Can Prevent Children" and "Of all my relations I like sex the best." T-shirts printed with the anti-nuclear peace symbol and with "Black is Beautiful" are also out. Greeting cards essaying double entendre are proscribed, like the one reading, "On your birthday I'm going to give you something big, red, and hard." A jigsaw puzzle depicting a nude Marilyn Monroe is forbidden; so are the luscious calendars found normally in garages and workshops. And of course "sexual aids": vibrators, dildos, penis rings, life-size rubber female dollies, "condoms with offensive attachments." An "Adam and Eve salt and pepper set" must be very dirty, for it is prohibited. So is the periodical *Gay News* (London), together with *L'Humanité* (Paris). The print of the famous Modigliani reclining nude—a favorite of artistic college boys everywhere—was proscribed for years, but recently it has been removed from the prohibited list, despite its stylized pubic hair. (We are to infer that an accepted masterpiece may exhibit a little such hair, but that a run-of-the-mill painting may not. A young woman not too long ago had four of her paintings of studio models removed from a group show in Johannesburg for this offense. Purged from the same exhibition were some etchings by a local practitioner showing nude young men engaged in housework, gaily plying feather dusters and vacuum cleaners.)

But most of the items listed in *Jacobsen's Index* are books, and it's here that the Afrikaner mind most interestingly reveals its sensitivities. The whole corpuses of sly pornographers like Gershon Legman and Gordon Merrick are prohibited, together with most of the pseudo-hot fictions of hacks like Jack Woodford and Carter Brown, and the perhaps more valuable works of William Burroughs. Of course sex guides like Alex Comfort's *The Joy of Sex* are forbidden. (The Pretoria smut-hounds have not yet encountered *The Joy of Gay Sex* and *The Joy of Lesbian Sex*. These, we can be sure, will shake them badly, confirming them in their conviction of the wickedness of the rest of the world.) In publishing its weekly list of books and authors, the Directorate can't avoid using authors' names as they appear on title pages. The *Gazette* will earnestly inform its readers that they must not peep into a certain work by "Roger Shaft," or by "Nona Coxhead," or by "Lance Horner," thus providing the pornographers with a slight comic revenge. We are not surprised to find the works of Linda Lovelace and Xaviera Hollander forbidden, but we may be taken aback to learn that the Directorate has proscribed Mimi Sheraton's *The Seducer's Cookbook*. Gore Vidal's *Kalki* is prohibited because it violates, among other things, the blasphemy clause of the Publications Act, going so far in one passage as to point to a resemblance between the male genitals and the Holy Trinity.

Sodomy is the problem in Mailer's *An American Dream*. Wit about diaphragms is what earns Mary McCarthy's *The Group* its place on the list. Edmund Wilson's *Memoirs of Hecate County*, John Updike's *Couples*, and Lawrence's *Lady Chatterley's Lover* are all there for deviating from the Afrikaner image of wholesome wedded coitus. The same is true of Philip Roth's *Letting Go*, although *The Breast* may offend through sheer outrageous wit and wealth of literary allusion. Nabokov's *Ada* is on the list, together with James Guetti's novel about compulsive gambling, *Action*. Malamud's *The Assistant* is forbidden, and so are Martin Amis's *The Rachel Papers* and *Dead Babies*. His father Kingsley's *I Want It Now* may not be imported (perhaps because the "It" is too readily fleshed out by the heated Afrikaner imagination); neither may *The Green Man*, presumably for blasphemy. *Jacobsen's Index* contains such old standbys as Apollinaire, Swinburne, de Maupassant, Zola, Robert Burns, Daniel Defoe, Boccaccio, John Addington Symonds, Aubrey Beardsley, Stekel, and Krafft-Ebing. But most of the proscribed authors are contemporary, and Americans can feel proud that so many of their current writers have made the list. Prohibited works include at least one book by Leonard Cohen, Robert Penn Warren, Jack Kerouac, James Baldwin, Joan Didion, Kurt Vonnegut, Joseph Heller (*Catch-22* was recently cleared after many years; *Something*

Happened is still banned), James T. Farrell, John O'Hara, Nathanael West, William Faulkner, Karl Shapiro *(Edsel),* Tennessee Williams, Maxine Kumin, George Garrett, R. V. Cassill, John Cheever, Paul Theroux, James Jones, Truman Capote, Thomas Pynchon, Richard Brautigan, Angela Davis, Erskine Caldwell, Howard Hunt (!), Nelson Algren, Ken Kesey, Tom Wicker, Walker Percy, Rona Jaffe, Alison Lurie, Shelby Foote, Alan Lelchuk, Richard Wright, Frederick Prokosch, Robert Coover, Herbert Gold, Leslie Fiedler, John Hawkes, and John Irving *(The World According to Garp).* We must be doing something right.

Even scholarly works are occasionally proscribed for political suggestiveness, like John Hope Franklin's *From Slavery to Freedom.* Of course the writings of Lenin, Engels, Trotsky, R. Palme Dutt, Marcuse, and Malcolm X may not be imported; but forbidden likewise are learned analyses of Marxism in relation to the history of ideas like Sidney Hook's *From Hegel to Marx,* or even unsympathetic treatments of Marxism and some of its results like the anti-Soviet books of Robert Conquest. Scholarly writings that seem to touch on sex are banned as easily as lubricious fictions or naughty rubber goods. The Princeton historian Lawrence Stone's *Family, Sex, and Marriage in England, 1500–1800* was declared undesirable in the *Gazette* for December 21, 1979, following on the prohibition of Nick Reynolds's *The French Orgasm,* the pamphlet *Sept. 12: Steve Biko Day,* and a "vibrator in the shape of a tongue."

The Afrikaners seem especially sensitive to writings implying that war is either boring or dangerous. Thomas Heggen's *Mister Roberts* has been on the list since the 1950's, and so has Dalton Trumbo's jolting version of the consciousness of a World War I basket case, *Johnny Got His Gun.* Even Audie Murphy's naïve memoir of his heroic performance in World War II, *To Hell and Back,* is forbidden, perhaps for bad language. The censors also seem to keep a sharp lookout for works implying some relation between military training and homosexuality. Calder Willingham's *End as a Man* has finally been cleared after many years on the list; Lucian K. Truscott's *Dress Gray* went on the list as soon as it hit the Republic, which requires two years of compulsory military service, widely hated.

Bernard DeVoto's *Portable Mark Twain* (1946) is on the list, and the censors give as the reason "falsified contents," referring presumably to the scholarly dispute about the authorship of some of the writings DeVoto includes. But since the Directorate of Publications does not normally trouble itself about the authenticity of texts, we may suspect that the real reason is the volume's containing the prose satire "The War Prayer": "O Lord our God, help us to tear their soldiers to bloody shreds with our shells; . . . help us to wring the hearts of their unoffending widows with unavailing grief; . . . we ask . . . in the spirit of love, of Him Who is the Source of Love. . . . Amen." Novels morally harmless which nevertheless tend to discredit the military or to suggest that high officers are fallible have a hard time in South Africa. Thus Stuart Cloete's sentimental middlebrow novel about World War I, *How Young They Died,* is prohibited—but perhaps the real reason is to punish the author (he is South African) for his disloyalty in once publishing *Mamba,* a novel touching on indigenous black life.

Some of the prohibitions will strike the non-Afrikaner as odd. Orwell's *Down and Out in Paris and London* was on the list for years, although now it may be imported freely. Did it go too far in discouraging tourists by exposing luxury hotels and restaurants as filthy and bogus? Or was its mild socialism thought inflammatory? Alec Waugh's innocent novel *Island in the Sun* may not be sold, and neither may his *A Spy in the Family.* Peter Benchley's *Jaws* is conceived to pose a threat, like Hiram Haydn's *The Time Is Noon* and such thoroughly dated goods as Cyril Connolly's *The Rock Pool* and Dorothy Baker's *Young Man with a Horn.* One would think John Livingston Lowes's *The Road to Xanadu,* his classic (1927) scholarly study of the sources of Coleridge's "Kubla Khan," unlikely to occasion a blush anywhere. But the edition of 1978, we learn from *Jacobsen's Index,* may not be distributed in South Africa. This edition is published in paperback in London, and although I've been unable to find a copy I can imagine that the problem—barring an anomalous anti-Apartheid introduction by a manic young person—must be an inappropriately lewd cover designed by some brightie at Pan Books to make the product "go" among the uninstructed.

If the occasional scholarly or polemical book is stopped, most

of the books banned are novels, a genre apparently assumed to
pose special risks. The hard-working civil servants of the Directorate of Publications are so busy reading questionable novels that
they don't notice the streams of filth pouring into the Republic
in the form of memoirs, letters, poems, literary criticism, biographies, and social histories. J. R. Ackerley's *My Father and
Myself* circulates freely, and so does Isherwood's *Christopher and
His Kind.* Both are memoirs and thus not immediately suspected
as vehicles of nastiness. Isherwood's novels *The Last of Mr. Norris*
and *The World in the Evening,* being fictions, have been easily
discovered to be undesirable. The indecency of Tom Driberg's
posthumous memoir *Ruling Passions* has been called to the
Directorate's attention, and it has taken action there; but because
South Africa is not a notably bookish place no one's ever complained, apparently, about Ginsberg's *Howl,* Robert Creeley's
A Day Book, the works of Paul Goodman, or R. W. B. Lewis's
responsible biography *Edith Wharton,* which offers as an appendix
(pp. 547–48) a hitherto unpublished passage by Wharton warm
enough ("His head bent lower, and with a deeper thrill she felt
his lips pressed upon that quivering invisible bud," etc.) to make
Genet (proscribed, of course) seem like Lydia Huntley Sigourney
(1791–1865). The Directorate appears to be especially nervous
about the act Wharton describes, and if Lewis's book has so far
escaped proscription, Richard Ellmann's *Selected Letters of James
Joyce* (1975) has not.

But if the censorship prevents public access to the rich modern
literature of sex, it also bars loonies and the violently mad from
items like the pamphlet *The Negro a Beast,* issued by the South
African Anglo-Nordic Union. The grossly anti-Semitic *Protocols
of the Elders of Zion* is prohibited, and so are *This Time the
World* and *White Power,* by the late American Nazi George
Lincoln Rockwell. If the Publications Act forbids anti-apartheid
pamphlets and brochures and handbills focusing on the scandals
of Sharpville and Soweto, it also forbids Terry P. Edwards's *The
Mercenary's Manual.*

Attitudes toward the censorship vary. The majority Afrikaner
middle class is pleased with it, although some Afrikaans authors
like the novelist André Brink have discovered that they can be

banned like anyone else. Intellectuals of British background are
infuriated with it and deeply ashamed of it, although none
entertains hopes that it will soon be done away with. The booksellers, obliged to tread carefully, consulting *Jacobsen's Index*
every step of the way, deplore it both as bad for the trade in
general and as a costly bore. But some booksellers have grown
shrewd in defying the Directorate, at least for the brief time it
takes for a questionable book to be unloaded on the docks and the
Directorate to be informed by the local committee that the book
should be scrutinized for undesirability. The Cape Town booksellers rush the copies off the dock and sell as many as possible
before the Directorate can act. Thus one enterprising bookstore
in Cape Town got off fifty copies of Styron's *Sophie's Choice*
before the censors could get through it and, arriving at pages
496–98, forbid it.

Banned South African authors, deprived by the Publications
Act of any local readership, complain that their British and
American publishers let them down by supinely accepting the
censorship. One embattled novelist has asked, "Why don't American publishers protest more strongly when their books are banned
here, even though sales might amount to only a couple of hundred
copies?" I'm afraid the last part of the question answers the first
part. But sometimes publishers go to bat for their books, the way
the Cape Town representative of a British house recently did.
A historical novel of theirs, *Now God Be Thanked,* by John
Masters, was banned, presumably for a persuasive scene of deflora-
tion (pages 320–26), although the novel's touching on the military
screw-ups incident to the British First World War can't have
endeared it either. The publisher's representative journeyed to
Pretoria and argued the book's case before the Publications
Appeal Board, pointing out that the novel was the first volume of
a projected trilogy and that it seemed unfair to ban a work
destined to run to over two thousand pages because seven of them
delivered a sexual scene. The Appeal Board was persuaded and
lifted the ban.

Some South Africans have allowed themselves to hope that the
administration of Prime Minister Botha will gradually loosen the
censorship, in practice if not in theory. They point to several
successful appeals and reversals in 1979 and 1980: Irwin Shaw's

The Top of the Hill was cleared, together with Pynchon's *Gravity's Rainbow,* Jacqueline Susann's *The Valley of the Dolls,* Gordimer's *A World of Strangers,* Tennessee Williams's *A Street-car Named Desire,* Alan Sillitoe's *Saturday Night and Sunday Morning,* and James Jones's *From Here to Eternity.* Even *New Approaches to Sex and Marriage,* by John E. Eichenlaub, M.D., may now circulate. But other citizens of the Republic, noting the undiminished power of the Afrikaner majority and the traditional rigidity of its outlook, despair of change. "It's a Calvinist country," observed one Johannesburg skeptic. Sitting on the time bomb of revolutionary racial violence, the heirs of the Dutch pioneers continue worrying about the threat of vibrators and outré sexual images, devoting that energy to literal-minded acts of classification that could be spent on social reform before it is too late.

Literary Biography
and Its Pitfalls

The problem for any biographer of an imaginative writer is that writers pursue their mystery by telling great resounding inventions, or lies. The more important of these are called novels, plays, and poems; the less important, letters, prefaces, memoirs, journals, and diaries, and we can add essays and travel books as well. When an amateur or a literalist gets hold of any of these and, avid to write a biography of their author, pores over them with care, look out.

What we actually know about Shakespeare as a person can go on a 3 × 5 card without crowding. But the writings confidently telling his life story and delineating his personality, morals, temper, and character would fill moving vans. The comic and pathetic distance between fact and fantasy is the subject of Samuel Schoenbaum's *Shakespeare's Lives,* a book which will delight the sophisticated, outrage the sentimental, and instruct everyone who reads.

Beginning with a recital of all we know about the man Shakespeare—little more than that he was born in Stratford, married a pregnant local woman, went to London, wrote poems and plays there, made quite a bit of money, and finally returned to Stratford—Schoenbaum goes on to survey 354 years of myth-manufacture designed to flesh out these meager data and in the process to supply "The National Poet" with a moral personality appropriate to the mythmaker's idea of the dignity of literature.

Schoenbaum examines the accretions of legend in the seventeenth century; and then the gestures toward responsible biography beginning in the eighteenth, with the simultaneous development of the traffic in fake relics—many of them imputed to that True Cross of a mulberry tree in Shakespeare's alleged garden, now cut up into thousands of snuffboxes, little chests, door-stops, and pipe-tampers—and the forgeries of Shakespeare documents by William Henry Ireland (preposterous) and John Payne Collier (cunning). He examines the motives and results of romantic and Victorian sentimentalizing of The Bard; anatomizes Baconian, Oxfordian, and similar heresies; and finally celebrates the establishment of documentary biography—E. K. Chambers is the hero —in the twentieth century. Along the way he introduces us to scores of eccentrics, drunks, spirit mediums, cryptanalysts, frauds, losers, and plain fools. The scene is as lively as a Dickens novel.

Like all good scholarly books about literature—and there aren't many—Schoenbaum's is something more than it seems. F. O. Matthiessen's *American Renaissance* was apparently an essay in literary analysis and the history of ideas: actually it was a moving personal testament of faith in American liberalism. Northrop Frye's *Fearful Symmetry* purports to be "A Study of William Blake": actually it is a brilliant personal deposition about theory of knowledge. Schoenbaum's book seems to be a history of Shakespeare idolatry and a disclosure of the pitfalls awaiting those who try to write literary biography without a grown-up's sense of evidence. But actually it is a satire which uses "scholarship" only as its medium, the way a poet uses metaphor and cadence and a painter line and color. In the early eighteenth century, before there was such a thing as "English scholarship," it would have taken the form of Swift's *Tale of a Tub*.

The butts of Schoenbaum's satire are numerous. Social snobbery is one of the funniest. Animating those who devote their lives to arguing that the plays must have been written by Lord Bacon or the Earl of Oxford is the assumption—belonging, ironically enough, not to the socially stratified eighteenth century but to the assertively egalitarian nineteenth and twentieth—that the writer of great works ought to be a fairly classy person, like Lord Lytton, say, or Sir Walter Scott. How could a grammar-school product write *Hamlet* or *King Lear?* Impossible. Hence the necessity of finding an aristocratic and thus admirable author. If the author can be associated in any way with royalty—didn't Shakespeare once (it is said) pick up Queen Elizabeth's glove for her?—so much the better. According to one such theorist, the plays are so good that only James I could have written them. King James himself was the real poet who used the nom de plume

Shakespeare. King James was brilliant, and the greatest king ever to occupy the British throne. Who else even among royalty, in his time, would have possessed the talent to write Shakespeare's works? Is the person reasoning this way some mean little British snob, some sniveling jumped-up Victorian worshipper of the aristocracy? No, he is Malcolm X, and he is putting his mind to the Shakespeare problem while confined in a prison in Massachusetts.

Another target of Schoenbaum's satire is the incapacity of most people—including many who imagine they have something to contribute to the interpretation of literature—to read except with a dogged literalmindedness. "My mistress's eyes are nothing like the sun," says Shakespeare (apparently) in Sonnet 130:

> Coral is far more red than her lips' red;
> If snow be white, why then her breasts are dun;
> If hairs be wires, black wires grow on her head.

Faced with these lines, one William Jordan posits in 1861 that this girl must be a "mulatto or quadroon"—those brown breasts, that kinky hair.

A century later, Ivor Brown, noticing all the images of "ulcers, abcesses, boils, and plague sores" in Shakespeare's work of the early seventeenth century, suggests—what could be more reasonable?—that "in the early years of the century Shakespeare himself suffered from a severe attack of staphylococcic infection and was plagued with recurrent boils and even worse distresses of the blood and skin." Sonnet 78 speaks of an "alien pen." Aha, concludes one nineteenth-century critic: the Rival Poet must be a foreigner, doubtless an Italian, very likely Torquato Tasso, in fact.

To the eighteenth-century critic Charles Gildon the reason Shakespeare provided *Hamlet* with the ghost scene is that while writing it he was also staring at the charnel house in Stratford churchyard. He knows so much about Italy, say Charles Armitage Brown, that he must have traveled there, especially to Verona to get inspiration and local color for *Romeo and Juliet*. Act IV of *King Lear* must have been written while the Bard was actually pacing the Dover Cliffs.

This sort of imbecile literalness belongs, of course, not merely to a past that didn't know any better, that still believed in God, that knew nothing of double entry bookkeeping, etc. It is exactly what lies behind silly, pretentious, illiterate sensations like Velikovsky's *Worlds in Collision* or James W. Mavor's *Voyage to Atlantis*. These operate on the assumption (shared, of course, by the poor unschooled reader) that literature is documentary, that if the Old Testament or Plato says that something happened, it must have happened. Any day now someone will start excavating in England, seeking the location of Alexander Pope's Cave of Spleen (*The Rape of the Lock*, IV, 11–88).

By numerous comic-sad examples Schoenbaum exposes the domination of three centuries of literary understanding by the childish notion that literature is openly self-expressive and sincere. Since what we want is an honest and genteel and high-minded person named Shakespeare, and since there's nothing in the biographical facts to supply one, we have to make one up out of the writings. The result is that during the nineteenth century, as Schoenbaum says, "The divinity of Jesus was rather less universally acknowledged than that of the Bard." This assumed simple one-to-one correspondence between the non-literary identity of the author and his management of conventional symbols on a page is a superstition which has entered Shakespearian biography everywhere, and it would be interesting to launch a deep inquiry into why most human beings seem to require this belief—is it to persuade themselves that in real life duplicity is as rare?

Are many of the sonnets undeniably homoerotic? Then they, perhaps, may be allowed to be conventional and not entirely a registration of Shakespeare's experience. But the plays surely—especially the good ones—are sincerely self-expressive. But what about the nasty ones like *Troilus and Cressida* and *Titus Andronicus?* Well, they must be mistakes of some sort, or at least expressions of the National Poet in the dumps (everyone gets depressed from time to time), out of which he finally arose to give us, all passion spent, the lovely Late Romances. It's clear that all along he had our comfort and well-being in view.

In *Literature and Sincerity*, Henri Peyre points out that "Victor Hugo . . . wrote his poems describing the winter during the summer months, those which conjured up vernal raptures during the autumnal season, and . . . his most heartrending pieces on the death of his daughter . . . alternated, in their dates of composition, with songs of sensual love." In the same way

"Palestrina composed his funeral laments, supposed to have been inspired by his wife's death, not as he was afflicted by his bereavement but just as, eight months after her death, he had arranged to marry a widow, enriched by the fur trade, at substantial benefit to himself."

Schoenbaum is instructive too on "the mirror effect" in Shakespearian biographical procedures, which tend, he finds, "toward oblique self-portraiture." He recalls "once mentioning this pattern to . . . John Crow on the porch of the British Museum, and he reminded me that Desmond McCarthy had said somewhere that trying to work out Shakespeare's personality was like looking at a very dark glazed picture in the National Portrait Gallery: at first you see nothing, then you begin to recognize features, and then you realize that they are your own." To the Romantic poets, Shakespeare is a god; to Carlyle, a prophet; to the Victorians, a property-owner and recipient of interest, but with unexceptionable morals; to Frank Harris, he is a sensualist; to Oscar Wilde, a pederast.

A schoolmaster writing a life of Shakespeare will generally conclude that Shakespeare must have been a schoolmaster. Lawyers writing lives of Shakespeare unerringly find that he was a lawyer. "In *Sergeant Shakespeare* (1949) Duff Cooper develops an idea that first came to him amid the gas shells and stench of the Flanders trenches during the First World War. Shakespeare . . . enlisted in the army for service in the Low Countries . . . and was promoted to the rank of sergeant." Schoenbaum concludes: "The biographer of Haig goes on to demonstrate Shakespeare's martial experience from episodes and allusions in the plays."

Schoenbaum is entertaining as he analyzes this "familiar pattern of self-projection," but in his demonstration there is ample pathos as well. What he shows is the sad inability of the mind to operate reasonably, to overcome its built-in impulse to self-aggrandizement even when performing "objective" inquiries. If like other satirists Schoenbaum smells out knaves and fools everywhere, he is at pains to understand the sad, deceived creatures he ridicules. Even while he's gleefully exposing his gallery of sentimentalists, paranoids, liars, forgers, fabricators, and fantasists, he is appreciating their pathetic motives: their lust for meaning; their desire that literature make some sort of useful sense; their hope that human happiness and illumination will ensue if only Shakespeare's full secret can be disclosed—surely this man has something to *tell* us. In short, their touching faith in literature, which seems entirely consistent with their lack of faith in imaginative invention.

We expect satirists to imply some moral norm, as it has been called, against which we are to measure the deviations they depict. Schoenbaum celebrates intelligence and discipline and self-distrust whenever they make their rare appearances in the persons of Edmond Malone, Halliwell Phillipps, the Wallaces, and Chambers. Their achievements as scholars, antiquaries, and skeptical biographers help redeem the otherwise ludicrous history of Shakespeare biography. It is not wholly a Paradise of Fools.

Schoenbaum's book is a model for literary scholarship, and by that I mean that in addition to being learned and sparsely annotated it is frank, unpretentious, skeptical, ironic, and vastly amusing, with not a single dull page among its 838. Nor has Schoenbaum repressed his personality in the interests of either pseudo-objectivity or "good taste":

> Away from the academy, whether in the Bar de l'Atlantique of the S.S. *France* or in the shadow of the Moorish wall in Algeciras or on an Intourist bus on the road to Sevastopol, the professor of English (once his identity has been guessed by fellow holiday-makers) will be asked, as certainly as day follows night, "Did Shakespeare really write those plays?"
>
> He will do well to nod assent and avoid explanation, for nothing he says will erase suspicions fostered for over a century by amateurs who have yielded to the dark power of the anti-Stratfordian obsession. One thought perhaps offers a crumb of redeeming comfort: the energy absorbed by the mania might otherwise have gone into politics.

For some reason, literal-mindedness in the interpretation of biographical data seems especially prevalent among physicians and surgeons, with the result that over the years members of the medical faculty have covered themselves with about as much glory interpreting literature as literary critics have earned curing impetigo. Confronting *Hamlet* sixty years ago, Dr. Ernest Jones betrayed a sense of evidence and a capacity for reasoning so shaky as to be frightening. "The intrinsic evidence from the play," he wrote, "decisively shows that Shakespeare projected into it his inmost soul." *Decisively shows:* imagine allowing a mind like that access to your varicose veins. More recently another practitioner entirely misses the comic irony in a letter of Samuel Johnson's, misunderstands Johnson to say the opposite of what he's saying, and then promotes this misapprehension into a whole solemn essay, brought to the attention of the entire medical fraternity in the *Journal of Nervous and Mental Disease* for August, 1962.

William B. Ober, M.D., has caught the flame. He is a histopathologist from New Jersey, and he has sated his need to perform biographical interpretation by writing *Boswell's Clap and Other Essays: Medical Analyses of Literary Men's Afflictions.* As a representative of a profession which for ten years has been stumped to diagnose a mild tropical disease I picked up somewhere in the Near East, even with my person and its effluents available for empirical scrutiny, he proposes to diagnose and interpret the ailments, or causes of death, of a number of prominent wits and authors running all the way back to Socrates (d. 339 B.C.) and Rochester (d. 1680), and to diagnose by means of documentary attestations, gossip, memoirs, letters, biographies, philosophic dialogues, poems, satires, and other rhetorical phenomena. Like Ivor Brown diagnosing Shakespeare's loathsome infections from the "plague sores" in his plays, in his attempt Dr. Ober is not intellectually compelling.

There's nothing wrong with his scholarship and learning, which, all things considered, are impressive. It's his power to use knowledge that's weak. Consider his essay "Did Socrates Die of Hemlock Poisoning?" (He concludes he did, and speculates that Plato refrained from depicting him throwing up or going into convulsions because "he wanted no undignified details.") Dr. Ober alludes to Jacques Louis David's neo-classic painting *The Death of Socrates* and recognizes that since David was not present at the scene his painting does not "pretend to verisimilitude." All very well, if very simple, so far. But as the reader goes on his eyebrows begin to ascend, for Dr. Ober is next asking, why did David depict as so large the prison chamber in which Socrates is reaching for the hemlock? Why did he make it large enough to hold comfortably a dozen or so people, plus the condemned? "To be sure," he writes, "we do not have floor plans of the jail at Athens, but as a general rule rooms in Greek buildings and houses were smaller than rooms used for similar functions today. . . ." Furthermore, "It is difficult for anyone familiar with prisons in any period to imagine a cell commodious enough to hold the prisoner, the jailer, and 11 or 14 witnesses. A possible solution is that the execution took place in a special chamber. . . ." If, like Dr. Ober, you can't distinguish between history-painting and ex post facto photography, you'd better leave the arts alone. The solution to the non-problem raised by Dr. Ober is of course that David gave Socrates ample architectural space because that's a standard late-eighteenth-century way of conferring dignity upon a noble character arrested in a noble moment.

That's a sample of the way Dr. Ober frequently goes wrong: his mind does one thing while imagining it's doing something else. But his most common technique for getting things wrong is to assume that works of fiction, including poems, constitute all-but-direct autobiographical registrations. Thus Lord Rochester is said to have "painted directly from life" in his poem "The Imperfect Enjoyment," actually a standard, traditional late-seventeenth-century comic-porno complaint about premature ejaculation. Ignoring its taking place in heroic couplets (surely odd!), Dr. Ober conceives the *ejaculatio praecox* to be actual, and goes on to explain: "Caught in a conflict between female and male object-choice, Rochester's psyche demanded retreat to infantile behavior in the form of premature ejaculation."

(VOICE FROM BACK OF CLASSROOM Dr. Ober?
DR. OBER Yes?
VOICE I didn't know infants ejaculated prematurely.)

The same illiterate use of evidence could diagnose Robert Graves's trouble as priapism. Look at "Down, Wanton, Down."

Dr. Ober is at his worst psychoanalyzing authors across great divides of time, invoking the most tired metaphors of early twentieth-century mechanics and hydraulics like "repression," "bursting out," and "emerging into consciousness." D. H. Lawrence comes out badly, stigmatized as a "latent homosexual" purely on the evidence of fictional passages. Dr. Ober lacks sufficient literary instinct to know that a person of imagination, let alone genius, is a latent everything. Shakespeare is a latent Iago, not to mention a latent Weird Sister. Keats, reported to "conceive of a billiard ball that it may have a sense of delight from its own roundness, smoothness, volubility, and the rapidity of its motion," is a latent billiard ball. A corrective to Dr. Ober's silliness is Robert Conquest's spoof critical article, "*Lady Chatterley's Lover* in the Light of Dürfian Psychology," which infers from Lawrence's imagery his "repressed wish to be an airman."

Not all Dr. Ober's essays are ridiculous. Some are pointless, like the one on Thomas Shadwell, which conjectures that he died not of an overdose of opium but of a heart attack. The one on the three mad eighteenth-century poets, Collins, Cowper, and Smart, is better: it does discriminate their three kinds of distress and even offers a just appraisal of Smart's poem *A Song to David*. The essay on Boswell, with its brilliant title for which Dr. Ober deserves praise, lacks point but does perform the service of tabulating Boswell's outcrops of urethritis during his life—he suffered nineteen separate attacks of gonorrhea. The Boswell essay also contains two valuable paragraphs on the eighteenth-century condom and its deployment.

In dealing with Boswell, Dr. Ober is on fairly firm ground, for he is working from the journal entries of a man devoted to getting things down with "authentic precision"; he is not working with satires or lyric poems. With Swinburne, on the other hand, poems are the evidence, and only the poems seeming to involve "masochism" are invoked; the others are ignored. I'm not saying that Swinburne was not wiggy. I'm saying that the poems he wrote are no way of ascertaining his condition, let alone "diagnosing" it. To Dr. Ober Keats's poems are equally autobiographical. Thus the "Ode to the Nightingale" contains "imagery and ideational content" betokening the effects of opium on its author. Dr. Ober doesn't know, or can't understand, that in the early as well as late nineteenth century when you want to sanction a far-out fiction you report it as a dream. Thus "Kubla Khan." There's a crucial intellectual and even "scientific" difference between saying, as Dr. Ober does, "Like Coleridge, DeQuincey, and Crabbe, [Francis] Thompson suffered from nightmares" and saying that they *said* they suffered from nightmares and sometimes wrote about them. Anyone who doesn't see the difference simply must abstain from literary scholarship and criticism.

Dr. Ober likes to drop names like Xenophon and Mozart and Pirandello to show that despite his barbarous diction and insecure grammar and clumsy sentences and pretentious jargon he's really a man of broad "culture," not just the hick technologist we took him for. His hurling himself all unready into humanistic criticism is a bit like Dr. Albert Schweitzer's not being content to cure yaws: he had to come on as a philosopher and a Bach organist as well. It seems a syndrome—as Dr. Ober would say—in the medical profession, and we need a study, based on the sort of evidence his performance provides, of the social and cultural insecurity there. I'm ready to believe that Dr. Ober is an able pathologist, but as a perceiver of what writers do, and as an interpreter of literature, he's a quack.

Nabokov as "Comparatist"

The traditional non-book is large and full of pictures; Valdimir Nabokov's *Notes on Prosody* is small and full of tables, numerals, and funny words. These "notes on English and Russian tetrameters" originally—and appropriately—served as an appendix to Nabokov's translation-edition of Pushkin's *Eugene Onegin*. Detached now from the only context that could give them meaning, Nabokov's observations on Russian and English verse structure flagrantly lack point. Gertrude Stein is reported to have told Hemingway that remarks are not literature; someone should tell publishers that an appendix is not a book. If this volume were titled *Pyrrhic Substitution in "Eugene Onegin"* and emitted by a sincere old-lady candidate for a doctor's degree from a bad American university press, how we should rail. How we should mock its pedantry and pity its insignificance. And yet for all the energy and bustle Nabokov musters, and for all the undeniable gaiety of his performance, his demonstration leads exactly to this small point—that Pushkin is a master of pyrrhic substitution.

But pedantry (at least of the standard kind) and insignificance cannot be accepted by Nabokov as his *métier*: everything must be twisted into at least a simulacrum of idiosyncrasy and portent. Distressed like everyone else by the inadequacy of the received English prosodic terms, Nabokov has programmatically obscured matters further by contriving his own terminology. "I have been forced," he says with an irony which becomes more apparent as we press forward, "to invent a simple little terminology of my own." Thus what a mere graduate student, in the simplicity of his heart, would call a pyrrhic foot Nabokov calls a "scudded foot," or a "scud "; what everyone else has for centuries been calling a trochaic foot, or in a predominantly iambic poem even an "inversion of stress," Nabokov calls a "tilt." Whatever their necessity, these terms have at least the merit of comedy, and Nabokov, wit that he is, revels in manipulating this mock-pedagogic language and thus playing out the role of farcical pedagogue, as he has earlier delighted to play literate nympholept (*Lolita*) and mad scholarly annotator (*Pale Fire*). Here, as if we were listening still to the wildly intelligent but fatally disordered zany presiding over *Pale Fire*, we hear of "semiscuds" and "split tilts"; we are vouch-safed words like "scuddable" and fruity formulations like "a surge of scuds."

Sometimes the idiom of the bird-watcher, or even of the lepi-dopterist himself, takes over, as when we are invited to scrutinize "the rare 'long tilt.'" This calling ordinary things by funny or magical names has always been part of Nabokov's happy stock in trade when he has appeared in his various comic guises: in *Pale Fire* it is the lowly blackhead which is elevated to mock-consequence by being denominated a comedo. But when, impa-tient of the ingenuousness of his predecessors in prosody, Nabokov finds it necessary to speak of the "false spondee' and the "false pyrrhic," he conducts us into something very like the world of Sick Fiction, the place where the farcical Guru-Daddy at the end of *Candy* assures Candy that what she is about to experience may resemble—deceptively—"the so-called 'orgasm.'" We have had lots of Camp humor in the past few years: this is the first time we have had Camp prosody. It is as if William Beckford had essayed a treatise on metallurgy or Ronald Firbank a manual of operating-room practice.

And yet for the reader willing to plough through this wild heap of wit Nabokov provides compensations. When he tires of being cute, his awareness of metrical context is sensitive and instructive. As he says, "An iambic foot cannot be illustrated by a word unless that word is part of a specific iambic line." And valuable too is his brief discourse on the conventions and implications—largely whimsical or burlesque—that have attended the iambic tetrameter line in English. In Russian it became in the nineteenth century the staple medium for serious verse, the equivalent in English of iambic pentameter or in French of the syllabic hexameter. Why, on the other hand, does the English tetrameter imply so readily a vacation from the rigors of heroic sobriety and serious commit-ment? One thinks of Prior, Gay, and Swift. Nabokov rightly lays a large part of the blame on the enormous popularity and staying power of Butler's *Hudibras,* which remained popular way past its artistic deserts because it was politically gratifying. It transformed a line capable of emotional range in the hands of Surrey, Shakespeare (Sonnet 145), and Milton into a vehicle more fit for, as Nabokov says, "boisterous and obscure topical satire, the dismally comic, mock-heroic poem, the social allusion sustained through hundreds of rhymed couplets, the academic tour de force. . . ." Although Nabokov forgets one fairly recent master of the tetrameter—Yeats, not mentioned in the book—his point is important, even if it is a little hard on eighteenth-century English poetry.

Prosodically the Augustan Age is Nabokov's black beast: it is always "the pedestrian eighteenth century" or "that most inartistic of centuries." But this automatic, old-fashioned disvaluing of Augustan poetry is all based, apparently, on the eighteenth-century performance in tetrameter verse. This is about as fair as judging twentieth-century poetry by its performance in, say, the limerick or the clerihew or the double-dactyl and then condemning the "century" (what's that?) for lacking emotional and aesthetic depth and range. Everyone knows that in the eighteenth century the tetrameter line was conventional for songs, fables, and various kinds of drollery; and that it was a line with a much wider spectrum of conventions, and strictly decasyllabic pentameter of the *Dunciad, The Vanity of Human Wishes,* and *The Borough,* that poets of that moment wielded with such memorable grace, wit, and power. All this is to be misrepresented because Nabokov, urged by his ambition to "compare" across literatures, must collect some English tetrameters to compare with Russian ones.

And it is here that we are brought face to face with the hazards of the "comparative" method in criticism and literary understanding. The comparative method has enjoyed considerable vogue in the United States ever since the Second World War, which brought here numerous brilliant young people adept in more than one European language. These were sufficient to staff numerous university departments of Comparative Literature and to perform some impressive cross-national critical operations. But these "comparatists," as some call them, are now aging, and barring another flux of highly educated refugees to this country, they are unlikely to be replaced. Although not strictly an academic, Nabokov participates in the comparatist tradition, and his dual focus on English and Russian tetrameters offers a way of seeing what's wrong with the method.

The fact is that literatures, at least when regarded not thematically but technically, are not comparable, not if we know a language sufficiently to have become really adept in its idiom and its nuances. Perhaps novels in different languages can be talked about comparatively since to most critics scrutiny of their finest textures seems a less pressing obligation than consideration of their characters, themes, architecture, and social-political leanings. Consider what Nabokov does when he ventures technical comparisons of poems even within one literature: he compares apples with camels. He offers a few lines of—among other poems—Johnson's *On the Death of Dr. Robert Levet,* Keats's *The Eve of St. Mark,* and Tennyson's *In Memoriam* as somehow related prosodically and somehow all prosodically relevant to Pushkin's verse-making. But these English examples are only very dubiously comparable in texture, for one is a domestic elegy in a version of hymn-stanza replete with overtones of the English Protestant sense of duty; another is a romance in couplets bearing entirely different, pseudo-medieval implications deriving from the "folk"-dimension of Bishop Percy's ballad revival and its prosody; the last is a significantly redundant personal elegy in a very special stanza which determines powerfully the special metrical techniques of that one poem. All three poems are "written in iambic tetrameter," but that's the sort of formulation we might hear in a high-school classroom. It is of little use if we are even minimally interested in the details of poetry. To be told by Nabokov of the *In Memoriam* extract that "I have chosen this as a particularly brilliant example of scudding (based mainly on monosyllables and partly owing to the repetition of a specific split tilt)" is to have the rhythm described but not interpreted. It is to abandon criticism for science, or rather pseudo-science. Prosodic talk ends as a mere pastime unless it finally locates specific links in specific poems between semantic and metrical meanings. Nabokov tells us of *Eugene Onegin* that "There are several stanzas containing as many as five ["second-foot scudders": read "pyrrhic feet in the second position"]; and one stanza (One: XXI, Onegin's arrival at the theatre) breaks the record with six." But what we want is not the record-keeping of the hobbyist but the criticism of the expert. Nabokov does not tell us what relation there is between Pushkin's sense of Onegin at the theater and a spate of unaccented syllables. If there is none, the prosody is accidental, insignificant, or inept, and critically undiscussible.

Nabokov's elaborate comparative and "taxonomical" procedures do yield some conclusions no one is likely to quarrel with. He finds that Russian prosody is different from English because the languages are quite different. Russian abounds in polysyllabic words having only a single accent. Russian poets are thus able to make omission of stress ("scudding") a common technical device. English poets, on the other hand, managing a language rich in monosyllables, have developed more fully than the Russians what old-fashioned people would want to call spondaic substitution. But we have always known that the two languages, not to mention the two cultures, are not the same. We would expect their poetries to be different.

Actually even in what appears to be one language, different poetries are not close enough to be comparable in the Nabokov way except for purposes of the coarsest kind of description. The idioms and genres, and therefore the prosodies, of Donne and Arnold—two of Nabokov's authors of "tetrameters"—are comparable only by the most generous courtesy. It is all so much harder than Nabokov makes it out to be, with his amateur's unsteady tone, now airy and inconsequential, now perspiring and statistical. Early on he says that his researches have turned up not "a single work that treated English iambics—particularly the tetrameter—on a taxonomical and comparative-literature basis," and here he imagines that he is scorning the past instead of saluting its admirable sense of the uniqueness of separate languages and its wise disinclination to press specious and irrelevant comparisons.

But to say this much risks breaking a butterfly-collector on a wheel. An appendix, no matter how skilfully excised, preserved, and displayed, remains an appendix; whimsy, no matter how artfully disguised as scholarship or criticism, remains whimsy. And it is the whimsicality of Nabokov's approach to poetic technique, his constant pursuit of the *outré,* his late-romantic impressionism and idiosyncrasy, that finally are the most striking things about this little volume. He has always enjoyed parody, and what we have here is like a parody of an academic dissertation or a text-book. The genre he is working in seems close to that of Pound's *ABC of Reading,* but if in Pound's work we catch the tones of an angry midwestern Populist of the late nineteenth century, Nabokov's spiritual ancestry goes even further back, extending through Lewis Carroll and Thomas Love Peacock to Laurence Sterne himself.

Can Graham Greene Write English?

A while ago the *New Statesman* invited readers to impersonate various contemporary writers making statements on their art. One of the winning entrants did Graham Greene:

> "How is it, Mr. Greene, you're able to turn out novels so regularly?"
> "Oh, that's easy. I just make each one a little worse than the one before."

Scandalous, to be sure. But that does register a widespread feeling about Greene. It might be thought that it's only the current absence of Faulkner and Waugh and even Hemingway that makes Greene seem a novelist of consequence instead of, say, a fourth-rate Conrad. Is Greene not really a writer whose conceptions, plots, and style, are, if the truth were told, as seedy as his famous settings? Can he construct? Can he imagine plausible characters and deliver believable images of their behavior in an efficient style? Is not his melodramatic, Manichean vision of life less a sign that he is "a Catholic novelist" than evidence of a coarse intelligence? Are not his psychological studies of fear and guilt forced and fraudulent? Is there the qualitative difference he imagines between his novels and his "entertainments"? Does not his instinct for spy and detective adventure betoken a literary sense considerably short of subtle? Finally, can he really write English? These are the troubling questions that arise whenever Greene is put forward as a major writer. They arise again when we open *Ways of Escape,* the second volume of his memoirs.

The first volume, *A Sort of Life,* appeared a decade ago. It dealt with his life only up to his twenties. Here we have the rest of it, from 1929 to 1978. As Greene admits, "rather less than half" the

book has been cobbled together from the introductions he's provided for the collected edition of his works. These bits are now
arranged chronologically and bridged by new passages. There is
thus an air of pastiche and incoherence about the whole, although
the parts are often attractive.

"I grew clever at evasion," Greene wrote of his youth in *A Sort
of Life*. "Truancy was impressed as the pattern of my life." (More
later about muddy metaphors like *was impressed*.) This action of
repeated escaping is now promoted to the theme, or pseudo-theme,
of *Ways of Escape*. Travel is an escape from boredom and England.
Novel-writing is an escape from newspaper work. Film-reviewing,
an escape from novel-writing. The short story is an escape from
longer fiction. Playwriting is an escape from filmscript writing,
etc. Here escape is like other big "themes" in Greene: it seems to
illuminate and unify, but actually it's just another way of escaping—escaping precision. As in: "A friendship can be a way of
escape, just as much as writing or travel, from the everyday rou-
tine. . . ." (I can understand how travel can be considered a form
of escape, even if that idea is more complicated than Greene is
able to register; but I can't see how a writer escapes anything by
writing. Writing is supposed to be what he does. You see what a
morass we're stuck in here?)

But if Greene's run-through of his literary career is dominated
by this kind of thematic hokiness aspiring to an ultimate vagueness, when he forgets his fake unifying theme of escape (and what
an adolescent idea that is, really), he offers some interesting things.
Like his account of libeling Shirley Temple. Her attorneys
brought an action which closed down forever the London magazine *Night and Day,* which might have become the British *New
Yorker*. (In his review of *Wee Willie Winkie* Greene had suggested that the moppet's manner was that of an experienced little
tart. "A Gross Outrage"—*London Times*.) Valuable too are his
accounts of anti-colonial uprisings he has seen, in Malaya, Kenya,
and Vietnam. His interpretation of what happened at Dien Bien
Phu is masterly. So is his version of being deported from Puerto
Rico as a onetime college Communist during the days when the
McCarran Act was still without loopholes. He is startling and
funny on Batista's Havana, in its day porn capital of the Free

World, startling and not so funny on Papa Doc's Haiti. There are hints that he's been engaged in more espionage than we have known about, for sometimes he has the greatest trouble explaining his motives for being in a certain crucial place at a certain crucial time, and has to fall back on his "escape" justification. He is pleasant and perceptive about the fondness of American Foreign Service officers abroad for reactionaries and militarists. He provides a warm portrait of Evelyn Waugh: seeing past the satirist and stage Tory, he dwells on Waugh's charity, bravely, loyalty. And he ends with a characteristically melodramatic account of "the Other"— an imposter calling himself "Graham Greene" who pops up all over the world, introducing himself as the famous writer, making time with women, and borrowing money. Greene's closing words give off a final whiff of evasiveness, lodging with us the suspicion that perhaps his problem is that he has the soul of a spy. "I found myself shaken by a metaphysical doubt. Had *I* been the imposter all the time? Was I the Other?"

Who is he anyhow? He seems by this time so conspicuously an international figure, with his Harry Limes in Vienna and Orient Expresses and Stamboul trains, his travels everywhere, his exotic locales, his residences abroad in Antibes and Anacapri, that it's surprising to be reminded by *Ways of Escape* how intensely British he remains. His mind and psyche were formed by Rider Haggard, *Diary of a Nobody*, and Beatrix Potter; by Hardy and Kipling and Dickens; and by Wordsworth, astonishingly present here by frequent quotation and allusion. Greene's subject is justice, and he comes from the very British world of Blackstone and Fielding, Cobbett and *The Secret Agent* and Orwell. He writes in that quintessentially British genre, the detective story, only once-removed.

His frequent success with the nasty has tended to conceal the terrible truth that he's seldom written carefully. The very first sentence of *A Sort of Life* offers a freshman howler: "An autobiography is only 'a sort of life'—it may contain less errors of fact than a biography, but it is of necessity more selective. . . ." For *less,* read *fewer*. But Greene's winning quality is his modesty. He knows he doesn't write very well, although he thinks his main trouble is ineffective metaphor and blurred visual perception. It is true that his metaphors are very often skewed and vague, but actually his main handicap is his inability to master English syntax and the fine points of English sentence structure.

Like many another OK writer, his publishers have oversold him. The jacket copy of *Ways of Escape* proclaims that Greene is "the most distinguished living writer in the English language." That's not merely hard on Philip Larkin, Kingsley Amis, Christopher Isherwood, Gore Vidal, Tom Wolfe, and dozens of other impressive managers of the English sentence. It's impertinent and illiterate, and the evidence to refute it is so palpable that it's embarrassing. Actually Greene's writing is so patently improvable that it could serve pedagogic purposes, as follows.

EXAMINATION

English 345: Expository Writing (Intermediate)
(One hour. Write in ink on one side of the paper only.)

The following passages have been written by Mr. Graham
Greene in his book *Ways of Escape*. They have been passed by
his editors and approved by his publishers, who assert that
Graham Greene is "the most distinguished living writer in the
English language." Rewrite each passage as indicated.

---

1. *Correct the grammar:*

   a. "I am not sure that I detect much promise in [*Orient
      Express*], except in the character of Colonel Hartep, the
      Chief of Police, whom I suspect survived into the world
      of Aunt Augusta and *Travels with My Aunt*."

   b. "In my hotel, the Ofloffson . . . , there were three guests
      besides myself: the Italian manager of the casino and an
      old American artist and his wife—a gentle couple whom
      I cannot deny bore some resemblance to Mr. and Mrs. Smith
      of [*The Comedians*]."

   c. "The day of the Lee-Enfield and the Maxim gun were more
      favorable to the European than those of the dive-bomber
      and the Bren."

2. *Shift the misplaced modifier to the right position:*

   "It is only since the Revolution that the Pole, I believe, has
   changed his habit of only communicating on certain major
   feast days."

3. *Eliminate the jargon:*

   "What the [Polish] authorities had not realized was the
   effectiveness of this play [Eliot's *Murder in the Cathedral*], at
   this moment in time, in modern dress. . . ."

(over)

4. *Suggest alternative phrasing to eliminate the clichés:*

   a. "The game . . . was not worth the candle."
   b. "These men [at Dien Bien Phu] were aware of what they resembled—sitting ducks."
   c. "Resettlement was a turn of the screw of discomfort."
   d. "A Gurkha patrol worked by the compass and not by paths. It moved as the crow flies."
   e. "For me to describe Brighton was really a labor of love. . . ."
   f. "The sudden arrival in 1931 down a muddy Gloucestershire lane of a Norwegian poet whom I didn't know from Adam seemed unaccountable. . . ."

5. *Eliminate the awkwardness:*

   "A writer's imagination, like the body, fights against all reason against death."

6. *Eliminate the redundancy:*

   "Next day [in Israel] I met a Burmese officer, a Frenchman, a Swede and a Finn (English was the common language they all spoke)."

7. *Reconstruct the sentence to eliminate excessive prepositions:*

   "Suicide was Scobie's inevitable end; the particular motive of his suicide, to save even God from himself, was the final twist of the screw of his inordinate pride."

8. *Give the sentence a backbone and eliminate the awkwardness:*

   "Some critics have found in [*Travels with My Aunt*] a kind of resumé of my literary career—a scene in Brighton, the journey on the Orient Express—and perhaps a hint of this did come to my mind by the time Aunt Augusta arrived at the Pera Palace, but what struck me with some uneasiness, when I reread the book the other day, were the suggestions I found in it of where the future was going to take me."

   (Be sure your name is on your paper.)

Being Reviewed:
The A. B. M. and Its Theory

Ever since the seventeenth century, when authors began soliciting customers to buy their books and thus confer money and fame on them, vanity and vainglory have been their constant temptation, neglect or contempt their frequent reward. Thus, as Samuel Johnson says in *Rambler* 106,

> No place affords a more striking conviction of the vanity of human hopes than a public library. For who can see the wall crowded on every side by mighty volumes, the works of laborious meditation and accurate inquiry, now scarcely known but by the catalog . . . , without considering how many hours have been wasted in vain endeavors, how often imagination has anticipated the praises of futurity, [and] how many statues have risen to the eye of vanity. . . .

When Johnson came to write *The Lives of the Poets,* one of his themes was the disappointments of authors and the comic-pathetic dynamics of their expectations dashed by the disdain of the world. The scholar Walter Harte is for Johnson a case in point. In 1759 he published an immense book, the *History of Gustavus Adolphus.* "Poor man!" says Johnson. "He left London the day of . . . publication . . . that he might be out of the way of the great praise he was to receive; and he was ashamed to return when he found how ill his book had succeeded." When in the early nineteenth century Isaac D'Israeli compiled a series of anecdotes about writers, he titled it *The Calamities of Authors.* A few items from his index will indicate the tenor:

> *Drayton's* national work, the *Polyolbion,* ill received, and the author greatly dejected
> *Hume,* his literary life how mortified with disappointments
> *Walpole, Horace,* his literary mortifications.

Contemporary writers have their calamities too, and their complaints are legion. Their manuscripts are rejected, sometimes not even with a letter of explanation or criticism. If they do achieve a contract with a publisher, when publication day arrives he swindles them by issuing a tiny pro forma edition, announced at the very bottom of his spring or fall list. He ostentatiously refrains from advertising the book, and his visible contempt for what he has unwillingly published results in no invitations for the author to appear on talk shows or to sign his book at literary fêtes. The final calamity for the author is to pass through crummy discount bookstores and see great piles of his masterpiece stacked up on the remainder tables, marked down from $14.95 to $1.95, and moving sluggishly even then. He will feel worse when he gets home and finds that his contract specifies that he gets no royalty on copies sold at remainder prices. That is the nadir, that discovery.

We should not be ashamed of ourselves if we find these misfortunes essentially comic. After all, no one is obliged to become an author. Every author is, in a sense, showing off; and in the view of the world he has elected a very easy job: he works at his own pace and on his own schedule, supervised by no boss and under no obligation to be nice to people he doesn't like; he pursues his trade comfortably sitting down in private while others are carrying hods or sweating in front of klieg lights while forgetting their lines, or arguing in a courtroom or being squirted with blood at an operating table or being beaten up every Sunday on a football field. The writer has it soft, and his moans must strike the more active part of the world as funny. The news that few authors earn any real money is not likely to strike the great audience as a very sad thing. And news of authors' hardships will always find delighted readers for a further reason, one Alberto Savinio has thought about: "The hatred of writers," he points out, "is universal and everlasting," and it's entirely to be expected: "Why shouldn't someone who *makes a profession of intelligence* be hated? There will be no end to this variation on the class struggle, because men never tire of hating in others what they would like to be and cannot be themselves. And who does not want to be intelligent, or at least to seem so?"

But the most crushing calamity for authors, and the one that gratifies their audience most, is bad reviews. An author's relations with a publisher are largely out of sight, and the relation of his hopes to actuality is secret; but bad reviews broadcast news of his ineptitude to that very world whose admiration he has labored to extort. As Virginia Woolf perceived, what an author is tormented by when confronted with a bad notice is less the damage he fears to his sales than the damage suffered by his social sense. All these years he's been talking about his forthcoming book and coming on as something special before his friends and acquaintances, and suddenly someone announces to the whole country that he's a phony—a slob, actually, lazy and ignorant, pretentious, tasteless, and inept. Woolf probes into the heart of the matter:

> What part [of the author] is affected by [the reviewer's] bite? —what is the true nature of the emotion he causes? That is a complex question: but perhaps we can discover something that will serve as answer by submitting the author to a simple test. Take a sensitive author and place before him a hostile review. Symptoms of pain and anger rapidly develop. Next tell him that nobody save himself will read those abusive remarks. In five or ten minutes the pain which, if the attack had been delivered in public, would have lasted a week and bred bitter rancor, is completely over, the temperature falls; indifference returns. This proves that the sensitive part is the reputation; what the victim feared was the effect of abuse upon the opinion that other people had of him. He is afraid, too, of the effect of abuse upon his purse. But the purse sensibility is in most cases far less highly developed than the reputation sensibility. As for the artist's sensibility—his own opinion of his own work—that is not touched by anything good or bad that the reviewer says about it.

As Woolf sees, the sensitive part is the reputation, and few authors, no matter how grand, rich, and famous, seem immune to some distress when faced with an unfavorable notice. Even Woolf herself, who felt some tremors while waiting for the reviews of *Jacob's Room*—not all of them, only one: "The only review I am anxious about," she tells her journal, "is the one in the *Times Literary Supplement*: not that it will be the most intelligent, but it will be the most read and I can't bear people to see me downed in public." Some authors are so sensitive in their reputation part that in their view a hostile notice implicates in caddishness not just the one who writes it but the editor who prints it. Kingsley Martin, editor of the *New Statesman,* tells of lunching amiably with H. G. Wells and telling him how good it was to see him again. "It happened," says Martin, "that that very week we published a savage review of H. G.'s latest novel—one of a number of pot boilers that he wrote at that time. On Monday morning I found a card from H. G. which began: 'So you really had that stinker up your sleeve when you greeted me so warmly last Tuesday,' and ended by saying that I was a cad." For illuminating the psychology and ethics of the whole business of being reviewed Martin's reply deserves classic status:

My dear H. G.,

With your note in front of me it takes some effort to recall that you are not really the vain and abusive little man that its petulance would suggest. . . .

When I saw you . . . , I was friendly because I felt friendly to H. G., whom I have always admired and to whom I owe a great deal of my mental furniture. I knew nothing of your new book . . .; I did not know to whom it had been sent for review or whether a review had been written. It was not in my mind. Why should it be? I did not actually see the review until it was in page-proof after I had seen you.

But that is not the point. The important question is how you can think that if I had seen the review or known that we were printing an unfavorable review of your book, I would somehow have behaved differently. Do you mean to suggest that because a reviewer had written something unfavorable to you . . . I should therefore cut you when I met you? Or that I should be in tears or blushing from shame? Or what *do* you suggest? Or can it be that you imagine that when I saw that an unfavorable notice of your book had reached the paper I ought to have said "My old friend H. G. Wells will not like this review, and therefore I cannot print this reviewer's honest opinion of his book." If I had done that, I should therefore have blushed when I saw you. . . . What would you say, supposing you had written a review and then the Editor explained that he could not print your criticism because he was a friend of the author or did not like to hurt his feelings?

Martin grasps entirely the principle about the ethics of author-ship enunciated by Johnson over a century and a half earlier: "An author places himself uncalled before the tribunal of criticism, and solicits fame at the hazard of disgrace." (Only genuinely se-cure people can say things like that: consider also Harry Truman's remark about staying out of the kitchen if you can't stand the heat.) But even though in their more lucid moments of moral understanding authors would agree with Johnson, in practice vanity and the affectation of delicate sensibility frequently hustle them into intemperate despair over bad reviews. Tennyson, Woolf reminds us, at one point was so cast down by reviews of his work that he "actually contemplated emigration." More recently May Sarton, novelist and poet, felt herself so damaged by an abusive notice of one of her novels in the *New York Times Book Review* that she suffered something close to a nervous collapse, culmi-nating in a sarcoma of the breast and a mastectomy—"I know that the amount of suppressed rage I have suffered since last fall had to find some way out." She has recorded her year-long agony in *Recovering: A Journal.* Sorry as one is for May Sarton's illness and surgery, it must be said that her book makes an instructive document for the pathologist of literary vanity.

For years May Sarton has chosen to solicit fame by positioning herself uncalled before the tribunal of criticism, and for years the *New Times Book Review* (some tribunal, but let that pass) has been handing down unfavorable verdicts. As she says, "The *Times* has sneered at or attacked every book of mine since *Faithful Are the Wounds.* . . . So the effect of this last public beating was as bad as it was, I think, because it was cumulative. You can rise above one or two public humiliations such as this, but finally after ten or more it gets to you . . . I felt like a deer shot down by hunters." Sarton pretends that she's bothered because the bad notices have imperiled her livelihood—"A bad review keeps read-ers from buying a book, it's as simple as that"—but her adversion to "public humiliations" suggests that it's not as simple as that. It's only her reputation part that's been injured, and as for what Woolf calls "the artist's sensibility," she seems not to have one. John Keats (to compare great things with small) had one, and instead of being thrown into a funk by contemptuous notices in *Blackwood's* and the *Quarterly Review* and the *British Critic,* he wrote an acquaintance who had defended him: "Praise or blame has but a momentary effect on the man whose love of beauty in the abstract makes him a severe critic of his own works." But Sarton lives in quite a different atmosphere, where attention to the distinction of one's works yields to concerns over "loss of identity," as she puts it, or "the sense I had of myself," or "how to build back to a sense of . . . valuing myself again." Her difficulty is the *myself* problem, and the example of Keats suggests how little necessary it is to the genuine lyric sensibility. She could profit no end from a reading of *The Boy Scout Handbook*.

Since May Sarton has no visible sense of humor or irony, it's doubtful that she could ever understand some things about reviewing that seem largely the possession of the ironic and skeptical classes. Johnson is a memorable spokesman for these, and he knows that looked at correctly—that is, without personal vanity—there's no such thing as a bad review. Boswell reports: "He remarked that attacks on authors did them much service. 'A man who tells me my play is very bad is less my enemy than he who lets it die in silence. A man whose business it is to be talked of is much helped by being attacked.' " Traveling in Scotland, Johnson heard Sir John Dalrymple complain about some bad reviews of his *Memoirs*. Johnson said: "Nay, sir, do not complain. It is advantageous to an author that his book should be attacked as well as praised. Fame is a shuttlecock. If it be struck at only one end of the room, it will soon fall to the ground. To keep it up, it must be struck at both ends."

Another source of comfort for authors smarting under a bad notice is to realize that not all readers are so dull as to ignore context. There is always a chance of a backfire. It was an unfavorable notice of E. E. Cummings's *The Enormous Room* in the old *Times Literary Supplement*, in the days when it was a byword for stuffiness, that sent Anthony Powell out to buy the book. "I was pretty sure," he says, "the *TLS* being what it was in those days, that I should like the book. This turned out to be a correct guess; incidentally highlighting an aspect of unfavorable notices to be borne in mind both by writers dispirited at receiving them and reviewers hoping to do damage."

In addition, a little experience in reviewing is a great help to authors in learning to survive bad reviews. Not that the trade is as corrupt or lazy as outsiders sometimes imagine. Sidney Smith's witticism, "I never read a book before reviewing it; it prejudices a man so," remains a witticism. But authors of some rhetorical sophistication know that a reviewer has an obligation that goes beyond deposing accurately and justly on the contents and value of the book in hand: he has an obligation to be interesting, which means, variously, funny, dramatic, significant, outraged, or winning. The reviewer is writing an essay, and the book in question is only one element of his material. No editor wants to publish a dull review, no matter how just. A veteran reviewer like Edmund Wilson knew this, and knew the implications: "The author has no justification," he said without qualification, "for expecting serious criticism from reviewers, and . . . in becoming elated or indignant over anything that is written about his books, he is wasting his nervous energy."

It is easier for an author to refrain from elation over the good reviews the more he sympathizes with the predicament of the reviewer. Reviewers who feel their authority and celebrity slipping very often seek to restore their positions by praising a book so that their juicy little phrases will find a place in the publisher's blurbs. This is an important reason why we encounter in reviews brief quotable phrases like "the best novel of the season," "a gripping experience," and "Miss —— is an artist of the first rank." Knowing that there's no book so bad that some part of it can't be made to serve this purpose, an author should find as little cause for ecstasy in such self-promoting reviewer's clichés as despair in their absence.

Furthermore, experienced authors know that it's less the tenor than the length of the review that counts. I've winced at a hostile review ("a sad disappointment"; "well-informed fatuity"; "chirpy facetiousness"; "prissy hauteur") and a few hours later met people who've read it and remembered it as highly laudatory. What they're remembering is the size of the review and its position in the format, and they will hasten to buy the book and expect to find great merit in it, recalling that some national periodical took it seriously, that is, gave it a lot of space. Empirically, it's generally true that unfavorable observations in reviews are remembered only by authors or reviewers, very seldom by readers. But the May Sartons of this world are too fascinated with the state of their

feelings to notice what really goes on in the world out there, including the book business. There is an objective dynamics operating in the trade which has little to do with real human hopes
and fears or with real human admirations and disgusts. To say
that it's all show business might be going too far, but on the other
hand it might not.

While abandoning a multitude of former literary genres, like
the sermon, the theatrical prologue in verse, the ethical essay, and
the Arthurian narrative poem, our age has formulated very few
new ones. One generic invention we'll probably be credited with—
if that's the term—is the "documentary" novel about real-life
murderers, like Capote's *In Cold Blood* or Mailer's *The Execu-
tioner's Song*. In addition we have devised two brief prose genres,
and I can't find any precedents for them in earlier literary history.
Neither, I am afraid, does us much credit.

The first is the little self-celebratory classified ad in the Per-
sonals column of outlets like *The New York Review of Books*
offering one's body genteelly for sexual uses. Here the convention
is unstinted praise of oneself for being exceptionally sensitive and
spirited, for liking music, "books," and "art," and for not smoking.
Like this:

UNIQUE INDIVIDUALIST MALE, 6–1, 170 lbs., well-built, said
to be handsome, non-smoking. Boston area. Into jogging, Picasso,
Ravel's *Bolero*, white wine, sun. Seeks equally original young lady
to share these pleasures, and others. Box 507.

The other brief prose genre belonging to the later twentieth
century also finds its home in *The New York Review of Books,*
although it's also to be seen in the *Times Literary Supplement*
and the *New York Times Book Review,* as well as the British *New
Statesman* and *Spectator*. This is what I'd call the A.B.M.—the
Author's Big Mistake, that is, the letter from an aggrieved author
complaining about a review. He has sent out his book for acclama-
tion. Encountering contempt instead, he has instantly taken pen

in hand to right this great wrong. The little lyric Personal ad and the letter from an ill-reviewed author are not as distinct generically as one might imagine at first glance. They share the convention of shameless self-satisfaction. Each constitutes a little arena of a very twentieth-century sort of insecure egotism and self-concern, and a critic would be hard pressed to decide which bespeaks the more pitiable dependence on external shows of esteem.

Just as the abuse sometimes visited upon authors gratifies many readers, so these letters have something irresistibly comic about them. Sputtering away, the veins of their foreheads standing out, these little compositions generally deliver the most naked view of the author's wounded vanity. And never with subtlety, for they are conceived in fury and scribbled in haste. The dynamics are as follows: The author reads the review, at first with disbelief, then, as he realizes others will read it too, with passion. Instead of sleeping on the matter a week or so, or better, simply getting on with his next book, he rushes to his typewriter and vents his sense of injured merit in five hundred or a thousand words. He is too impatient to revise, and he certainly feels no impulse to keep his piece nine years. Rage propels him out to the mailbox, and for the next few weeks rage causes him to tap his foot and with knitted brows to make sudden little sideways movements of his head, incomprehensible to his friends, few of whom have seen the review. (Among those who have, half have mistaken it for a good notice; the other half secretly agree with most of it, while still liking the author just as much as before.) Finally there arrives a copy of the offending periodical, and in it is the author's letter of complaint. Only now it doesn't look the way it looked in the author's typewriter. It's not been altered at all by the editor, or even shortened. But now it reads as if some puling adolescent, cut from the high-school basketball team, has published a letter about how good he really is, and written it not very well. All the author's sarcastic rebuttals now seem both too broad and too lame, inviting the reader to regard him as an even greater ass and loser than before.

There are certain inviolable conventions in these letters. The main one is to open by asserting that one doesn't write them. Thus:

To the Editor:

A copy of the review of _____ has just reached me in Australia. It is not my practice to comment on a review. But. . . .

(New York Times Book Review)

To the Editors:

Generally speaking one does not answer hostile reviews, especially self-refuting ones. But it would be a pity if readers. . . .

(New York Review of Books)

The tradition is that authors should not question too much utterances of those who review their books. Normally, I adhere to this tradition. But a review of my latest book . . . raises an issue of principle which. . . .

(New Statesman)

Other conventions of the A.B.M. are self-pity and self-praise. A classic performance in self-pity is the opening chord of Jan Morris's letter about her memoir of her gender change, Conundrum:

Sir,—Your cruel review of my Conundrum (April 26) reduced me to tears, of course, as its author doubtless intended: but I comforted myself with the thought . . . that. . . .

(Times Literary Supplement)

Sometimes the self-pity is more subtle, while aspiring to be as heart-rending. Thus:

I accept full responsibility for the too numerous misprints, explaining only that the proof-reading had to be undertaken while I was in hospital.

(Times Literary Supplement)

Sometimes the letter opens with a would-be ingratiating display of wit, as if to demonstrate that the writer is not really so angry as to be disabled from generating a little playful sarcasm:

Sir,—I am sorry that one of the grounds on which your reviewer . . . objects to my book . . . is that it is weighty. That however is probably the reason that, far from being unable to put it down, he was hardly able to take it up. It may account too for the inaccuracies and ineptness of his complaints—though not excuse them any more than it excuses the ill-tempered dismissiveness which they make evident. . . .

(Times Literary Supplement)

In these letters a favorite form for self-praise is the citation of an authority greater than the reviewer. So:

> To the Editors:
>
> _____ accuses me of attempting to go behind _____'s poetry, so I will refrain from speculating what could lie behind her extraordinarily vindictive review of my book. . . . For whatever it's worth, [the poet in question] liked the portions of my book that he read in manuscript; thought that my style was "fine"; and in his last letter to me, written weeks before his death, wished me "good luck with your book." That matters infinitely more to me than the polemics of his posthumous spokesman. . . .
>
> *(New York Review of Books)*

Sometimes other reviewers can be invoked, so that the reader will carry away the impression that this one bad review is merely an aberration, that indeed, the whole reviewing fraternity has not agreed that your book is terrible:

> This kind of reviewing, unfortunately now too common, which in effect helps to bar a writer's communication and denies his right to it, is intellectual hooliganism. I am happy that two other reviewers, _____ and _____ who, one cannot doubt, know what they are talking about, have actually discussed my thesis and arguments, putting forward reasoned criticism while maintaining a favorable account.
>
> *(Times Literary Supplement)*

Here's another nice one, so good, indeed, that the reader may suspect, unjustly, that I have made it up. Now the complainant is not the author of the book reviewed, but merely someone patronized in passing. But notice that this writer, in addition to delivering a full measure of self-praise, also honors the convention, "Ordinarily, I wouldn't think of replying, etc."

> To the Editors:
> In his review of _____'s _____, _____ referred to and used my critical study . . . , noting that I

was not "competent to discuss the classical background" of
_____'s fiction. Ordinarily such an outrageous charge
would not merit a rejoinder. However, since I was trained
as a classicist who taught his discipline and published in the
field before moving into Comparative Literature, I cannot
allow _____'s irresponsibility to go unchallenged. . . .

My greatest satisfaction comes from the fact that I pleased
the late Gilbert Highet, to whom the book was dedicated
and who was not above sending me *errata*. Gilbert Highet is a
name to reckon with. Frankly, I never heard of _____.

(New York Review of Books)

It's clear that editors are very fond of printing these letters. One
reason is fairly obvious; they add the drama of personal conflict
to their normally gray pages. Another reason is that the letters are
almost always funny, offering readers the spectacle of some pomp-
ous self-celebrator given ample ironic room in which to parade
his self-solicited hurt. But the main reason editors like these letters
is that by their means they get a lot of signed copy without having
to pay for it. The principle has been thoroughly mastered by the
publishers of sex magazines like *Forum*. They have learned that
once you establish for the magazine a tradition of lubricious self-
praise, you can fill a third of a monthly number with fascinating
copy at no cost whatever. The same principle operates with more
genteel people. If sufficiently angry, an author who normally
wouldn't think of writing a thousand words without payment is
delighted to supply them for nothing so long as in these words he
can engage in his little dance of self-justification. To eke out their
free copy further, editors often try to cajole the original reviewer
into composing an "answer" to the complaint. But the best advice
to reviewers is that ascribed to the British Foreign Office: never
explain, never apologize. And in addition, never write without
payment. If ever tempted to a comment, reviewers should be ada-
mant about responding to an author who complains that he's been
"misunderstood." If he has been, it's his fault, and no comment is
called for. It's his fault because he's supposed to be adept in matters of lucid address and explanation, and if he's failed there, he's
failed everywhere.

But what should an author do if he receives an ecstatic review,
one he imagines fully "understands" him and values his book at

its true worth? Should he write a different kind of letter, this one to the reviewer, thanking him and praising him for his perception? The answer is precisely the same as with the bad review: never. As usual, Johnson, the first professional writer to think seriously about the ethics of the trade, has the best word: "Such acknowledgements . . . never can be proper, since they must be paid either for flattery or justice." Silence is the author's only proper recourse, unless he wants to publish a letter like this, which I have never seen and never expect to see:

> Sir,—Decent reviewing is something every author has a right to expect, and consequently I was distressed to read Mr. _____'s laudatory review of my *Sanitary Engineering in Belgium and the Low Countries,* which entirely fails to mention the clumsy prose in which much of my book is couched—I was not feeling well two summers ago—and wholly overlooks the slick reasoning by which I make the transit from Part I to Part II, not to mention the inadequacies of the Index, which I made myself, and the pretentiousness of the jacket-blurb, which your reviewer ignorantly imputes to the mendacity of my publisher but which is actually of my own composition. Your readers deserve better than this. I am, sir,
>
> Yours faithfully,
>
> _____.

III
GOING PLACES

Terrors and Delights
of the Traveler Abroad

Terrors:

That the hotel will never have heard of one's reservations, and will be full.

That the prices quoted in the letter of confirmation will no longer apply.

That one's travelers checks will be lost or stolen, together with the little slip indicating their numbers.

That one will come down with malaria/fevers/diarrhea/cramps and that no doctor will speak English or have gone to a decent medical school.

That one will have to eat nasty food.

That the bar will be closed.

That one will miss the plane/boat/train and that there will not be another for a very long time.

That one will run into terrible people from whom there will be no escape.

That one will be lonely.

That the hotel will supply no soap, and that one will discover this after all the shops have closed for the weekend.

That servants will be insulting.

That since one's departure one's own country will have fallen into grave international discredit bringing unexpected contempt upon the traveler.

That since one's departure one's own currency will have been ludicrously devalued.

That only vile pipe tobacco will be available, or none at all.

That one will be struck from behind by a silent bicycle coming from the right while one is assiduously peering left.

That one will be seen to be assiduously peering left.

That one will be set upon by touts so persistent and agile that the only escape will be immediate costly flight from the country (Egypt? India?) in question.

That one will be arrested on frivolous charges.

That one's bribe will be disdained.

That one's consulate, hearing of one's arrest, will disclaim all responsibility and instead lecture one on duty and prudence.

That one will be unable to read street signs in the local language or alphabet.

That one's French/German/Italian/Spanish will be openly ridiculed.

That it will be impossible to acquire any small change, obliging one to tip exorbitantly with large notes.

That the hotel concierge habitually throws away the postcards consigned to him for mailing, or gives them to his children to play with.

That one's passport will expire while one is not looking.

That when one returns the man at immigration who looks into his computer to find something nasty about one will find it.

Delights:

Finding that it is a custom among Filipinos to applaud when the plane touches down.

Finding that if Iran is a loathsome place, Isfahan is not.

Finding in Tahiti that the "No Trespassing" signs say "Tabu."

Finding in Japan that the better sort of bus and truck drivers wear white gloves.

Finding for the hundredth time that alone among living creatures the French make real bread.

Finding that the 747 will be virtually empty.

Finding that, through some anomaly of international regulation, Singapore Airlines, Air Pacific, and Cathay Pacific charge nothing for their copious drinks or for wine with meals and cognac after, and that Singapore Airlines gives out free four-color ballpoint pens as well.

Finding that the Turkish island of Buyuk Ada has carriages which for a trifling fee take one around the island on a thyme-bordered little road.

Finding that New Caledonia, a speck in the Pacific, is a perfectly equipped, rational mini-France, with blue workman's clothes; draconic, Cocteau motorcycle police; Kronenbourg and Müt-zig Pils beer; Pernod, baguettes, and pâté; good roads, brilliantly sign-posted and furnished with classic red and white *bornes;* and Tour-de-France aspirants pedalling furiously in correct costume.

Finding that the bar opens at ten in the morning.

Finding that nothing on the Greek island of Spetses has changed in twenty years.

Finding that the restored Leningrad looks exactly like Dostoev-sky's.

Finding that the policemen in London liked to be addressed as Constable.

Finding that old men in minor French towns wear berets.

Finding in Tokyo that on the FM radio one can hear a half-hour of birdsong daily.

Finding that enlisted personnel of the armed forces of the Republic of India, while walking the streets in uniform, tend to hold hands.

Finding that the tufts of straw worn behind by residents of northern Papua New Guinea are called, in Pidgin, *arse-grass.*

Finding that the beer in Munich really is extraordinary.

Finding that there are swans on the Thames, and that they belong to the Queen.

Finding in Mexico that young people congregate at a waterfall near Palenque and swim naked.

Finding that the pyramids look exactly as they're supposed to.

Finding in the Solomon Islands that the evening broadcast of local news is in Pidgin, spoken with impressive formality and dignity: "One fella good policy," "one fella new legislation," etc.

Finding that an unlikely bookstore in Athens is stocked with excellent English books.

Finding that the scarab one has bought in Luxor is real.

Finding that the car-rental charges are lower than expected.

Finding that *The Observer* is sold on the beaches of Rhodes.

Finding that at Japanese wedding receptions the guests bow to the various principals so deeply that for some seconds their upper bodies are parallel with the surface of the earth.

Finding that despite rumors Corfu has not been spoiled.

Finding that the cold lobster in Lisbon is still served with exquisite mayonnaise.

Finding that in rural Russia people meeting relatives at railway stations present them with large bouquets of flowers.

Finding that Baedeker's *Paris and Its Environs* (1907) will do perfectly well today.

Finding that Schliemann's "Troy" may actually be Troy.

Finding that all the clichés about a place are true.

Finding that when one comes home, one is ready to.

Footwork as Scholarship

During the past two centuries exploration has largely diminished to travel; and during the past fifty years travel has attentuated to tourism. One important difference between these things, as Morse Peckham has noted, is the kind and amount of knowledge thought appropriate for each. The explorer must be thoroughly learned, a master of ancient and modern languages as well as of historical topography understood from original sources. The traveler must at least be literary, knowing history from guidebooks and previous travelers' styles of perception from travel books. Finally, the tourist, if the industry devoted to him is to function well, must know nothing. "Explorers are to the ordinary traveler what the Saint is to the average church congregation"—thus Hugh and Pauline Massingham in *The Englishman Abroad*. If any explorer ever deserved canonization as a hero of learning he is Sir Aurel Stein, the dapper, courageous little magister of Central Asian archeology.

The writer of a full and richly detailed account of Stein's life and work must be almost his equal in Central Asian learning, and Jeannette Mirsky, who worked almost twelve years on *Sir Aurel Stein: Archeological Explorer*, is eminently qualified to interpret Stein's achievement. Her feel for landscape matches Stein's; and her learning in wide historical and geographical contexts equips her to write here what is virtually a history of Central Asian archeology, with Stein at the center.

He was born in Budapest in 1862 and named Marc Aurel after Marcus Aurelius. Born a Jew, he was baptized a Protestant because his parents wanted him to succeed in one of the learned professions, then largely closed to Jews. As a child he spoke Magyar and German, to which he added French and English, and finally Greek, Latin, Sanskrit, and Persian. He was the lucky recipient of a German education at Dresden, Vienna, Leipzig, and Tübingen (Ph.D.,

1883) in the days before current events was considered a university subject. His subjects were comparative philology and Sanskrit, ancient history and historical geography, and he developed early a devotion to three heroic travelers: Alexander the Great, Marco Polo, and Hsüan-tsang, the Chinese pilgrim of the seventh century whose accuracy in describing the overland route from China to India prompted Stein to call him "the Buddhist Pausanias." He capped his preparation by further linguistic, archeological, and numismatic studies in London and Cambridge. His luck held even during his year's compulsory military service back in Hungary. He might have wasted the year sweating on the parade ground and listening to bawdy stories. Instead he was sent to map-making school, where he mastered surveying and the niceties of topographical representation.

He knew he somehow had to get to India to investigate on the ground the ancient cultural, commercial, and religious intercourse between China and India. To this end he got a job as an educational administrator in Lahore, a convenient venue for his real work: the discovery and interpretation of Sanskrit manuscripts and the exploration of Buddhist architecture Like all successful explorers and like most successful travelers, he was mighty tough and stubborn. When Freya Stark encountered him in Baghdad thirty-five years later, she noted his "gentle deceptive manner," the "manner of those who always get their own way." He finally got his own way in India. In 1900 he set off on a fully mounted fourteen-month expedition, supported by the Indian government, to Khotan in eastern Turkestan, where his studies had told him there were Buddhist landmarks in the desert waiting all these years to be excavated. Assisted variously by ponies, yaks, and camels, Stein and his party cheerfully braved glaciers and avalanches and subzero temperatures (Stein's ink froze constantly, impeding his evening note-taking in his tent). They climbed twenty-thousand-foot mountains without oxygen and arrived finally at the torrid desert, where Stein located and excavated numerous Buddhist shrines buried under the sand, just where he knew they would be.

Returning from these happy exertions in 1901, he was appointed an education inspector in the Punjab and three years later became a British subject. In his letters, as Mirsky says, "educational work

is always accompanied by the adjective 'tiring,' whereas his stren-
uous assault on mountains is 'invigorating,' 'refreshing.' " His most
famous Central Asian expedition was his second, from 1906 to
1908. After discovering numerous first-century documents at the
site of a wall marking the western frontier of ancient China, in a
cave at Ch'ien-fo-tung he came upon a hidden library of ancient
Buddhist documents guarded by a Taoist priest whose determination never to part with these sacred materials equalled Stein's
determination to secure them for Western scholarship. After weeks
of cajolery, bribery, and pressure, Stein bought and came away
with some three thousand text rolls, together with innumerable
silk paintings, banners, and emboideries. It was a triumph less
perhaps of "archeology" than of patient, single-minded diplomacy.
Stein's thinking, Mirsky notes, "was colored by his unshakeable
belief in the primacy of Western scholarship. It justified everything"—even depriving a monk of his holy treasure and whisking
it off to the British Museum.

Carrying this hoard back to India, Stein suffered the only severe
physical misadventure of his career. On a twenty-thousand-foot
glacier in a temperature of 16 degrees (F.) below zero, his toes,
frostbitten, turned gangrenous. After a month's painful journey
to a hospital, he lost to the surgeon two toes on his right foot and
the tips of the others. But he was now a hero, promoted from the
education department to the Indian Archeological Survey, and
his name was coupled with Nansen's, Peary's, and Shackleton's.
Back in England to deposit and catalog his finds at the British
Museum, he was elevated to the status of Commander of the
Indian Empire and soon became a knight of that order—hence the
"Sir."

A third Central Asian expedition followed in 1913. As usual,
Stein exhibited his command and his cool by keeping in order
forty people and twenty-six camels while he headed for the Afghan-
Russian border and eastern Persia, hot on the trail of Buddhist
survivals. During the day he traveled with his caravan or supervised excavation; at night he took notes, wrote his books, and read
proofs by lantern light. The fruits of this assiduity were the seven
major works he published from 1907 (*Ancient Khotan*) to 1940
(*On Old Routes of Western Iran*). The loss of his toes slowed him

down not at all; in his mid-sixties he walked hundreds of miles to inspect a wild mountain pass where Alexander was reputed to have conducted a defense.

He was really frustrated only once. This was in 1930, when his carefully planned expedition, financed by Harvard, to survey Inner Mongolia and pick up artifacts for the Fogg Museum turned into a fiasco. Politically conservative and convinced of the superiority of Western learning and occidental usages, he failed to notice that the rise of xenophobia in the new China gave his pokings around there the appearance of a threat, at least to the new Chinese self-respect. He brushed aside warnings that trouble lay ahead. As Jeannette Mirsky says, "His dogged persistence, honed sharp by his long apprenticeship in learning not to take No for an answer, had hardened into willfulness." The Chinese finally tired of hearing him insist on his prerogatives and expelled him.

Today the sort of scholarly questions Stein sought to answer by means of footwork look luxuriously liberal. A typical one: Where exactly did Alexander cross the Hydaspes? An expedition to Iran in 1932 gave the answer. Another: Where were the Roman roads and military outposts in Syria and Iraq? Airplane flights over the desert (courtesy of the RAF) helped Stein make out the traces. The spry old party lived until 1943, and his refusal ever to fold his tent or his hands makes him seem an exemplary senior citizen. On one of his late expeditions to a remote part of what is now Pakistan, he came upon a number of ancient sites, but wrote—he was then eighty—that he was "reserving trial excavations for later" because he had to dash off "to the southwest mainly with a view to tracing the exact route followed by Alexander on his march into Gedrosia." After years of solicitation he finally received permission to explore in Afghanistan, and his heart leaped up. But "dyspepsia" and old age intervened, and he died suddenly at Kabul on his way in.

He can stand as a permanent model of intellectual curiosity, useful to those who pursue knowledge on foot as well as in libraries. Notably a man of his historical moment, he adhered to the tradition of high-minded strenuousness associated with Theodore Roosevelt and Robert Baden-Powell. His almost mystical fondness for mountains and high altitudes is an index of his Germanic brand of late romanticism. Although he deplored Hitler, he would have adored a mountain retreat like the Berghof near Berchtesgaden, situated so like the tents he loved to erect on mountaintops. There, "in absolute Purdah," and dressed in jacket and tie, he would write his books in total silence, his dog Dash curled at his feet.

An Impediment to Pilgrimage

At roughly the moment the British vacated Suez, the volumes of the World's Classics and Everyman's Library, which in their millions once conveyed British literature to the United States, began to take on the status of rarities here. With the decline of British political power, British literature has seemed more and more irrelevant, until now you can bring a dinner party of university-trained people to a dead stop by dropping a name like Sidney or Landor or Patmore or Firbank. Recently, a friend of mine who teaches English in the Middle West wrote me in despair: "A blow today: I have been informed that *The Voyage Out, Jacob's Room,* and *The Waves* are all out of print in this country, in either hard-back or paperback. A nice way to gut my second semester Virginia Woolf seminar before it begins." And a seminar of mine was gutted in the same way when I discovered that for the first time in thirty years no edition whatever of Sir Joshua Reynolds's *Discourses on Art* was in print here: there used to be three or four. If the actual works of British writers seem not much wanted, gossip about them, like the current obsession with the Bloomsberries, is at a peak, and picture books flourish about the writers' "worlds" —actually their clothes and houses and gardens and friends. Thus we have *Lewis Carroll and His World,* even *Somerset Maugham and His World*. It is as if everything about British writers fascinates except their words.

A recent climax in the process of replacing authors' works by their associations was achieved by *Literary Landscapes of the British Isles: A Narrative Atlas,* a curious bit of book-making by David Daiches, formerly professor of English at Cornell, and the cartographer John Flower. Daiches is responsible for the first 227 pages, a series of essays with numerous illustrations calculated to show how "a sense of place was important in the literary imagination of some major writers." His essays deal with Chaucer's "world" and the London of Shakespeare, Johnson, Dickens, and Woolf; Bath and the Lake District; the Brontë country and Hardy's "Wessex" and the Midlands under Victorian industrialism; Scotland in literature; and the Dublin of Yeats and Joyce. And there's an anomalous essay on "The Romantic Poets Abroad," which, despite the assurance of the book's title that it is the literary topography of the British Isles that's at issue, gives us Wordsworth in the Alps, Keats (all too briefly) in Rome, and Shelley and Byron in Italy. In addition to contributing maps to Daiches's part of the book, Flower has provided at the end a disjunct twenty-five-page literary atlas of the British Isles as well as more detailed literary maps of Edinburgh, Dublin, Oxford, Cambridge, and central London. He has included an eighteen-page gazetteer indicating where over two-hundred authors were born, lived, and died. There are also lists of those buried or memorialized in Westminster Abbey and St. Paul's, those who lived at the Inns of Court (Sir Thomas More to Rider Haggard), and those who attended the main Public Schools (a school qualifies for listing if it has produced at least two "literary figures"). Because, as Flower acknowledges, most of his data derive from Dorothy Eagle and Hilary Carnell's *Oxford Literary Guide to the British Isles,* we are to suppose that the superadded essays by Daiches make this book special.

They do, but in a melancholy sense. It is sad to see "a founder of the University of Sussex" (jacket blurb) and the author of the best modern book on Robert Burns reduced to such unsophisticated procedures. Throughout, literature is assumed to be a branch of photography, bearing a wholly representational relation to actuality. Daiches makes much, for example, of Wordsworth's notice of daffodils and implies that you have to perceive them in the Lake District to depict them persuasively. The fact is that Wordsworth's daffodils do come from the Lake District, but they come also from Pliny and ancient myth, from Spenser and Shakespeare and Herrick and Milton, and from Dorothy Wordsworth's notebook. In the same way, pictures are assumed to be essentially representational, and engravings by Doré and after Turner are offered without stylistic analysis as depictions of real scenes.

In the writing there is constant incoherence and waywardness, and some of the essays are barely about literature at all, as if they'd been thrown in from some other book. The one called "The

Blackening of England," about the Midlands, is a brisk classroom survey of economic conditions with only a glance occasionally at Carlyle and Dickens and Disraeli. D. H. Lawrence, the laureate of the industrial nasty in *Sons and Lovers* and *Lady Chatterley's Lover,* is accorded one brief clause, and the main work of "description" is entrusted to Engels. In dealing with such matters as capital punishment in the eighteenth century and the plight of the London poor in the nineteenth, Daiches give us the usual late-twentieth-century self-righteousness and seems to assume that the task of imaginative writers is to expose social wrongs. Thus he writes of Virginia Woolf:

> In her novels she recognizes the existence of poverty and gives us glimpses of it every now and again to support the structure of mood and feeling she is building up, but she does not explore it (as Gissing had done, for example, in *The Nether World*).

Which is to expect a tetrahedron to be a billiard ball.

The chapter on Bath is representative of Daiches's method, which is to invoke the most obvious sources (here, Goldsmith and Christopher Anstey and Smollett and Austen) and to quote them for pages without analysis, as if they were trying to describe Bath rather than generate compelling fictions. All the clichés find a comfortable home here, and it doesn't matter whether they're related to literature and topography: we have Beau Nash, Bath Oliver Biscuits, the prohibition of dueling. And sometimes the clichés yield to stubborn irrelevance, as when we are told that George Saintsbury chose to retire to Bath. Where the essays are not canned literary history with special resort to place-names, they are shallow biographies of writers or gravely reductive plot-summaries of novels. We are taken along on Mrs. Dalloway's and her acquaintances' London walks and on Bloom's wanderings in Dublin without learning anything but inert lists of street names.

Since Daiches is a Scot, we'd expect something original and interesting in his essay "Scotland and Literature." What we get are conventional remarks about Burns, Scott, and Stevenson, and a translation of *Kidnapped* into tedious topographical notation (David Balfour and Alan Breck "cross Loch Ericht by night and proceed 'down its eastern shore to another hiding-place near the head of Loch Rannoch.' They cross Loch Rannoch and move south to the Braes of Balquidder. After a night at Strathyre they push on southward and eventually reach Allan Water and follow it down"). That's what most of the book sounds like, although sometimes it sounds like this too:

> Coleridge was born at Ottery St. Mary, Devonshire, in 1772, and was educated at Christ's Hospital, London, and at Jesus College, Cambridge. . . . In 1795 he was living in Bristol with Southey. . . . In October 1795 he married Sarah Fricker and settled in Clevedon, Somerset, on the Bristol Channel. In 1797 he moved to a cottage at Nether Stowey, Somerset. . . .

This from a work said by its publisher to constitute "a landmark in literary criticism," to offer "literary criticism at its most readable." Readable? It's not even publishable.

Let's posit a couple of innocent young college English teachers embarked on their first literary visit—pilgrimage, really—to the British Isles. They have been saving for years for this, and although their budget is tight, at the last moment before leaving New York they've bought this book, attracted by its pretty jacket. Its subtitle, *A Narrative Atlas,* seems to promise just what they need, and the jacket assures them that the atlas and gazetteer part will serve as "an invaluable reference for travelers." These young people are devoted to A. E. Housman (their tastes are somewhat retrograde), and their new book tells them that he's buried in Ludlow, Shropshire. (They are even so old-fashioned that they remember the text of "When smoke stood up from Ludlow.") They want to visit Housman's grave, and on their fourth day in England they set off from London northwestward in their (viciously costly) rented car. The man drives, and the woman sits in the strange left-hand front seat (spooky at first) proposing to direct him to Ludlow from Flower's maps. She quickly finds Ludlow in the Geographical Index, but when she turns to Map 7, Square A3 (nervously, for her partner is already beginning to panic in the traffic on the Edgware Road and is bellowing for instructions), she finds Ludlow all right, but no indication of the numbered highways by which you reach it. After some hours of angry, fruitless tooling around, they stop at a fair-sized market town, find a bookshop on the High Street, and with a sigh get *The Oxford Literary Guide to the British Isles,* which they can't help noticing costs the same as the Daiches and Flower book. The *Oxford Guide* informs them instantly that Ludlow is on the A49 about twenty-eight miles north of Ross-on-Wye, which you reach by taking the M50 off the M5. Once they get to Ludlow, the *Oxford Guide* tells them that Housman's ashes are buried outside the north door of St. Laurence's Church. From Daiches and Flower they'd know only that Housman is buried somewhere in Ludlow, and we can easily imagine the time our young people would be in for, asking repeatedly in their American accents of everyone on the streets, "Where is A. E. Housman buried, please?" "Who, dear?"

Returning, they decide to stop at Pembroke College, Oxford, to pay their respects to another of their favorites, Samuel Johnson. (I have said that this is a very old-fashioned pair of young people.) By this time they are getting adept at comparing Daiches and Flower with Eagle and Carnell, whose names, they observe with some ribaldry, are given by Daiches and Flower as Eagle and Correll. They work their way back to Oxford easily, following the numbered highways on the maps in the *Oxford Guide.* In Oxford Daiches and Flower prove not entirely useless: their map of Oxford does show the locations of the colleges. But the material on Pembroke tells them only that Johnson was there for some time beginning in 1728. Where was his room? There's no answer in *Literary Landscapes of the British Isles,* and our young folks don't want to risk rebuff from the snotty porter. No need: Eagle and Carnell give them exactly what they want. "Johnson came up in 1728 and had rooms on the second floor over the gateway." Furthermore, he stayed only fourteen months.

On the drive back to London, the woman navigating skillfully now with the maps at the end of the *Oxford Guide,* they agree to throw the Daiches book out the window, tearing out and retaining only the two pages not better done elsewhere, the plans of Oxford and Cambridge. This done, they hurl the book out near Hendon, and it falls with a satisfying splash in the middle of the River Brent. They feel cleaner and more intelligent now, a feeling, they conclude, almost worth the more than thirteen dollars (New York sales tax included) Daiches and Flower's book has cost. They are growing up. Next time (and let us hope always) they will look inside the poke before purchasing the pig.

Latin America Defeats
Intelligent Travel Writer

One of the casualties of travel by jet, together with honest cuisine and the concept that people are not sardines, is the old-style travel book, the sort that used to be written by Norman Douglas and D. H. Lawrence and John Dos Passos and Graham Greene and Evelyn Waugh. The guide book, compiled by committees under the supervision of Eugene Fodor or Temple Fielding, has "replaced" the travel book, just as, according to Ezra Pound, the pianola has "replaced" Sappho's barbitos. We now have books instructing us how to save money and time; but with rare exceptions, such as Herbert Kubly's *Stranger in Italy* (1956), we have few any more satisfying the requirements laid down by Norman Douglas fifty years ago:

> The reader of a good travel-book is entitled not only to an exterior voyage, to descriptions of scenery and so forth, but to an interior, a sentimental or temperamental voyage, which takes place side by side with that outer one; . . . the ideal book of this kind offers us, indeed, a triple opportunity of exploration—abroad, into the author's brain, and into our own. The writer should therefore possess a brain worth exploring; some philosophy of life—not necessarily, though by preference, of his own forging—and the courage to proclaim it and put it to the test; he must be naïf and profound, both child and sage.

A book Douglas would have liked was Paul Theroux's *The Great Railway Bazaar,* his account of a rail trip from London to Japan and back again, full of characters, scandals, and disasters.

In *The Old Patagonian Express* Theroux has attempted a replay, offering a narrative of a masochistic two-month rail journey from his parents' house in Medford, Mass., all the way through Mexico and Central America to the southern tip of South America, the remote and barren Patagonia celebrated by Theroux's friend Bruce Chatwin in his excellent *In Patagonia,* another book Douglas would approve.

If this sequel—it must be called that—is not so delightful as *The Great Railway Bazaar,* the fault is as much geography's as Theroux's. Europe and Asia seem to be a richer venue for this sort of thing than Latin America, which by contrast lacks *timbre,* deep literary and historical associations, and variety. For anyone experienced with Europe, it is boring. Squalor in Mexico is identical to squalor in El Salvador; the ghastly Mexican town Papaloapán is too much like the horrible Costa Rican town Limón, 600 miles farther south. Illiteracy here is like illiteracy there, and variety enters only in the ways allusion and subtlety are absent in different places. As Theroux proceeds, things do get worse, but not dramatically worse: "Since leaving the United States," he writes, "I had not seen a dog that wasn't lame, or a woman who wasn't carrying something. . . ." He seems aware that his sequel isn't quite up to the original, referring to poor old Jack Kerouac, fat and fifty, trying to re-experience *On the Road* by hitchhiking West many years later: "Times had changed. The lugubrious man reached New Jersey; there he stood for hours in the rain, trying to thumb a ride, until at last he gave up and took a bus home."

Theroux does not give up, although often he is brought close to despair. On a Mexican train he experiences "Two classes: both uncomfortable and dirty. No privacy, no relief. Constant stopping and starting, broken engine, howling passengers. On days like this I wonder why I bother: leaving order and friends for disorder and strangers. . . . Impossible to get comfortable in this seat. A jail atmosphere: the brown walls and dim light of the condemned cell." He is proud to be traveling alone, but now and then he miserably confronts his loneliness, as when he reads Donne and finds him saying, "The greatest misery of sickness is solitude. . . . Solitude is a torment which is not threatened in hell itself."

In addition, Theroux is crawled over by flies, roaches, and rats; he cuts his hand and is stricken with a diarrhea so violent that even his British "cement" won't arrest it; he suffers agonies from altitude-sickness crossing the Andes and finds relief only by squirting into his mouth the contents of an oxygen-filled toy balloon,

purveyed by a vender on the train. By the time he's descended to
Ecuador he perceives that all decent people either drive or fly:

> I had been in Latin America long enough by now to know
> that there was a class stigma attached to the trains. Only the
> semidestitute, the limpers, the barefoot ones, the Indians,
> and the half-cracked yokels took the trains, or knew anything
> about them.

In northern Argentina his train sits at a deserted platform. "There
were orange peels and banana skins under every window . . . water
poured from beneath the coaches, and there were heaps of [excre-
ment] under each toilet pipe. The sun had grown stronger, and
flies collected. . . ." A woman walking along the platform says to
her nicely dressed friend: "This is the train to Tucumán—it
came all the way from Bolivia. Aren't you glad we came by car?"

Like good conversation, a good travel book consists of two kinds
of materials: narrative (or dialogue) alternating with comment.
Theroux's comments come in the form of little three-hundred-
word essays: on the Chisholm Trail, the ghastliness of Fort Worth,
the wetback problem, the career of Juárez, the inferiority of
Ambrose Bierce to Jonathan Swift (why the surprise?), and the
comic inappropriateness of Latin American place-names, like Pro-
greso in Guatemala and La Libertad in El Salvador. We are given
essays, some of them a bit stiff and self-righteous, on the history
of Guatemala, human sacrifice in nineteenth-century El Salvador,
the curious secularism of Costa Rica, American colonial life in
the "company town" of the Panama Canal Zone (it's like being in
the army), the building of the Canal, Inca culture, and the drug
traffic (all-encompassing) in Barranquilla, Colombia.

Interesting as some of these excursions are, Theroux's narrative
is better—his rendering of a combined soccer game and riot in San
Salvador is superb—and his dialogue is best of all. In Veracruz he
meets a middle-aged American divorcée who tells him about her
terrible husbands, one "violent," the next "a bum" who has tried
to squeeze alimony from her, because she has the money. *"I'm*
supposed to pay *him!"*

"What sort of business are you in?" Theroux asks.

" 'I own slums,' she said. 'Fifty-seven of them—I mean, fifty-
seven units. . . . God's been good to me.' "

In Costa Rica he meets a traveling American, Mr. Thornberry, who can't resist designating aloud everything visible through the train window: "Sawmill." "Pool of water." "Pipeline." "Poverty." "Bananas." "Pigs." "Pretty girl." "Kids playing." "Pipeline again."

But the finest dialogue of all is Theroux's conversation with Jorge Luis Borges. On his appalling trains Theroux has been solacing himself by reading Boswell's *Life of Johnson*. (It's wonderful, by the way, how popular as a traveler's *vade mecum* that book is. As he records in *The Road to Oxiana*, the great British traveler Robert Byron carried it all over Persia and Afghanistan in the 1930's and drew much comfort from it.) The *Life of Johnson*, says Theroux,

> became my life line. There was no landscape in it. I had all the landscape I wanted out the window. What I lacked was talk, and this was a brilliant talk, sage advice, funny remarks. . . . I think if I had not had that book to read as I made my way through Colombia, the trip would have been unendurable.

Looking out the window, he calls up such Johnsonian observations as this: "Where a great proportion of the people are suffered to languish in helpless misery, that country must be ill-policed and wretchedly governed: a decent provision for the poor is the true test of civilization." Agonizing on the hard railway seats, hot, half-starved, and wholly miserable, Theroux agrees with Johnson's finding that "there was more to be endured than enjoyed in the general condition of human life." In Buenos Aires, Theroux is thoroughly primed to play Boswell to Borges's Johnson, and the resulting conversations provide a delightful climax, a triumphant overflow of civility, intelligence, and wit after all the brutality and stupidity.

Borges is happy to meet Theroux because he admires an essay on Kipling Theroux has published. And Theroux realizes the magic of walking down a street in Buenos Aires with the blind Borges, "like being led through Alexandria by Cavafy, or through Lahore by Kipling. The city belonged to him, and he had had a hand in inventing it."

Theroux may Boswell-Johnsonize Borges a bit, but he reports him saying some fine things: "People respect soldiers. That's why no one really thinks much of the Americans. If America were a military power instead of a commercial empire, people would look up to it. Who respects businessmen? No one. People look at America and all they see are traveling salesmen. So they laugh." On the Peróns: "He looted the country. His wife was a prostitute." "Evita?" Theroux asks. "A common prostitute," Borges replies. (Cf. Johnson: "The woman's a whore, and there's an end on't.") "As he fished out his door key," says Theroux, "I asked him about Patagonia."

" 'I have been there,' he said. 'But I don't know it well. I'll tell you this, though. It's a dreary place. A very dreary place.'

" 'I was planning to take the train tomorrow.'

" 'Don't go tomorrow. Come and see me. . . .'

" 'I suppose I can go to Patagonia next week.'

" 'It's dreary,' said Borges. He had got the door open, and now he shuffled to the elevator and pulled open its metal gates. 'The gate of the hundred sorrows,' he said, and entered chuckling."

Theroux finds that Borges has been quite right about Patagonia when he comes to the end of his journey, the town of Esquel, in southernmost Argentina. He arrives there on the final "teeny-weeny steam train," the "Old Patagonian Express." He has arrived precisely at Nowhere, at "enormous empty spaces," the sort of scene Australian and New Zealand troops used to be fond of designating as "miles and miles of bugger-all." "The nothingness itself," he concludes, "a beginning for some intrepid traveler, was an ending for me. I had arrived in Patagonia, and I laughed when I remembered I had come here from Boston, on the subway train that people took to work."

But except for the Borges oasis, the reader gets little relief from the horrors and boredom. He misses the sheer joy of the anomalous, which surfaced frequently in *The Great Railway Bazaar*. Here Theroux is exhausted. Outraged by Latin America, he picks unfunny quarrels, depicts himself winning arguments, allows his liberal moral superiority to grow strident. He seems to think we have to be told that people should not starve or live in filth. Even though he knows he's doing these things ("I was sick of lecturing people on disorder"), he can't help himself, and sometimes the sound of an angry person shouting shakes the reader's pleasure in Theroux's sharp eye and shrewd perception: he notices, for example, that an American on the train is wearing "the sort of woollen plaid forester's shirt that graduate students in state universities especially favor." In Peru, "the Indians have a broad-based look, like chess pieces." The terrain outside the train window, at one low point, looks like a "world of kitty litter." In the dark once, "in one field, five white cows were as luminous as laundry."

In the former days of the travel book, Greene and Waugh could tour through horrors and make them something other than occasions for mere superior disgust. Their sympathy was wider than Theroux's, their involvement in history was deeper, their belief in the redemption of mankind by good sense was less certain, and perhaps their knowledge of themselves was more profound. Theroux never says of the messes he observes: "That's me." And thus he fails to take us a sufficient distance (as Douglas would require) into our own brain.

Latin America has defeated Theroux, assaulting him until in self-defense he has grown superior and morally facile. And as Lawrence and Greene and Waugh and Robert Byron show, and as Douglas pre-eminently recognizes, the morally facile tone is not found in travel books which remain of permanent literary interest.

A Place To Recuperate

Our condition is best understood by imagining an alternative. What would be an alternative to the shopping malls, the slimy artificial fibers, the rotten trains, the boring frozen food and the boring packaged politics, the one-liners replacing wit and the intense perspiry harangues replacing conversation? What would be the alternative to the uniform placeless national highway, its language (*Motel, Furniture, Hot Tubs, Gourmet Dining, Bowling, Adult Books*) betraying with every mile the local perversion of the once-dignified bourgeois ideal? What would be the alternative to the systematic rape of Atlantic City? to the banks where no one knows the customers' names; the bookstores selling nothing but calendars, cards, and the books on the *New York Times* best-seller list; the hotels where a paper strip across the toilet brags of advanced sanitation but where the staff treats the clients with open disdain?

A while ago my wife and I were touring Israel. One morning in Jerusalem I woke with an inexplicable insistent pain in my side: I felt as if during the night someone had kicked me in the ribs very hard. But the pain wasn't bad enough to interfere with our touring schedule for the day, which involved an overnight bus trip to the northern part of the country, including the Sea of Galilee and the Golan Heights, and a stay at a kibbutz which runs a motel and restaurant. At dinner that night my pain worsened, and now I found it hard to breathe. I assumed that somehow I'd broken a rib or pulled a muscle humping our heavy suitcases. A possible alternative explanation was that my years of wine-bibbing had finally paid off in a monstrously swollen liver which was now obtruding anomalously up into my rib cage. I couldn't see the kibbutz physician because he was on vacation. The solution to my problem, it was indicated, was to be examined at a hospital some thirty miles away. A taxi took us there—by this time I was groaning and thrashing about in the back seat—and within an hour I was scrutinized, thumped, X-rayed, and, encased in blue pajamas made of some canvas-like material, installed in a bed in a ward. I hurt like hell. For no reason at all, I had achieved a severe case of pleurisy. I would recover, I was told, but the treatment would take two weeks. And after that, I was warned, for an additional week I would have to convalesce somewhere.

Somewhere. "Where do you want to go?" my wife asked when I was ready to leave the hospital. Where indeed did we want to spend a week?

> The world was all before them, where to choose
> Their place of rest, and Providence their guide.

I could have said I wanted to go to Baden-Baden or a Greek island or Juan-les-Pins, or even Oaxaca or Tahiti. Then I realized where I wanted to go.

I wanted to go to a certain small European provincial city on a large lake. The population is about eighty thousand. A Romance language is spoken there, and the prevailing religion is Roman Catholic in a serious but never solemn way—lots of processions and frequent public blessing of objects like fishing boats and municipal vehicles. Everyone greets the priests in the streets, and the priests (who wear soutanes and birettas and never smoke cigarettes in public) smile back. Almost every week there is a fête celebrating some saint's day. This begins at dawn with a great echoing explosion from the eighteenth-century cannon on the lakefront, proceeds through a day of municipal sports programs accompanied by many drinks, and ends with fireworks over the lake at night, with tired children, unwillingness of friends to part, and universal satisfaction that the day has been spent so well. On this day the police all wear white gloves, and as you walk home you smell tobacco, wine, coffee, and flowers.

Events like that take place near the town center, laid out as an oval sloping slightly uphill one and a half kilometers, from the hotel at the bottom, on the lake, to the municipal building at the top. The architecture here actually dates from the last third of the ninteenth century, but the style is either Palladian or Romanesque or Baroque. A gently curving main street encloses the central grassed area containing a large fountain, never out of order and lighted at night; statues on pedestals, some classical nudes, some fully dressed local worthies of the last century like doctors, composers, and minor authors; curving walks with green slatted wood benches where the elderly rest and admire the beds of red flowers against the grass; and, in the center, a covered band-stand with a wrought-iron railing around it featuring lyres. Around the band-stand are hundreds of quite comfortable folding chairs, and from it twice weekly (Wednesday evenings, Sunday afternoons) issues three hours of band music like *Poet and Peasant Overture,* "Waltz" from *The Merry Widow,* and the "Anvil Chorus" from *Il Trovatore,* with real anvils sending up real sparks when struck with hammers by members of the percussion section. The band, supported by the city, has mastered the complete oeuvres of Romberg and Sousa and Strauss, with the result that if you stay a week you never hear the same "selection" played twice.

On the main street around this oval-shaped central park there is no building taller than three stories, and the ground floors are occupied by shops, restaurants of all categories, and cafés. The shops sell no cameras or electronic equipment, and of course they sell no would-be comic T-shirts, no cocaine or dildos. They sell good-looking clothes and luggage and fine small leather goods, chess sets and interesting playing-cards and dice beautifully machined, antique jewelry and chrome-plated corkscrews that work, snuffboxes and good sandals and surprising things made of marzipan, like little pork chops and slices of salami. There are many bookshops carrying works in the local language as well as stationery and school texts. But there's one shop which stocks all the Penguins and Pelicans, and in addition has all the volumes of Everyman's Library, the Modern Library, and the World's Classics as they existed in 1949.

Each restaurant, whether modest or grand, posts a menu outside, and it is lighted at night. Because the provision of public music is regarded by the municipality as one of its prerogatives and a public trust, mere street musicians are prohibited, and the playing of music inside restaurants, whether by the living or by record or tape, violates a city ordinance which is rigorously enforced. Although this place is neither in nothern Italy nor anywhere in France, the food is a combination of northern Italian and French. You can have *prosciutto e melone* and *fettucine al burro,* and you can also have *truffes en croute, poulet d'estragon,* or trout from the lake, and finish with a soufflé Grand Marnier. And there's a nice local slightly sparking white wine. The waiter, who would rather die than say something like "Good evening. I am your waiter. My name is Dimitri," leaves the wine in a bucket by your table, assuming that you will want to pour it yourself. After dinner you stroll out to a café, where you have coffee and cognac and perhaps a little pastry or ice cream and watch the young people go by, some slowly in cars, some on foot, but all very attractive and all, boys and girls alike, wearing tight white trousers. They seem very happy. If café musicians are prohibited, lottery-ticket sellers, shoe-shine boys, and itinerant peanut venders are allowed, but they are a very nice type who smile and go away immediately when you shake your head ever so slightly.

It is at the café especially that you'd do well to master the local currency and coinage. You get four of the monetary units to the dollar. Coffee at the café costs half a unit, beer two, the wine in the restaurant four or five, depending on whether it's 1976 (a nice year) or 1978 (a not so nice one). A large, satisfying meal costs about eighteen units. The coins are cupro-nickel all the way through (no tacky sandwiches) and of satisfying and even comic design, like the Irish. And the sizes make sense: for example, the "nickel" is not twice the size of the "dime." The banknotes reveal their value instantly by being of different sizes and colors, like the French. There is a 15 percent service charge everywhere. You leave a tiny tip over that only when the waiter has told you something really funny (and funny by international standards) or the chambermaid in the hotel has flirted with you. You also might leave a small tip (an eighth of a unit would do it) with the attendant always on duty at the impeccably tidy public conveniences in the center of the park. A man once tried to make a pass at another man there, but he was summarily deported, and there's been no trouble of that kind for years. From the café you can see the taxi rank, with four or five cabs always waiting. They are built on the British model with lots of room and so tall that you look not only out but down. They have entirely trustworthy meters, and the driver will expect a tip only if, when the ride ends, he jumps out and opens your door, or carries suitcases into the hotel. Here and there you find kiosks on corners: they sell tobacco and matches and combs and papers of pins and soap, and postage stamps so tastefully designed you hate to stick them on and mail them away. The kiosks also stock a full line of newspapers, weekly journals of opinion, and illustrated magazines from all over. You can stroll slowly around the whole central oval in less than an hour, sampling the various cafés and making small purchases. In the daytime you are likely to pass or be passed by a crocodile of schoolchildren in blue and white carrying little briefcases. A teacher or nun is at the head, and while she's leading them in public, the pupils conduct themselves with the dignity appropriate to learning. You will arrive ultimately down at the lake front, where you will often see fishermen making for their vivid little boats and wearing their traditional outfits, including long knitted caps with tassels, like the Portuguese.

The glory of this city is its renowned hotel on the lake. The citizens are proud of it, and they like the people who come there. This is where I'm going to get my strength back. Architecturally the hotel resembles a large British country house dating from the early part of the nineteenth century. Outside, stucco and stone, roofed patios with Palladian balustrades, ferns and hanging baskets. Inside, the atmosphere is that of a well-run London club of sixty years ago. There are public rooms for specialized purposes: billiard- and card-playing, letter-writing, reading. Downstairs there is a cigar stand which sells cigars. When you arrive the people at the reception desk are not engaged at the telephone.

The elevator closes with a sliding bronze gate finished in faded gilt, and there is a small upholstered bench to sit on. There is no piped music for the same reason there is none in the restaurants. Your guest room will have flowers and fruit in it, as well as a small sewing kit. When you look into the bathroom, you will find a tub over six feet long. It is made of porcelain. Above it is a small drying line. There are more towels and soap than you will need and two extra rolls of toilet paper. The bed is double and the two reading lamps are fitted with hundred-watt bulbs. There are extra bulbs in a drawer of the dresser, whose mirror is unostentatiously arranged so that if so minded a couple can watch itself performing sexual intercourse. The closets contain an excess of quite stealable broad wood hangers, which the guests do not steal. In the guest rooms as everywhere in the hotel there is moulding at the junctions of walls and ceilings, and there are moulded panels (six or eight) on the doors, which are of oak or similar hardwood. Door fittings are of brass, and the doorknobs have things like lion heads in bas-relief. A search of the bed-table drawers will reveal no Bible, the management entertaining sufficient respect for its clientele to let it select its own reading matter without suggestions clients might find impertinent or, if Moslem or Hindu, provincial, impious, and offensive.

When you go down for drinks and dinner, you will find everything nicely arranged for the convenience of the guests rather than the staff: it's as if these people had never heard of the modern world. Drinks can be had immediately on any one of the covered patios by sitting at one of the low tables and simply ringing the little bell. With the drinks arrive, unfailingly, salted peanuts and sometimes the splendid local potato chips and olives. After 5:00 p.m. one is offered tiny hot hors d'oeuvre such as midget weenies in blankets made of memorable crust.

The hotel restaurant: thick white tablecloths and twenty-four-inch napkins at every meal, including breakfast. Flowers on the table always. The cutlery is heavy nickel silver, the waiters aged and serious. They wear black and white. You are hardly seated at breakfast before someone arrives to pour coffee or tea. The bread and rolls are superb.

On the beach side of the hotel there's a simpler restaurant with light meals and snacks at all hours and a bar with waiters who with the greatest good humor will bring things to your place on the beach. There is no sign on the beach prohibiting anything. When you look across the lake you look not upon emptiness but at boats and, far away, the dim outlines of the distant other shore with light-blue mountains rising behind. While you're here the weather is bright and clear, warm in the daytime but at night cool enough for good sleeping.

This is the place where I wanted to go to recuperate. But we did not go to this place. After a day or two in Tel Aviv, which resembles this place in no respect, I felt perfectly well, and we resumed our trip and flew on to Central Europe. And by the time we returned to the United States, and to our condition, this place was only a memory.

IV

BRITONS,
LARGELY ECCENTRIC

Boswell and His
Memorable Scenes

The spirit of James Boswell is always with us, lurking in the most surprising places. Consider the art dealer Ambroise Vollard, depicted by Jean Renoir in the act of "interviewing' Renoir *père:*

> He had a talent for putting his adversary off the scent by asking idiotic questions, half naïve, half specially fabricated. For example: "Tell me, Monsieur Renoir: what are bloomers for?" Renoir: "For horses." He began every sentence with a "Tell me." "Tell me, Monsieur Renoir: why is the Eiffel Tower built of iron, and not of stone like the Tower of Pisa?" "Tell me, Monsieur Renoir: why don't they have bull-fights in Switzerland? With all those cows, you know. . . .

And Tom Driberg unwittingly discloses Boswell up to his old tricks at one of Edith Sitwell's evenings. Once one of the guests was, unaccountably,

> Dr. Frank Buchman, founder of Moral Rearmament, then in its early days as the Oxford Group. [Geoffrey] Gorer teased Buchman a good deal, and after Gorer had left, Buchman insisted that his hostess should join him in prayer for Gorer's conversion and in seeking divine guidance on the best means of bringing this about. Edith said afterwards that she disliked being forced to her knees and also disliked Buchman's handshake, which she found clammy.

Driberg asks: "Who can have been so inept as to bring Buchman to Edith's flat? Gorer thinks it was 'a young Scotsman.' Whoever it was, it is unlikely that he was asked again.''

Wherever social scenes are not only enacted but sparked and stage-managed, there harbors the spirit of Boswell. Wherever calculated encounters between notorious incompatibles leave little ripples of hostility and embarrassment behind, there Boswell chiefly lives. For he is much more than a case. He is a type; and it is the special privilege of types to indulge in successive metempsychoses. He is the eternal fixer and manager and inquirer and seeker of clear answers to dumb questions. Later avatars are Bouvard and Pécuchet and Dick Cavett.

The modernity of the man, for good or ill, is incredible. He is after all the sole inventor of that peculiarly contemporary exercise, the "interview," especially the hard as opposed to the soft kind. Here the straight-faced interviewer poses the most vexing questions to elicit the maximum rise from his subject and thus guarantee the most dynamic copy: "If, Sir, you were shut up in a castle, and a newborn child with you, what would you do?" "Pray, Sir, can you tell me why an apple is round and a pear pointed?" "When we were alone, I introduced the subject of death. . . ." Even the cunning inquisitors of the *Paris Review* have been unable to improve on Boswell's technique:

INTERVIEWER Would you admit to there being symbolism in your novels?
HEMINGWAY I suppose there are symbols because critics keep finding them. If you do not mind I dislike talking about them and being questioned about them. It is hard enough to write books and stories without being asked to explain them as well.

Boswell is also modern in his sexual ambitiousness and self-consciousness. Except for Boswell, few before the age of Kinsey, Masters and Johnson, and Wilhelm Reich can have bothered to record for posterity the number of their sequential orgasms on given occasions. Pepys and William Hickey sometimes come close to Boswell in erotic frankness, but their enjoyments of the flesh are not, like Boswell's, a function of the delights of documentation. Very forward-looking too is Boswell's constant pursuit of "authenticity" both in his own experience and in his recording of it. When he carefully spreads his writing paper on the very slab covering the body of Melanchthon while writing about it to Johnson, he is engaged in prefiguring the whole modern idea of "documentary." And his sense of the necessity, and even the seemliness, of full literary publicity is our sense. He knows that the age of anonymous publication is past and that personality never hurt any piece of writing. He knows that a book succeeds only as it catches its audience in a receptive posture, prepared for relish by all the arts of reputation and publicity. Boswell thus did not let his Corsican book drop among those unprepared to consider it interesting: he provided the context for the book by puffing it himself anonymously, by making certain that everyone knew beforehand what a valuable and interesting person he was. The purpose of an author, as not only Boswell but also Johnson knew, is to be read. And Boswell was read. As Frederick A. Pottle says in *James Boswell: The Earlier Years:*

> By the publication of *An Account of Corsica* Boswell became
> at twenty-seven a literary figure of international reputation.
> . . . For a certain period of time far more people knew about
> him than knew about Goldsmith or Johnson.

Pottle has been meditating a biography of Boswell for well over thirty years, ever since his exemplary "bio-bibliography" of 1929, *The Literary Career of James Boswell,* where his focus, happily, was on his man not as a prodigy of fatuity but as an author. No one knows Boswell as well as Pottle, and his decades of intimacy have given him just the right approach, at once affectionate and ironic. Unpretentiousness is Pottle's charm, as well as a readiness to take the stylistic low road when appropriate. He speaks of Boswell's "Holland act"; people in his book "blab" and "guzzle" and "tattle." And his scholarly candor is as refreshing as his language. What must constitute an almost unique moment in contemporary literary scholarship is his thus characterizing one of his own early essays on Boswell: "Ill-informed and inaccurate, to be used with great care." No one can come to grips with Boswell at all who does not have a bent for quiet irony, and here Pottle is gifted too. "Boswell's sight-seeing in Paris was surprisingly restricted and conventional: he felt an obligation to explore it diligently on its wicked side only." Speaking of Boswell's new sobriety in Utrecht, Pottle says: "Even his schemes for publication took their color from the new and sober pattern of his life, became in fact quite Dutch."

But if style is the merit of Pottle's biography, structure is its defect. It has no dynamics: it starts at the "beginning" and proceeds doggedly onward, emphasizing everything equally. Why must a biography so rigorously enslave itself to chronology? Why can't it operate like other works of art and find its own kind of order for the job at hand? The claims of chronology must be recognized, of course, but they can be recognized in the notes, or an appendix. Why not organize a biography by themes or motifs? Or at least why not use the beginning for the most interesting matter and present the subject's ancestry and infancy—almost always the least interesting things about him—in a less conspicuous part of the book? Justin Kaplan's life of Whitman offers a good structural model. Kaplan begins by presenting the end of Whitman's life, performing a biographical version of what, in fiction, used to be called "the narrative hook" (at the beginning, hook the reader with compelling narrative). Only after he has engaged the reader in the image of the old, ailing Whitman and got him asking his own questions about why he ended that way does Kaplan go back to the beginning. Perhaps too "popular" a way of proceeding, but certainly one way to induce readers to open even learned biographies.

Boswell was luckier in writing the *Life of Johnson* than Pottle in writing the life of Boswell. He knew less about his hero's earlier years, and fortune, if not art, invited him to skimp the early part of Johnson's life for which documentation was scarce. Thus the emphasis falls as if naturally on the rich adult years beginning in 1763, when Boswell and Johnson (then fifty-four) met. The important part of the book becomes the longest part. What's wanting in Pottle's book, despite its lively texture and civilized tone, is the appearance of art. It is devoid of proportioning.

Pottle's Boswell, for all his gaucherie and self-concern, is essentially a writer. When a type like Boswell becomes a writer he is doubly destined to persist, for

> Time . . .
> Worships language and forgives
> Everyone by whom it lives;
> Pardons cowardice, conceit,
> Lays its honours at their feet.

His great work is his life-long journal, out of which he carved and fashioned the Johnsonian books. These, especially the *Life of*

Johnson, established a new genre for the nineteenth and twentieth centuries—the excessively full literary biography, overweight, obsessively "authentic," minutely detailed. A characteristic of the genre is that no one can work in it without ceding his identity to his subject and becoming forever the creature of his author. Obsession is inseparable from the genre; other characteristics are exhaustion, intemperate documentation, and artistic numbness induced by an overwhelming excess of material. Newman Ivey White's *Shelley,* Richard Ellmann's *Joyce,* Mark Schorer's *Sinclair Lewis,* Arthur Mizener's life of Ford Madox Ford, Pottle's Boswell itself—these weighty biographies constitute an important part of the legacy of Boswell. Before him there were what we would recognize as "biographical treatments." After him, the deluge, from Lockhart's *Life of Scott* to Carlos Baker's life of Hemingway.

Boswell wrote a journal in the first place because he was a natural writer and because, as Pottle says, "The accepted public genres of [his] day offered him none that quite suited him." If we knew less about Boswell, we might assume that his main motive in scribbling about his life and contacts was a mere lust for personal publicity. But David Hume, who knew him well, perceived that his ruling passion was "a rage for literature." He was a published author by the age of nineteen, and he grew to become the most conspicuous ornament on the list of the publishers Edward and Charles Dilly.

Boswell's invention of a new biographical genre is fine enough. But perhaps even finer is his stylistic achievement. At a moment when prose offered almost irresistible temptations toward either symmetry or décor, Boswell had the temerity to keep his writing clean and spare. As Pottle says, "In him we seem to see the past through no medium at all, or at most through plate glass." Not that he can't work out in practically any modish style when he wants to: the Gibbonian, for example. He reports to Rousseau from Rome: "I remembered the rakish behaviour of Horace and other amorous Roman poets, and I thought that one might well allow one's self a little indulgence in a city where there were prostitutes licensed by the Cardinal Vicar." But normally he pitches it low, and "it is because Boswell's style is so scrupulously low-pitched," Pottle perceives, "that it affects us like the writing of a contemporary."

Boswell would be ravished by Pottle's big book (and it's only the first half of his life: Frank Brady is working on the second half), for he lived always like a man hoping that his biography would be an exhaustive affair. We can now see that his "archives," all those monstrous bales and bundles braving time, were materials doggedly preserved for his inevitable biographer, whoever he might turn out to be. All he knew was that he would have one. He had done his part by making his life interesting—now let the biographer do his. Boswell seldom did anything without a consciousness that his future biographer's eye was on him. Uncertain whether to marry an Irish girl of promise, for example, he inclines toward her because "my Irish connexion [would] make a pretty anecdote in my life." This awareness that meaning attaches to his life only as he is able to enter literature as a character worthy of a future biographer motivates much of his eccentricity. In his own lifetime he became consciously a literary character. Or rather, a whole series of them. He is surely one of the first to realize Christopher Isherwood's point that "good autobiography is only achieved when its live original has qualities which would make him a suitable hero for a novel."

Or in Boswell's case, a play. Now he is Malvolio:

> I am always fixing some period for my perfection as far as possible. Let it be when my *Account of Corsica* is published. I shall then have a character which I must support. I will swear like an ancient disciple of Pythagoras to observe silence. I will be grave and reserved, though cheerful and communicative. . . .

Then again, as when he upbraids the actress Louisa Lewis for clapping him, he is Hamlet confronting Gertrude in her closet:

BOSWELL Do you know that I have been very unhappy since I saw you?
LOUISA How so, Sir?
BOSWELL Why, I am afraid that you don't love me so well, nor have not such a regard for me, as I thought you had.
LOUISA Nay, dear Sir! (*Seeming unconcerned.*)

BOSWELL Pray, Madam, have I no reason?
LOUISA No, indeed, Sir, you have not.
BOSWELL Have I no reason, Madam? Pray think.
LOUISA Sir!

Part of the richness of this derives from Boswell's doubtless knowing that Gertrude was one of Louisa's roles: she'd played her at
Covent Garden just a few months before. Another time, traveling
with Johnson near Loch Ness when both inadvertently frighten
an old woman fearful of rape, he is (as Pottle says elsewhere) an
unlikely Prince Hal to Johnson's Falstaff:

> A good way up the Loch, I perceived a little hut with an
> oldish woman at the door of it. I knew it would be a scene
> for Mr. Johnson. . . . She . . . was afraid we wanted to go to
> bed with her. . . . Mr. Johnson and I afterwards made merry
> upon it. I said it was he who alarmed the poor woman's
> virtue. "No, sir," said he. "She'll say, 'There came a wicked
> young fellow, a wild young dog, who I believe would have
> ravished me had there not been with him a grave old gentle-
> man who repressed him. But when he gets out of sight of his
> tutor, I'll warrant you he'll spare no woman he meets, young
> or old.'" "No," said I. "She'll say, 'There was a terrible
> ruffian who would have forced me, had it not been for a
> gentle, mild-looking youth, who, I take it, was an angel.'"

It is Boswell's turn to play Falstaff when he answers a letter from
Johnson directing him to empty his head of Corsica: "Empty my
head of Corsica? Empty it of honour, empty it of humanity, empty
it of friendship, empty it of piety?" And if he plays in and out of
various Shakespearian roles, more uniformly he enacts a genteel
version of Captain Macheath, with conscious traces of Joseph
Addison (elegant sentiment), Sir Richard Steele (gaiety), and
Samuel Johnson (judiciousness). Sensing his identity as a literary
character, he contrives the events of his life to fill it with dramatic
materials, most of them the fruit of his talents for gross incongruity and wry self-scrutiny and self-criticism. And this is another
reason for his literary success: the duality of his character, his
capacity to act with one part of himself and to record with another.
When afire and at the top of his form, he becomes playwright,
actor, director, critic, and historian of the drama all at once. Thus
the series of great Boswellian moments which Pottle delivers.

Consider, for example, Boswell the university student, destined, as we know—and surely he has some inkling of it—to become one of the most memorable satyrs of all time: afflicted at once with the adolescent sexual development of his person and at the same time with a Calvinist conviction of the sinfulness of it all, he meditates self-mutilation as a solution. "The example of Origen" is his inspiration. But, he assures us, "that madness passed." Or consider Boswell, in Scottish blue bonnet, soliciting the King of Prussia's notice on His Majesty's own parade ground at Potsdam. Frederick the Great managed to contain his curiosity. Again, Boswell gains admittance to Rousseau, who has hidden himself in an obscure Swiss valley specifically to avoid this sort of thing, by sending in a note telling Rousseau how interesting he is: "Though I am still a young man, I have experienced such a variety of existence as will strike you with wonder." Triumphant with Rousseau, he next crashes Voltaire's residence to dispute with him about the immortality of the soul. Voltaire, bored and exasperated, finds his only defense in affecting a fainting fit. Boswell patiently sits by and awaits his recovery. He then renews the attack. We have Boswell reverently on his knees at Horace's presumed villa and leading a window-smashing mob in Edinburgh to celebrate the final success of the Douglas Cause. Terrified at the possibility of rejection in courtship, he performs the eighteenth-century equiv- alent of Whitman's "I think I could turn and live with animals, they are so placid and self-contain'd": he entertains images of fleeing to America and harboring with the Indians ("I had great thoughts of acquiring strength and fortitude"). Just before his marriage to his respectable cousin, he flies to London to clear away his gonorrhea with a course of Kennedy's Lisbon Diet Drink. Again, depressed by a severe gonorrheal attack, he cheers himself up by dashing off to Stratford to appear at Garrick's Shakespeare Jubilee in the costume of an armed Corsican chief, wearing the words *Viva la Libertà* on his hat and passing out copies of his own poem on the occasion. He carried with him to Stratford "a large wig and some rouge for disguise": those who don't realize the inten- sity of his role-playing will assume that these properties were part of his Corsican costume. But no: their purpose, it proves, was to prevent his being recognized in Stratford as James Boswell, Attor- ney, until he could assume his role of Boswell-as-Corsican-publicist.

"Corsica Boswell" he was called, and this was the identity he wanted to assume unmixed at the Jubilee.

All his life he adored rituals and memorable scenes in which he played conspicuous parts. Had he not contrived all these scenes, he would have risked a life of placid uniformity, unattractive to a biographer. Leaving Edinburgh for London as a youth, he must ritualize: he decides to bow three times to the palace of Holyrood-house, the emblem of ancient Scottish self-respect. At Utrecht, deep in a fit of melancholy and all but convinced that he is a toy of Necessity, he walks out to the fields, draws his sword "glittering in the sun," and swears on the hilt to endure and not to babble about his depression. He loved contrasts and oppositions, the more egregious—and touching—the better. What he noticed on Corsica was the incongruity between the primitive setting and the elegant usages of the inhabitants. At a house in Morsiglia, a vile rustic backwater, he records with relish the presence of a Raphael copy: "There was no necessity for its being well done. To see the thing at all was what surprised me." And at Pascal Paoli's head-quarters,

> When [my] passport was finished, and ready to have the seal put to it, I was much pleased with a beautiful, simple incident. The Chancellor desired a small boy who was play-ing in the room by us, to run to his mother, and bring the great seal of the kingdom.

Most young men who have spent weeks preparing a seduction would want to get on with it immediately when the opportunity for consummation was at hand. Not Boswell: he must do it his way. While Louisa undresses, he stalls. He takes a candle and strolls out to the dark inn-yard, in a very cold mid-January. "I experienced for some minutes," he records, "the rigours of the season, and called into my mind many terrible ideas of hardships, that I might make a transition from such dreary thoughts to the most gay and delicious feelings." An awareness of incongruity is indispensable to his identity: not to "make a transition" on this occasion would be to risk nullity.

It is out of such oppositions and incongruities, whether ob-served or contrived, that Boswell makes his literature. His aim in focusing on the incongruous—and this is what distinguishes him from his contemporaries—is never satiric. It is instead profoundly sympathetic. He welcomed incongruities in the world around him as a way of persuading himself that his own painful internal divisions had really a counterpart in the objective world outside and were not the deforming secret singularities he feared they were. His eye for incongruity originates in an impulse of rationalization and self-protection. But it ends as the moving spring of *The Life of Samuel Johnson, LL.D.*: all that wisdom combined with all that sloth! all that charity together with all that coarseness! all that intellectual beauty emanating from that hideous twitching frame! Boswell is true to his singularity to the end. Perhaps what makes him, finally, so much resemble a modern writer is just this self-division in him, a sickness which he, at least, managed to redeem if not to subdue by transmuting it into something very like art.

Kingy and Some Coevals

Why are we now so fond of contemplating everything Victorian, Edwardian, and Georgian? Why the current enthusiasm not merely for Woolf and Strachey and Wilde but for such phenomena as TV's *Upstairs, Downstairs?* Is it because as the dull, corporate late twentieth century grows more drab and uniform and dreary and programmed, more joylessly food-franchised and supermarketed and box-architectured, we hanker after at least a glimpse of class and elegance and real food and real leisure, as well as real eccentricity and real freedom? What is supplied by a couple of recent books about King Edward VII ("Kingy," as one of his ladyfriend's adoring children liked to call him) is vicarious swank, and it can clearly minister to our need.

What slave of the supermarket shelves, bored by synthetics and "additives" and anxious about cholesterol, will not relish being told by Christopher Hibbert, in *The Royal Victorians: King Edward VII, His Family and Friends,* that at house parties at Sandringham the king weighed each guest at departure, recording the augmentations in a record book? Or that when Edward visited Egypt as Prince of Wales, the Khedive supplied "six blue and gold steamers" for the trip up the Nile, each towing "a barge packed with provisions including 3,000 bottles of champagne, 4,000 bottles of claret, and 20,000 of soda water"? (It's as if you can pull off things like that only on the Nile:

> The barge she sat in, like a burnished throne
> Burned on the water. The poop was beaten gold;
> Purple the sails, etc.)

What reader driving herself toward anorexia would not be transfixed to hear that when the king attended the opera at Covent Garden he was preceded by "a chef and six footmen and by nu-

157

merous hampers filled with cloths, silver, gold plate, and food for
the ten- or twelve-course meal" to be consumed during the inter-
mission? And that sort of thing, a supper, really, took place only a
couple of hours after a stupendous dinner. Once the king got home,
there was the cold chicken always ready on the bedside table "in
case he woke up hungry in the night." At middle age, Edward,
although only 5 feet 7 inches, weighed over 225 pounds and had
a 48-inch waist. A friend who called him "Tum-Tum" was once
asked to leave the house.

"What a pretty boy!" people said when he was born, in 1841. It
was his mother's desire that he be brought up to resemble "his
dearest papa" Albert "in *every, every* respect." But by the age of
two he was already a very different sort. He hated his tutors and
studies, developed a stammer, flew into fits of stamping and scream-
ing. Victoria was appalled, anxious that in a moment of republi-
canism or even revolution the heir not betray signs of George IV's
madness. If the monarchy was to be saved, the future monarch
must be a man "of calm, profound, comprehensive understanding,
with a deep conviction of the necessity of practical morality." But
Edward remained ungovernable, and pressure and punishment
only made him worse. "A very bad day," one of his tutors wrote
in his diary. "The P. of W. has been like a person half silly. . . .
He was very rude, . . . throwing stones in my face. . . . Later in the
day he became violently angry because I wanted some Latin done."
Edward never became really literate, later writing one of his children from India about the leeches there that "climb up your legs
and bight you." But in his good moments he was affectionate and
gregarious, and on his early travels—attended by chaperons, tutors,
physicians, divines, and officers—he did not disgrace himself.

He was sent for a year to Oxford, and then to Cambridge, but
what he really wanted was to serve in the Army. Albert let him
summer with a unit encamped near Dublin, but disaster ensued:
he scandalized his parents by going to bed with the actress Nellie
Clifden. When Albert was carried off by typhoid in 1861, Victoria
let it be widely believed that worry over Edward's misbehavior had
hastened his end.

It was thought that only an early marriage would save him, and
there was general relief when at twenty-two he married Princess
Alexandra of Denmark. During the ceremony the four-year-old

kaiser-to-be perhaps foreshadowed future troubles by tossing Victoria's muff out a coach window and then addressing her as "Duck." The newly-wed Edward, fearing boredom acutely, lost no time in filling his house with wits and sportsmen and actresses while his mother grew more and more horrified. The sweet, thin, deaf, lame Alexandra stayed home while her husband dashed to races, nightclubs, bawdy houses, music halls, and constant parties. When these palled, there was yachting, shooting, masquerades, gambling, billiards, and more courtesans. Victoria was convinced that his pursuit of pleasure must bring on in England something very like the French Revolution, complete with guillotine. Warning him against raffish companions, she said in measured words that he would regret them "if ever you become King."

His popularity reached a low in 1870, when he was implicated in an adultery scandal, and after clearly lying on the witness stand he was jeered in the street and booed at the theater. But typhoid, that great Victorian *deus ex machina,* intervened melodramatically, striking him down after his disgrace; and his miraculous recovery generated renewed sympathy and helped restore his popularity. But he still had nothing official to do. His mother carefully kept everything public from him, and he did seem too indiscreet for serious responsibility.

When he was fifty-nine, in 1901, his mother died. The "arch vulgarian," as Henry James called him in a prissy moment, ascended the throne, where he would remain for nine years, becoming more impressive all the time and finally endearing himself as a peacemaking diplomat and distinguishing himself as a uniquely "European" British monarch. With his mum gone, he hurled himself into his new job, rapidly installing modern bathrooms in the palaces, cleaning out Victoria's bric-a-brac, signing with his own hand the thousands of military commissions, interesting himself in everything. He insisted that he be consulted and that his advice be sought, that he not be considered a mere puppet or "signing machine." He pressed for army and navy reform and for improvements in public health, and devoted himself especially to foreign affairs. His state visits to France and Russia, and his admirable tact in both places, have been thought instrumental in cementing the Entente Cordiale. There had been ill feeling between king and kaiser for years, and the Germans, impressed by

Edward's success in promoting alliances with France on one side and Russia on the other, now began to talk of "encirclement" and to foresee the nightmare of a two-front war. But by 1910 the king was almost seventy, and no one could go on much longer smoking twelve cigars daily and devouring those meals. When he died, people were astonished at how much he was loved and admired.

As he revealed in his excellent biography of Samuel Johnson a few years ago, Christopher Hibbert has a talent for understanding stout, funny, complicated men, and his biography of Edward and his near relatives does ample justice to the king's mixture of childishness and sophistication, selfishness and generosity, social sensitivity and fits of fury. No great reader, the king was an extraordinary public speaker, and he spoke without notes. He loved fast cars and fast people, chaffing, noise, and practical jokes. He was remarkably kind and open, with a unique fondness for pariahs like Jews and Americans. He once reminded the foreign secretary that "because a man has a black face and a different religion from your own, there is no reason why he should be treated as a brute." Edward was loyal to his friends, no matter what scrapes they got into. His own sexuality was so powerful and "normal" that when any acquaintance was caught in a homosexual scandal he regarded him as simply a lunatic and expressed profound pity for his "malady." He hated study and solitary thought, but few observed people more acutely. His contributions to modern Europe lie not merely in the ideal of peace-keeping by personally initiated alliances. He also popularized the homburg, the dinner jacket, and the custom of not buttoning the bottom vest button.

There is less about vest buttons than about the diplomacy of persuasion in Gordon Brook-Shepherd's *Uncle of Europe: The Social and Diplomatic Life of Edward VII,* as responsible a book as Hibbert's and as well researched: much valuable new material is drawn from the family papers of the Portuguese Marquis Luis de Soveral. In delivering a dramatic account of Edward's statesmanly and diplomatic achievements, Brook-Shepherd depicts this social king—who either knew or was related to all the crowned heads of Europe (and every country was then a monarchy except France and Switzerland)—as "a ruler who used dynastic diplomacy to place him in the front rank of the European statesmen of his day." The king's obsessions with protocol, including correct dress, made him virtually a charter member of the international *corps diplomatique,* and his fondness for travel and for Europe acquainted him with everyone rich or important. At spas and hotels, on shipboard and in automobiles and trains, he talked and listened and advised. What emerged between Kingy's courses and wines and cigars was the "Edwardian" stability based on alliances providing the crucial groupings when Europe went to war four years after he died and the Edwardian era officially came to an end.

If the term "Georgian" seems an invitation to patronize writers of floral poetry, "Edwardian" seems an invitation to see in the age's enjoyment of eccentricity a dangerous leaning toward madness. This at least seems the assumption governing *Eminent Edwardians,* by the British biographer and journalist Piers Brendon. He seems one of those who have trouble liking the people of the past. It's as if being alive while those others are dead confers some superiority on him. The title of his book evokes Lytton Strachey's *Eminent Victorians,* published over sixty years ago, and the evocation is not just intentional—it's complacent. Brendon imagines that he can reproduce something of Strachey's tone and method in his sketches of four worthies of Edward's age. Where Strachey deployed the irony and innuendo of genius to unmask four "representative" Victorians, Brendon more coarsely defames four eccentrics who flourished from 1900 to 1914 ("Each stamped the imprint of a monstrous personality on the modern world") and from their oddities affects to infer the spirit of the age.

His Edwardians are Lord Northcliffe, like Hearst an inventor of the popular (i.e., the low) press; the Tory dandy politician Arthur Balfour, prime minister from 1902 to 1905; Mrs. Emmeline Pankhurst, leader of the Suffragettes; and General Robert Baden-Powell, hero of the Boer War and founder of the Boy Scouts. Brendon's little biographies average sixty pages, and his commitment to "compact biography" is welcome in this day of the thoroughly documented but unreadable reference biography. But the size of his four biographies is more agreeable than their tenor. "Imitating" Strachey turns out to be harder than it looks. Those who think of Strachey as only a suave deflater of reputations may forget what he wrote in the preface to *Eminent Victorians:* "Human beings are too important to be treated as mere symptoms of the past. They have a value which is independent of any temporal

processes—which is eternal, and must be felt for its own sake."
Brendon succeeds in the easy task of patronizing his subjects. He
does not succeed in the harder work of locating their value through
an exercise of sympathy.

Not that, with the exception of Baden-Powell, they are easy to
like. Lord Northcliffe seems a gift to the satirist. He was hopelessly devoted to his mother, in the style of the period. He always
called her "darling" while his wife was only "dear." The Education Act of 1870 gave him his chance: it created a vast body of new
readers avid for trash. This he supplied tirelessly in a series of
pulp weeklies and dailies. He ultimately bought the London
Times, where the ferocious propaganda he caused to be published
greatly increased the savagery of the First World War. He was
tyrannical and rude and nutty, given to utterances like "You must
be a Jew, you have such a Scottish-sounding name." He was a
master of publicity and a crashing lowbrow with such influence
that the Great trembled, or so his parasites assured him. He lived
splendidly on the estate later inhabited by J. Paul Getty. He ended
quite mad. His last coherent message was, "Tell mother she is the
only one." Brendon's verdict, which seems too high-minded, if not
self-righteous, for the occasion, mistakes the amusing for the
menacing: "By confusing gewgaws with pearls, by selecting the
paltry at the expense of the significant, . . . by over-simplifying the
complex, . . . by presenting stories as entertainment, . . . Northcliffe titillated, if he did not debauch, the public mind; he pol-
luted, if he did not poison, the wells of knowledge." That's supposed to sound like Strachey. But actually, we've heard it more
recently. It's Aunt Sally tut-tutting over the influence of television,
which she is proud to say she "never watches."

Arthur Balfour is depicted as idle and frigid, a slick Mandarin
skilled only in equivocation. "Once he was sent an urgent minute
by his staff outlining two possible lines of action and asking,
'Which of these two courses do you wish us to adopt?' 'Yes,' replied
Balfour." Brendon delights perhaps a bit too much to emphasize
that the Balfour Declaration promising the Jews their own home-
land in Palestine was a shrewd anti-Semitic trick, designed to
cleanse Britain of "these outlandish figures," whom Balfour believed "could never, and should never, be assimilated into Gentile
society."

The beautiful but obdurate Mrs. Pankhurst is easily sent down for her puritanism, her noisy insistence not just on votes for women but on chastity for men. She was undeniably destructive, and she lusted for martyrdom. In 1914 she mutated without a pause into a tyrant of another kind, becoming "the flail of slackers, shirkers, and strikers," handing out white feathers and bawling for conscription.

Baden-Powell was also hung up on sexual purity, by which he meant total abstinence. He exhorted his Scouts to "douse the 'racial organ' regularly in cold water." He was also mad about "fun": one of his party turns was playing the piano with his toes. An innocent with extraordinary energy, he conceived of the Scouts as an antidote not just to sex but to socialism as well, which meant an antidote to strikes and loafing. He lived a very long time, and, says Brendon, even at the end "he did not enter a second childhood —he had never left his first." Although Brendon gives him a hard time, projecting him as a symptom of the Edwardian "nostalgia for the nursery," the reader may conclude that anyone who in a long if rather silly life commits as little evil as Baden-Powell deserves instead something close to celebration.

Eminent Edwardians, while often entertaining, leaves a sour taste, especially if we put it next to Hibbert's successful understanding of that oddity, the king. The style is too self-conscious ("Freud only knows"), too dependent on un-Stracheyan puns and mechanical allusions and elegant variations. Sometimes the fault is over-insistence: "Mrs. Pankhurst came not to bring peace but the sword. By now danger was her element. Excitement was her salamander's fire. Drama was her drug." If the style doesn't work, neither does the argument that these four are "in some way representative of the Edwardian era." Selecting four people as symptomatic of an age is an intellectual con-game. If ridicule of our age is your object, take as typical Richard Nixon, the Billys Graham and Carter, and General Westmoreland. If you want to give a different picture entirely, just shift sights and select Hannah Arendt, General Marshall, George Balanchine, and J. William Fulbright. If you write as well as Strachey you may be able to pull off the con. Otherwise, no.

Baron Corvo,
Sturdy Beggar

If you allow yourself to meditate on Victorian shell flowers, peacock feathers sticking up from behind picture frames, sentimentality about the Italian Renaissance, and artistic (and erotic)
religiosity, sooner or later you'll think of Frederick Rolfe, self-
styled Baron Corvo, author of those bizarre, over-ripe fictions and
fantasy memoirs, himself the subject of a masterpiece, A. J.
Symons's *The Quest for Corvo*. British eccentricity offers hardly a
more egregious exemplar, and for many years after Symons's inquiry in 1934, appreciation of Corvo seemed primarily a British
prerogative. But now, together with other rare, desirable things
like paintings and literary manuscripts, Corvine studies have
moved to the United States. Ten years ago the collector Donald
Weeks brought out his naïve *Corvo: Saint or Madman?* (False
Dilemma, anyone?), and now we have a much better book, Miriam
J. Benkovitz's *Frederick Rolfe, Baron Corvo: A Biography*, exploiting the rich holograph deposits of Austin, Texas, and New
York City.

Corvo offers a special *frisson* for Americans, whose tradition
offers few eccentrics in the grand style. Gross moral idiots like
Howard Hughes or Lee Harvey Oswald or the Rev. Jim Jones are
about all it can manage. Corvo also offers the American inquirer
the opportunity to tease that forbidden subject here, social class.
Benkovitz's life of Rolfe constitutes a tragi-comedy of money and
class, as well as a notation of a touching pre-Joycean moment
when Art was still not sure whether it was part of the official piety
or its resolute enemy.

Rolfe's origins in 1860 were "artistic" in exactly this sad "period" sense. He was the son of a broken manufacturer of pianos,
and little Frederick's early snob religiosity impelled him to play

"priest" at home, dressing up and conducting services which were liturgically very high indeed. He was energetically intelligent and persuaded himself early that his cleverness made him inestimably finer than his schoolmates. He left such *canaille* behind at the age of fourteen and himself commenced schoolmaster junior grade. This meant composing pederastic verses and toying with Roman Catholicism, with heavy emphasis on the imagined physiques of St. Sebastian and the Roman "boy martyr," Tarcissus. "Listen, boys, I tell the story," he wrote,

> Blazoned on the rolls of time,
> How a Boy, in bygone ages,
> Died a Martyr's death sublime.

In addition to producing things like that, he felt it incumbent on him to demonstrate his gentility by writing *shew* for *show* and using words like *persequent* and *purrothrixine*. Benkovitz performs a service by ascertaining that Rolfe's discharge from numerous teaching and tutoring jobs during the eighties had nothing to do with his fondness for boys: it was his lower-middle-class pride and his sense of injured distinction that made him unemployable. He desperately aspired to the priesthood, and his dismissal from the Scots College in Rome for debts, absences, and contumely was a blow from which his "regal dignity" never recovered. Henceforth, while vowing twenty years of "celibacy" to argue his sincerity, he became a violent enemy of Catholic institutions and a self-appointed scourge of that church's moral pretensions. His pride had already involved him deep in poverty, and obedience made him rave and rant.

Back in England in 1890, he projected countless Bouvard and Pécuchet schemes to establish himself as a valuable and up-to-date person: new methods for making lantern slides; bright ideas for underwater photography; improved stratagems for photographing boys in the nude. Now and then he got a menial job, but he always lost it in that affected high style he made his own. Fired once from a clerk's job for "messing about, coming and going when he liked, . . . and telling 'enormous yarns' to support condescension toward his fellow-employees," he "refused to be dismissed and returned for work each day." When the company wrote him a formal letter forbidding him to appear anymore, he answered:

It is a curious thing that at the moment I received your note I was about to carry out an intention I have been forming for some time—viz. to ask whether one would be allowed to invest a small sum say £1,000, in your business, and so secure a permanent and congenial appointment suited to my capacities. Perhaps it is inopportune now, but I think I had better mention it.

Next conceiving himself gifted as a painter, he spent a hopeful year at Holywell making ghastly arts-and-crafts banners to promote the local shrine of St. Winefride's Well. An estimate of his ability as a draftsman and painter can be gathered from his technique for overcoming his "difficulty with . . . drawing":

When he found in an illustrated paper, a magazine, or an advertisement, a figure which suited his needs, Rolfe pasted it on cardboard and cut around it. Then by means of a strong light [an assistant] cast a shadow of the figure on a sheet of white paper and Rolfe outlined it with a pencil. Figures in the foreground of one banner came directly from an advertisement for Scotch Whisky. . . . Rolfe talked grandly of his work. . . .

But this source of dubious income collapsed like all the others. The usual monumental quarrels ensued, and he found himself supporting life with nothing but cigarettes for two days. He also became acquainted with the Holywell workhouse. At one point he solicited commitment to an insane asylum: at least one could eat there. As Shane Leslie said, "He never lost his underlying belief that the artist should be supported by the unartistic."

Turning to writing, he finally found his métier. In the next sixteen years he produced with impressive application the exquisite fictions and imaginative histories that have fascinated posterity, although in their own time they merely impoverished their author. Rolfe could never get along with an agent or publisher, and his assumption that good writing results in instant riches, power, and ease embittered him while it beggared his creditors. He became perhaps the angriest writer in English. *Hadrian the Seventh* and *The Desire and Pursuit of the Whole* pay off old social scores with the brilliant high-class scornful Latinate diction that is part of the British autodidact's stock in trade: "perridiculous," "dirty Demos," "ostended," "ergastulum." To understand why only the half-educated lower middle class talks this way when it conceives its dignity affronted would be to understand some important things about the social history of the nineteenth century. Other words Rolfe overworked are those designating the costly Edwardian gems in whose light he is always seeing physical nature: amathyst, sapphire, topaz, jasper. Fantasies of Bond Street are always breaking in.

Rolfe is so closely associated with Venice that it's a surprise to find that he lived there for only his last six years. He went there for a brief "gorgeous holiday" in 1908 with Richard Dawkins and was left behind after the usual quarrel. In Venice the more and the better he wrote, the poorer he became. His suits turned into smelly strings, and he harbored under a thin blanket in various unpaid-for rooms. The uncelebrated hero of Rolfe's Venice years is Edward de Zucatto, His Majesty's Britannic consul there, who intervened many times on Rolfe's behalf and was always abused for his trouble. Typical of Rolfe's absolutism about everything was his assuming that the passport's words "allow ———— every assistance and protection" meant what they said.

He managed to annoy the whole colony of British "resident aliens" in Venice, and class was the reason. It was the spectacle of unearned money that infuriated him. In their turn the local British patronized him and wondered why he didn't get a job. A sturdy beggar, Edmund Gosse called him. Rolfe retaliated by sailing the lagoons with his gondolier boys in his extravagant boat, its mainsail painted with a nude St. George. He was impossible, but he was also the superior of the "artists," exquisites, and remittance-men then swarming in Venice. Something always propelled him, when he was in need, to the very worst people—horrible Anglican and Catholic divines, the daughter of the absurd American nut Horace Fletcher, at whose board he had earnestly to "Fletcherize"—i.e., chew each mouthful one hundred counted times.

Miriam Benkovitz seems not quite sure what to make of Rolfe's infamous "Venice Letters," those narratives of pederastic experience sent off to Charles Masson Fox to entice him to Venice, where Rolfe hoped to survive by pimping for him. She thinks them largely fictional. Perhaps: but I think they are largely real, just as real as Rolfe's hopes that Fox actually would come to Venice and pay him real money for providing real boys. Rolfe's character is quite complex enough to make such behavior compatible with his Johnsonian habit of praying aloud, quite sincerely, as he walked the streets. His last years in Venice are a reminder of how very nasty that version of pastoral can become for a foreigner without any money. He writes to Fox:

> No tobacco. Alps covered with snow . . . simply perishing cold . . . no privacy . . . *& no heating arrangements whatever.* And I have but one thin blanket. *My dear, I'm simply dying of cold and hunger.*

It was true. Pneumonia followed, and a heart attack finished him off in 1913.

Miriam Benkovitz has based her biography on Rolfe's letters, and this means that her focus is mainly on Rolfe's financial obsessions. The theme of her book is money, and the Rolfe it reveals is a man destroyed by fantasies about riches and aristocratic rarities. His ambitions of holiness, which were genuine, were inseparable from compensatory images of high rank and administrative dominion. It's a real nineteenth-century social-mobility story. If the actual Frederick Rolfe was ragged, nutty, stubborn, and disaster-prone, Baron Corvo had swank and elegance. The distance between these two images, that of the real loser and the fictive winner, is both funny and touching, and it is one of the things that make Rolfe so suggestive an index of an age when the old classes, institutions, churches, monarchies, and armies were beginning to confront the formlessness and uniformity that is the modern scene.

Poor Ivor Gurney

"They are getting at me through wireless." From *The Ordeal of Gilbert Pinfold*? No, from *The Ordeal of Ivor Gurney*, Michael Hurd's biography of the extraordinary insane World War I lyric poet and composer who died in 1937 after fifteen years in an asylum. Waugh's paranoid schizophrenia ended, we are assured, in a cure. Because he was a drunk, a pill-popper, a fatty, and a satirist, we think his affliction funny, and some would say he had it coming to him. Gurney's case is different, but not all that different; and Hurd, who has worked diligently through the whole Gurney archive, tells his sad story with just enough acid to make it credible.

Gurney's education in Gloucester was musical and poetic. Born in 1890, he went to King's School, which supplied choristers to the cathedral, and read privately with a gentle paedophile curate. At fourteen he was composing for piano and violin, ambitious to succeed as a professional like Vaughan Williams. As a boy he was outspoken, solitary, awkward, and sloppy. To his schoolmates he was already "Batty" Gurney. Later, his regimental sergeant major explained to a colonel appalled at Gurney's turnout: "Quite a good man, sir, but he's a musician, and doesn't seem to be able to get himself clean." Locally he was renowned for eccentric long-distance walks and sleepings-out, and for eating nothing for days and then gorging on half-pounds of butter and piles of cakes. The needs of his body embarrassed him: regular meals were an aversion, he was proud of his nightly resort to enemas, and early and late he seems to have repressed his sexuality entirely.

At the Royal College of Music, which he entered when he was twenty-one, he was a headstrong, impractical student, by now nicknamed "Schubert." He thought of himself as "an undigested clod," but his violin sonatas showed promise, and so did his settings of Elizabethan lyrics and of poems by Henley, Housman, and Bridges. Well before the war he was suffering from fits of suicidal depression and what Hurd calls "a marked emotional and physical instability" which troubled his friends. Just before the war he had a breakdown and returned to his beloved Severn—always magic to him—for therapeutic sailing expeditions in his tiny boat *Dorothy*.

Gurney's lunacy was a boon to between-the-wars pacifism. It has usually been understood that he is pre-eminently a monitory victim of the trenches, a sound mind done in by the horrors of the line, and even worse, an invaluable English lyric talent like Chatterton ruined by the cruel world. Hurd shows convincingly that we can't believe this anymore. As he finds, "illness would have declared itself, war or no war." Actually, life in the trenches as a private with the Gloucester Regiment did Gurney no end of good. He testifies frequently that the external distraction and fear in the line are wonderfully efficacious against his prewar aesthete's neurasthenia. What he means is that worrying with good cause is healthier than worrying without. "My mind is becoming saner," he notices, "and more engaged with outside things."

In the trenches he wrote better music than in London because he had no access to a piano, and the poems he sent back were now good enough to persuade Sidgwick & Jackson to bring them out in 1917 as a "war poet's" volume entitled *Severn and Somme*. Even a bullet wound in the arm, not quite a blighty but good enough for six weeks back in Rouen, left him cheerful. In September, 1917, however, he was gassed at Passchendaele and was adjudged to be suffering from shell shock as well. He recovered at a hospital in Scotland, where he fell, platonically, for a nurse. He was happy to be alive and proud to be known as "one of the war poets."

He snapped in March, 1918. His letters turned suicidal. After some months in a military asylum, he was discharged as cured and returned to Gloucester and then, vaguely, to the Royal College, where he resumed his pre-war eccentricities. His second volume of poems, *War's Embers* (1919), was much better than his first. Those who cared could find evidence in it of a rare lyric talent:

To His Love

He's gone, and all our plans
Are useless indeed.

We'll walk no more on Cotswold
  Where the sheep feed
  Quietly and take no heed.

His body that was so quick
  Is not as you
Knew it, on Severn river
  Under the blue
  Driving our small boat through.

You would not know him now—
  But still he died
Nobly, so cover him over
  With violets of pride
  Purple from Severn side.

Cover him, cover him soon!
  And with thick-set
Masses of memoried flowers
  Hide that red wet
  Thing I must somehow forget.

Gurney now played, as Hurd says, the role of Super Tramp, wandering the countryside from one friend's house to another and rapidly losing jobs as clerk and cinema pianist. He was now as impossible as before the war, and even worse: he was hearing voices and holding a pillow to his head to block the electric emissions aimed at him from nearby wireless sets. In 1922, after demanding a pistol at the Gloucester police station and then trying to gas himself, he was committed by his family and friends. He remained behind bars at the City of London Mental Hospital, Dartford, Kent, until he died of tuberculosis fifteen years later. His sufferings there he registered in thousands of lines like these:

    . . . there is dreadful Hell within me
    And nothing helps. Forced meals there have been and
        electricity
    And weakening of sanity by influence
    That's dreadful to endure. And there are orders
    And I am praying for death, death, death,
    And dreadful is the indrawing or out-breathing of breath. . . .

"The madman," says Chesterton, "is not the man who has lost his reason. The madman is the man who has lost everything but his reason." One of Gurney's symptoms was an intense belief in a

rational and just universe specializing in strictly logical compensa-
tion, where sacrifice is requited by "payment" and suffering recom-
pensed by happiness. A constant theme in Gurney's Dartford
poems is that England, whom he has served both as composer and
war poet, has shamefully neglected to offer him "pay for Lavantie."
He doesn't mean money; he means notice: "Soldier's praise I had
earned having suffered soldier's pain." This is also a theme in the
letters of appeal and grievance he poured out to strangers (some
in the United States), church dignitaries, and the London Metro-
politan Police, who, in his mad reason, he imagined would be
moved by the long Wordsworthian couplet-poems and plaintive
letters he addressed to them. In one of these, Gurney suggests that
even the unreason of the body can be tamed by scrupulous rational
observances:

> For 28 days I touched meat or bread only once, and little at
> that. Many people knew the truth and should have admired
> so good a life. . . . I drank much, not really too much, smoked
> much, ate as little as possible. Did gymnastics, digging, used
> an enema, washed my body every morning.

After all this, and the poems and songs as well, "Is there not
honour of war poet at rebirth, or in Heaven?"

One of the heroines of Hurd's biography of this annoying, pitiable man is Miss Marion Scott, who saw that his poems and music
were published while he was in France and who visited him constantly at Dartford. Another is Helen Thomas, widow of Edward
Thomas, who visited him during 1932. He told her, "It was wireless that killed Edward." Once she brought Edward's

> own well-used ordnance maps of Gloucester where he had
> often walked. . . . Gurney at once spread them out on his
> bed and he and I spent the whole time I was there tracing
> with our fingers the lanes and byeways and villages of which
> he knew every step. . . . It was most deeply moving.

A less attractive character is Gurney's brother Ronald, who was
always annoyed by Ivor's artistic pretensions and envious of his
classy London friends. He begrudged publication of his brother's
work until 1959, when he capitulated and lodged the manuscripts
in the Gloucester Public Library. Around 300 of the 900 poems

have been published and 82 of the 265 songs, constituting settings of poems by Hardy, Bridges, Yeats, Graves, and Thomas.

Michael Hurd understands music, but it must be said that Gurney the poet still awaits his critic. Although Hurd knows that pieces of music have models and use received styles, for him literature seems simply to photograph an actuality irresistibly and completely there rather than infusing it with form and thus half creating it. Gurney's odd, wrenched idiom does derive in part from his disturbed state of mind, but it also derives from Whitman and Hopkins and is received in turn by Dylan Thomas and Lincoln Kirstein.

One of the treasures Hurd has unearthed is an unpublished Dartford poem whose second half is incoherent but whose first half indicates abundantly that in his madness Gurney was gifted with uncanny prescience:

Time To Come

They will walk there, the sons of our great grandsons and
Will know no reason for the old love of the land.
There will be no tiny bent-browed houses in the
Twilight to watch, nor small shops of multi-miscellany.
The respectable and red-brick will rule all,
With green paint railings outside the front door wall,
And children will not play skip-games in the gutter,
Nor dust fly furious in hot valour of footer;
Queerness and untidiness will be smoothed out
As any steam-roller tactful, and there'll be no doubt
About the dust bins or the colour of curtains,
No talking at the doors, no ten o'clock flirtings. . . .

The same sensibility that contrived the line

Nor dust fly furious in hot valour of footer

also wrote this:

The Songs I Had

The songs I had are withered
Or vanished clean,
Yet there are bright tracks
Where I have been,

> And there grow flowers
> For others' delight.
> Think well, O singer,
> Soon comes night.

And this:

> Madness my enemy, cunning extreme my friend,
> Prayer my safeguard. (Ashes my reward at end.)

I think he's a poet worth celebrating.

Rider Haggard,
the Public Man

The eccentricities of Boswell and Northcliffe and Corvo appear in flagrant relief when placed against the normalities of Rider Haggard, the model public man. He was less dull than dutiful: the author of *King Solomon's Mines* could never be stigmatized as unimaginative. Indeed, it was precisely his ordinariness that taught him how much ordinary people enjoy fantasizing about violence. The large university library I use contains few books read virtually to pulp by the undergraduates. One is *King Solomon's Mines,* published almost a hundred years ago. Its pages are falling out and its binding has been worn to threads and cardboard. Clearly, students told off to go read Wittgenstein and George Eliot have been spending delicious secret hours enjoying Allan Quatermain's phlegmatic accounts of people crushed to death, impaled, dismembered, and beheaded. (Anyone imagining that "violence' in fiction and films is somehow modern or post-modern should re-read some Victorian male-romances of the Haggard kind. They seem to take up where the Jacobean drama leaves off, and some of them make snuff films look like *The Young Visiters.*)

Haggard produced almost sixty romances and novels, but he wanted to be something more than a writer of page-turners. He wanted to serve his country in a high-minded volunteer way. "I believe that public service is my true line," he wrote. "All the rest are side shows." After *King Solomon's Mines* and *She* had made him rich and famous, he devoted himself increasingly to agricultural reform and to service on Royal Commissions and committees of the Royal Colonial Institute. He was an Empire man and a thoroughly public person, frequenting a milieu defined by conferences, public statements, reports, clubs, societies, ceremonies, speeches, official dinners, the Athenaeum, and letters to the *Times*. It is largely these things that he chooses to record in his so-called private diaries, edited by D. S. Higgins as *The Private Diaries of Sir H. Rider Haggard, 1914–1925*. Here's a typical day (August 22, 1916):

> I came to town by the early train, went to the bank where they admitted their error in my accounts and then by a bright inspiration on to the *Field* office where I had promised to be interviewed. After lunch I went to the committee meeting at the Royal Colonial Institute where we got through a good lot of business. I hear indirectly that the Government is doing something about appointing a board, but I do not suppose I shall be on it.

Obviously readers whose notion of the "private" has been formed by, say, the diaries of Sir Roger Casement, or even the diaries of Evelyn Waugh ("Got very drunk in the evening"), will be disappointed by Haggard's entries. There are no secrets or scandals here, nothing to raise a blush or occasion any reassessment of Haggard's character or achievement. His diaries, all twenty-two volumes and two million words of them, have been known for years and have been drawn on extensively by biographers and historians. Higgins, a Haggard collector and enthusiast, has selected about one-fortieth of the text and made an edition which deserves to be called amateur. It is nevertheless a useful book, valuable especially to those interested in the history and mythography of the Great War.

When war broke out Haggard was in Canada as a member of the Dominions Royal Commission inquiring into natural resources and trade. He decided to keep a diary of public events to help him write a history of the war. This he never wrote, but he did continue the diary to his death, in 1925. His view of the war is that of an elderly patriot and *rentier*, a church-goer and Norfolk Justice of the Peace whose main work seems to have been fining violators of the wartime blackout regulations. Long before the Derby Scheme, he was an enthusiast for conscription, outraged to behold able-bodied young men lounging about London. He found the savagery of the war almost a justification of his own career in the fiction of violence:

> In some ways I think the war is doing good in England. It is bringing the people . . . face to face with elementary facts

which hitherto it has been the fashion to ignore. . . . How often have I been vituperated by rose-water critics because I have written of fighting and tried to inculcate elementary lessons, such as that it is a man's duty to defend his country, and that only those who are prepared for war can protect themselves and such as are dear to them. "Coarse! bloody! brutal! Uncivilised!" such has been the talk. Well, and today have I done any harm by inoculating a certain number of the thousands who are at the front with these primary facts, even although my work has been held to be so infinitely inferior to that of Oscar Wilde, Bernard Shaw, and others?

Public as he is, Haggard seems to occupy an intellectual and emotional backwater (the Athenaeum?) where the poems of Siegfried Sassoon never circulate and H. W. Massingham's liberal *Nation* never appears on the library table. Two years after the war, Haggard has still not heard of Sassoon. "I am not fortunate enough to be acquainted with the works of Siegfried Sassoon, who, from his name, I presume is a Jew of the advanced school," he writes; and when he does read Sassoon's poems, he pronounces them "feeble and depressing rubbish." (To the end of the war Haggard adhered to the diction of Rupert Brooke, passing the data of the trenches through such filters as *glorious, keen, plucky, gallant, honour,* and *God.*) In no sense was the modern for him. "There are two men left living in the world," he writes, "with whom I am in supreme sympathy, Theodore Roosevelt and Rudyard Kipling."

All this might seem pretty stupid and damning, but there's another element in Haggard's response to the war which complicates things. That is his capacity to be worn down by the grinding tragedy of it all. His nephews were killed. His godson was killed. His publisher's son was killed. Kipling's son was killed ("Poor lad!"). As the war proceeds, Haggard's initial complacent bellicosity yields to misery and despair, and that does him credit. And there's something more. Although he confesses his delight in being associated with "well-known and public people," at a memorial service for Kitchener, drowned on H.M.S. *Hampshire,* he is annoyed by the presiding bishop's dilating only on "Kitchener and his career." By this time Haggard has learned to extend his imagination and his sympathies: "For my part," he says, "I could not help thinking of the six or seven hundreds of good men and true who went to doom with him. But of these we heard little or nothing." Four years of ghastliness bring him to a state very like sensitivity, and by 1918 he has had enough of dismembering and impaling: "I see a new poster on the walls to encourage the buying of War Bonds which strikes me as more horrible and in worse taste than most of them. It represents a British soldier realistically driving a bayonet into the stomach of a German, and the legend underneath is 'The last blow tells,' or something of that sort. Its coarse brutality made me feel sick." Haggard, the renowned narrator of violent action, is confronting a characteristic of fiction noticed memorably by Samuel Johnson: "The delight of [stage] tragedy proceeds from our consciousness of fiction; if we thought murders and treasons real, they would please no more."

It has been observed that all twentieth-century wars tend to merge into one, at least in their imagery and mythology. Haggard's diaries provide an illustration. In 1972 a man named Colin Perry published his teenager's diary of 1940, titling it *Boy in the Blitz.* One interesting thing about it is the way it perceives the Second World War by means of the imagery associated with the First. Haggard's diaries uncannily seem to reverse this process, depicting the Blitz and blackout of his war in the terms of Colin Perry's war a quarter-century later. For example, it would be impossible to assign a date (or a war) to this passage:

> I have walked down Picadilly and seen some of last night's damage. A single bomb was drcpped near the Circus, opposite Swan and Edgar's. . . . The damage done is great; Swan and Edgar's windows and those of many other establishments are wrecked. . . . The roadway has a huge hole in it, and is blocked, so that the buses must go round by other routes; and the whole place is thickly strewn with fragments of glass.

That is Haggard writing on October 20, 1917. His version of the London blackout is likewise indistinguishable from an account of 1940:

> In walking to the Hampstead Tube at Charing Cross, . . . I fell over a high curb and was lucky to escape with a sprained or broken ankle. Also these wide crossings are dangerous to

negotiate in the gloom. It is strange to see the great search-lights wheeling about the sky in their quest for hostile aircraft. . . .

And here is his unwitting version (1915) of the Home Guard's determination to repel invasion in 1940:

> Yesterday I drilled with the Ditchingham and Bungay Volunteer Defense Corps on the Common, whereof I am a platoon Commander. The spectacle was distinctly funny— that of a lot of determined old gents stumping about and doing their best to execute manoeuvres which they did not understand. However, if only rifles and ammunition are given to them, I am convinced that they and tens of thousands like them would be most useful stuff in the event of invasion. Even if one is over 40 one can still hold a gun straight enough to shoot a German and we have the advantages of knowing the country.

And there is this startling off-hand prophecy of the Nuremberg Laws and the furnaces:

> *4th December 1919*
>
> Kipling, who has been lunching here today, is of opinion that we owe all our Russian troubles, and many others, to the machinations of the Jews. If . . . they are as mischievous as he believes, the evil that they do is likely to recoil on their own heads, since in extremity the world has a rough way of dealing with Jews.

But if passages like these seem to understand the future, there are others that most touchingly do not. The artistic disadvantage of a diary, as opposed to a memoir, is that its beginning doesn't know its end. But its advantage is that just this ignorance supplies ironies the more striking for being unwilled. "The war news seems better," Haggard is pleased to notice on June 29, 1916. Two days later the attack on the Somme will dash his hopes. Commenting on the extravagant public show of Princess Mary's wedding, a fairly minor royal occasion, he speculates with terrible vulnerability (thank God he didn't live to behold Wallis Simpson), "What will happen when the Prince of Wales's turn comes, I wonder!"

In the same way some of Haggard's unwitting juxtapositions

reveal much about universal social and political determinants of perception. On April 15, 1917, he converses with Lord Milner, just returned from Russia, about the revolution, and reports: "He is not sure where the revolutionary movement will end. Undoubtedly the hatred of kings is growing, in Russia and elsewhere, and I hear that our own George R. is very anxious about the Czar and 'much upset.'" Five days later Haggard is at St. Paul's attending the "solemn service to Almighty God on the occasion of the entry of the United States of America into the Great War for Freedom." George R. is of course present, and now Haggard writes: "I do not think that ever before I realised how small the King is. Beside the Queen, who after all is not so very large, he looked tiny and unimpressive. . . . To be frank, he did not look half an inch a king, notwithstanding his Field Marshal's uniform."

In addition, we find some unconscious but suggestive anticipations of future imaginative and literary history. One is Haggard's registration of his excitement at the relighting of the cities once the war has ended: "After more than four years of an abysmal darkness with the knowledge that often enough Death was floating overhead, I feel as though I should like to pass the rest of my days in a lake of light—as though night and day I could never be satisfied with brilliance." There he hints at something like the lust for the sun that enticed post-war dissidents and exiles such as Aldous Huxley and Norman Douglas and D. H. Lawrence and Osbert Sitwell to the hot beaches of the Mediterranean and the "lakes of light" in northern Italy and Mexico.

But Haggard was not their kind, and except for a trip to Egypt, after the war he stayed in England, attending his committee meetings, delivering his speeches, trying to organize a Liberty League to repress Bolshevism (a trusted reactionary colleague absconded with the funds), and watching everything get worse. Now he noted with upper-middle-class dismay the onset of what Kingsley Amis calls the modern "unchangeable crappiness"; the deterioration of the postal and telephone service, the decline of craftsmanship and the attendant rise of advertising and publicity, the vogue of strikes and slowdowns and quitting work early, confiscatory income tax and death duties, inflation, public sullenness and discourtesy, inexplicable "enormous crowds" of dreadful people everywhere bent on God knows what fatuous or sinister purpose, the collapse of manners, the disappearance of porters in railways stations, "the triumph of expediency over principle in high places," and the alarming increase in umbrella thefts by members of the better clubs.

"I am out of tune with the day," he writes: "I am a back-number." And even worse: "For me the world is largely peopled with the dead; I walk among ghosts, especially at night." And as he meditates on his own achievement and value, he concludes: "My talent may be of copper not of gold . . . but I have put it to the best use I could." He arranged that his epitaph describe him as one "Who with a humble heart strove to serve his country." It's a pity he can't be told that he's done so as fully by inventing the African witch Gagool and having her crushed to death with a great rock as by attending meetings and speaking at official dinners.

The Hearst of Literature

One bizarre feature of contemporary literary life is the assumption of famous authors that they have a right to posthumous privacy. After years of showing off by affixing their real names to books, after decades of courting the public by advertising and blurbs and photographs, after lifetimes spent totting up the totals of copies sold, just before they die they command the world, with a positively Hearst-like *chutzpah,* to treat them like sensitive plants again. Then they enjoin their acquaintances to burn their letters, withhold intimate anecdotes, and frustrate biographers. This lust to control future intellectual and artistic history in absentia by a final exercise of the senile *libido dominandi* is outrageous. It is also thoroughly "modern."

An author who's spent his life soliciting notice by offering the public images and ideas which he could easily keep to himself may have some legal right to final privacy. But he has no moral right, and that's as true of such high-class reticents as Eliot and Auden as of cads like W. Somerset Maugham, whose pride in being identified as a well-known best seller while alive was equaled only be his desire to take it all back again and regain privacy and innocence when dead. "He wanted to have his cake and eat it," Frieda Lawrence once said of him.

"I direct," Maugham wrote in his will, "I direct that there shall be no biography." With the complicity of Maugham's literary executor, the late Spencer Curtis Brown, a writer named Ted Morgan has ignored that preposterous injunction and written Maugham's life. "The whole story," S. N. Behrman said while Willie was alive, "is appalling and pitiful." Maugham was born in the reign of Victoria and survived into the reign of Elizabeth II, the only woman he ever really liked, her money and social position sufficing to repress his programmatic misogyny in her case. He was born at the British Embassy in Paris, where his father handled the embassy's legal affairs. His mother died when he was eight; his father, when he was ten. Like poor clubfooted Philip Carey in *Of Human Bondage,* he was bundled off to lodge with a horrible clergyman in England for seven years. He was miserable at school, and like so many of his contemporaries—Arnold Bennett, Churchill, George VI—became a stammerer. He had his first homosexual experience in Heidelberg with an older British aesthete, and at the age of eighteen found himself a medical student in London. "I became a medical student," he said, "because I could not announce to my guardian that I wished to be a writer." He was already writing naughty plays like Ibsen's and short stories like de Maupassant's and experimenting sexually with the occasional prostitute, one of whom clapped him. By now he knew he was homosexual, but when he was twenty-one Wilde was imprisoned, and ever after Maugham disguised his leanings with publicized heterosexual affairs and finally with marriage and parenthood. He became skilled in duplicity, and, as he looked out on the world, saw it with the eye of a cynic. Like most cynics he developed into a first-rate bridge player and frequenter of the Great. In his early middle age he was an immensely popular playwright and once had four plays running simultaneously in the West End, plays largely about marriage which took him only three or four weeks to manufacture. He was now Making It, hobnobbing with Churchill and Billie Burke and Edmund Gosse and Hugh Walpole. He lived in Mayfair and got into the Garrick Club.

In 1914 he was forty and too old for active service, but like everyone else he was intensely patriotic, and he joined an ambulance unit in France. There he fell for Gerald Haxton, a gregarious drunken San Franciscan who signed on as Maugham's difficult, erratic, unfaithful lover and secretary until his death in 1944, when he was replaced by the more compliant Alan Searle, destined to become, as Glenway Wescott says, "the nanny of [Maugham's] second childhood." In 1915 he published his masterpiece, *Of Human Bondage,* which got off to a great start in this country when Theodore Dreiser celebrated it in *The New Republic.* It is still a very good novel. Its treatment of London poverty and squalor, its exposure of the universal cash nexus, and its obsession with the pathos of bad writing (and bad painting) earn it a place on a line running from Gissing to Orwell, those other distinguished students of the down and out.

In the latter days of World War I Maugham transferred from ambulance-driving to intelligence-collecting in Switzerland while Haxton, back in London, found himself indicted on a charge of "gross indecency." Although acquitted, he was pronounced an undesirable alien ("a dreadful fellow," a spokesman for the Home Office called him) and forbidden ever to enter the United Kingdom again. Hence Maugham's extensive travels and prolonged residence abroad. After the war his need for a cover prompted him to marry Syrie Wellcome, the decorator who made her name by devising the all-white drawing-room. He had already impregnated her. For twelve years he was formally married to her until divorce ended his misery. The marriage provided a convenient façade for him, but for Syrie there was a problem: she loved him. "Willie told me himself," Wescott remembers, "that her physical demands were intolerable, inexcusable." He spent as little time as possible in her company, fleeing abroad to join Haxton at every opportunity.

He continued his spying career in Petrograd in 1917. His job was to channel British cash to Kerensky to keep Russia in the war. At the same time plays and stories and novels were streaming from his morning workshop, and in 1924 he received the ultimate accolade. A little book of his made it into what Forster calls the Queen's Doll Souse. Socially he was much in demand, with a penchant for slightly bogus hard-working climbers like Beverley Nichols and Chips Channon—and always the hordes of un-ideaed clever-shallow "attractive" young men.

After eleven novels, twenty plays, and three volumes of short stories, he was rich enough to buy the Villa Mauresque, on Cap Ferrat, where he lived to the end in an opulent, rigid, self-conscious high style, waited on by thirteen servants. The villa was his San Simeon, and there he behaved like the Hearst of literature, functioning virtually as a professional host because of his need to exhibit his riches. He entertained the Windsors and such, chatting bitchily while the increasingly embittered Haxton mixed the cocktails. Maugham estimated that during one three-week period his staff put out 1160 individual meals, not counting breakfasts. He no sooner had himself rejuvenated in Switzerland by the injection of matter from lamb fetuses than World War II broke out. He spent it in the States, propagandizing for the British cause and living with the Nelson Doubledays in South Carolina while Haxton did clerical work for the OSS, and drank heavily, in Washington.

He was seventy-one when the war ended, and his life henceforward makes unhappy reading. Technology had preserved his person but could do nothing for his mind and certainly not for his stubborn will. He grew to resemble one of Swift's never-dying Struldbruggs, snotty, rude, abusive, envious, mad. Secretly furious at the contempt of critics, he avenged himself by numerous acts of bitterness and fury. He hankered after the Nobel Prize. If he couldn't have that he wanted the Queen to give him the Order of Merit, as if he were Thomas Hardy. Instead she gave it to J. B. Priestley, whose conventional sexuality made him less of an embarrassment. Maugham had to settle for Companion of Honor, as if he were an orchestra leader or professor. He hit eighty in 1954, watched by all morbid eyes. "Maugham growing old," says Morgan, "was an international spectacle. No one since Dorian Gray had called so much attention to the aging process." He had earned four million dollars by writing, but when a book of tributes to his genius was proposed for his eightieth birthday, even his most loyal friends found excuses not to participate. By the end, at the age of ninety-one, he was sobbing, muttering, shouting obscenities. He would invite old friends to dinner and then, in a setting of black ties and shiny silver and footmen, scream at them, "Fuck you. Fuck you. Fuck you." Once he defecated on the carpet to show them all. He hated Syrie most, and in 1962 attacked her viciously in a memoir that startled even his most tolerant old friends. "Some evil spirit has entered his body," said Noel Coward. During lucid moments, he imputed the whole success-disaster of his life to his stammer, which obliged him to become a writer and spy instead of a lawyer, doctor, or public servant. He had to operate behind the scenes; or, in public, appear what he was not. Short and ugly, he detested tall people. He was shifty and sometimes quite dishonest, "a façade person," as Morgan calls him, eminently "social" in the unadmirable sense, a money snob with a powerful drive, physically brave, furtive, mean-minded, resentful of his sexuality, incapable of love.

Deficient, as he was the first to confess, in imaginative power, in his writings he stayed close to the materials and forms of actual life—medical studentship, the predicaments of lonely colonials, the behavior of Gauguin *(The Moon and Sixpence)* and Aleister Crowley *(The Magician)*—rather than the materials and forms of literature. Once when he wanted to acquire some exotic words to decorate his prose, he went off to scrutinize the gem collection in the British Museum instead of heading for the reading room and digging *jasper* and *jade* out of Shakespeare and Marlowe, Burton and Browne. He never cottoned to Eliot's and Pound's notion that literature feeds on literature rather than life, and without "material" from actuality, like scandalous "short stories" retailed by Malayan planters in their cups, he felt he had nothing to work with.

Or so he insisted, when accounting for his extensive travels in the East between the wars. His cordial welcomes at embassies we might attribute to his fame and his social pliability. But it's quite possible, even if Ted Morgan doesn't think of opening up the question, that he was still working for British intelligence as an aging but loyal Ashenden. As with Graham Greene, it's hard to believe that a man who's once worked successfully for The Firm is ever allowed wholly to resign—especially, perhaps, if his bosses know he's homosexual and the great public does not. (If Guy Burgess and Anthony Blunt are pure types of the modern British agent, so is Willie.) He admitted resuming intelligence work during World War II in the U.S.A., whence he secretly reported back on the attitudes and conduct of his fellow British subjects. I think it possible that he worked at the job fairly steadily from 1917 on. If so, this might go some way toward extenuating his more inert and mechanical works *(The Painted Veil, The Narrow Corner),* which are easily conceived as productions necessitated by his cover as "a writer."

Although Morgan's biography of Maugham is critically unsophisticated and superficial, it's not all bad. It contains lots of names and some juicy scandals, and the depositions about Willie which Morgan has solicited from Wescott are wonderfully bright, acute, and valuable. And there are some nice vignettes, like one of Robert Helpmann at a party at the Sitwell's country house. "Told that everyone would wear costumes . . . , he dressed up as Queen Alexandra, and made his entrance to find that none of the others had worn costumes." The worst thing about Morgan's biography is its disastrous language. The narrative pivots on words like "escalated," "prestigious," and "supportive," phrases like "male chauvinist," "radical chic," and "wheeler-dealer." These may do, alas, if applied to late-1970's American actuality, but they're quite incapable of getting at the essence of British social reality in the last half-century. But if his book is disappointing intellectually and artistically, Morgan has performed a distinct service by treating Maugham's final gesture of "directing" that no biography be written with the contempt it deserves.

Waugh in His Letters

One of the saddest of recent literary sights has been the stacks of unwanted copies of Evelyn Waugh's *Diaries* in the remainder bookstores all over the Republic. While the works of, say, James Clavell have moved briskly, Waugh's have languished, sad casualties of the apparent American war against wit. It's as if Waugh were too clever, as well as "too hard," for us. A pity, because he is much needed as an antidote to the current earnestness, literal-mindedness, and verbal slop.

Mark Amory, a friend of the family, has now edited *The Letters of Evelyn Waugh,* presenting 840 letters (selected from about 4,500) running from 1914 to 1966. He has omitted as little as possible and thus excitingly skirted libel in many places. He has supplied an appendix of brief biographies of persons mentioned, from which the shrewd reader can put together a skeleton social history of Waugh's time. And he has supplied footnotes sometimes as pointed and funny as if Waugh had written them himself: "Lord Derwent (1899–1949): Always called Peter although his name was George." It is fortunate for the reader that Waugh hated the phone (just as he hated Picasso, taxation, Le Corbusier, and "the bandying about of Christian names" on TV interview programs) and chose to transmit his vigorous comic views by letters, notes, and postcards. It is fortunate for the reader too that Waugh's great partner in wit, Nancy Mitford, lived in Paris, reachable only by post. "A letter should be a form of conversation," he insisted, and he demanded that a letter be interesting. Addressing his much beloved wife Laura from Dubrovnik during the war, he writes, "I know you lead a dull life now. . . . But that is no reason to make your letters as dull as your life. I simply am not interested in Bridget's children. Please grasp that."

Waugh is indispensable today because, for one thing, he is that rarity, a writer who cares about language. He knows that writing is an affair of words rather than soul, impulse, "sincerity," or an instinct for the significant. If the words aren't there, nothing happens. And in our atmosphere where verbal accuracy and elegance and wit seem virtually obsolete, Waugh appears as one of the heroes, perhaps one of the saints, of verbal culture. He is extraordinarily sensitive to idiom and its social and ethical implications, and in his letters he reveals himself to be, like Jonathan Swift, a master parodist of styles. He can do the novelist Henry Green by deploying *like* as a conspicuous illiterate conjunction. He can return to the idiom of nursery and schoolroom by using endless repeated *so's* as connectives between narrative moments. He can send up would-be colorful travel writing and would-be portentous military reporting. He is adept at Cockney rhyming-slang and at the slang of adolescent in-groups of the upper middle class, where a sinking ship is "sinkers," sleeping-draughts "sleepers," and congratulations "gratters."

He has frequent recourse to dictionaries and knows the difference between *pitiful* and *pitiable*. He is pained to have to inform Louis Auchincloss that he misuses *mutual* and to remind Nancy Mitford that *nobody* and *each* are singular. When Graham Greene sends him *The End of the Affair*, Waugh writes back that he greatly admired it but that Greene has written *cornice* when he means *buttress*. (Greene kissed the rod and made the correction in the next printing.) As a devoted friend he informs Harold Acton that he has committed the vulgar error of mistaking the meaning of "inverse ratio," and he pronounces himself "shocked" to find Tom Driberg "falling into the popular use of 'expertise.'" "In France," he writes, "the word does not mean 'skill' but the judgment of an expert on the authenticity of a work of art." He is sensitive to every pert or pretentious or fraudulent or cowardly usage. How he would gag at our *lifestyle*, how he would spew at our use of *fund* as a verb, how he would contemn our base, sentimental evasions like *low-income* and *senior citizens* and *slow learners* and *hearing impaired*. He would stick with *poor, old, stupid,* and *deaf* and would insist when he came to that condition that people describe him with honest adjectives.

All this may sound as if his letters reveal him as a terrible prig. "I am by nature a bully and a scold," he admits. "I am a bigot and a philistine." And indeed, there are some painfully embarrassing Catholic doctrinal letters to Clarissa Churchill abusing her brutally for her apostasy in marrying a divorced man, Anthony Eden. But there's another side, Waugh's vulnerable and tender one. He addresses his wife as "My darling love child," and, laying aside his elaborately constructed role of outrageous Catholic Tory, says to her again, "Darling Laura, I love you. Thank you for loving me."

His handicap was an excessive sense of honor. Carrying that baggage, no wonder he despised the world that first tried to buy off Hitler and then bought off Stalin. His sense of absolute moral principles provides the dynamics of idealism and disappointment in the *Sword of Honor* trilogy, and it led to his preposterous behavior as an officer during the war, when he stuffily insisted that everyone in the Royal Marines and the Army act all the time in accordance with their professed ideals of heroism and self-abnegation. The British rout on Crete, in which he participated, shamed him for life and served him as an unforgettable emblem of ignobility in politics, ethics, and social theory. In 1956 he writes his son Auberon: "You have a defective sense of honor." When in 1959 he writes his daughter Margaret, who has been having trouble at school, he makes us wonder how many fathers would choose to invoke the term *ignoble*—not to mention the words "I despise you"—in addressing a beloved child: "You wrote a very ignoble letter to your brother Auberon but since it was not addressed to me I will not tell you how much I despise you for your discontent, self-pity, detraction of others, etc., etc." That is strong stuff, but two years before that he'd written her: "I am absolutely confident that you will never never be dishonourable, impure, or cruel. That is all that matters." Waugh cared mightily about these things, and it is the ethical intensity, excessive and rigorous, indeed neurotic, as it sometimes grows, that makes these letters so instructive. He sees everything in moral terms, and his comedy is possible only because of his never-sleeping moral imagination. All delays in publication and mail delivery he imputes instinctively not to the innocent freezing-up of swollen bureaucratic mechanisms but to the "sloth" of printers and postmen. In this he is like a latter-day Swift. In 1965 he reads

Nigel Dennis's *Jonathan Swift: A Short Character* and observes to Diana Cooper: "I found many affinities with the temperament (not of course the talent) of the master."

His firm sense of what is morally right sustains his conviction of an author's obligation to write meticulously well. Nancy Mitford is the recipient of most of his strong views here. "It is the difference (one of the 1000 differences) between a real writer & a journalist," he informs her, "that she cares to go on improving after the reviews are out & her friends have read it & there is nothing whatever to be gained by the extra work." Thomas Merton also receives some much-needed advice, which he's let himself in for by sending *The Waters of Siloe* to Waugh for praise. "You tend to be diffuse," Waugh tells him, "saying the same thing more than once. I noticed this in *The Seven Storey Mountain* and the fault persists. It is pattern-bombing instead of precision-bombing. . . . It is not art. Your monastery tailor and bootmaker would not waste material. Words are our material." Laziness is the contemporary fault. As Waugh writes Robin Campbell in 1945, "I believe the sin the West is dying of to be Sloth not Wrath as is popularly assumed." Once writing is understood as an art and a craft rather than a mystery, one's obligation to do it well is clear. As he writes Lord David Cecil, writing differs "not at all from gardening or needlework."

But the moral sense propelling such axioms as the last issues more often in wit. He writes Nancy Mitford on Christmas Day, 1944: "I dined alone sitting opposite a looking-glass & reflecting sadly that the years, instead of transforming me into a personable man of middle age, have made me into a very ugly youth." Arguing with Penelope Betjeman about the meaning for Christian teleology of things like the crocodile, he asserts: "The crocodile serves man in many ways—his hide for note-cases, bags, and dago shoes, his name to enrich our literature with metaphor 'crocodile tears,' 'as warm & friendly as an alligator pool,' etc. Most especially he is a type & sign for us of our own unredeemed nature."

In 1950, feeling more feeble than usual, he consults a physician who takes his blood pressure and finds it "the lowest ever recorded—in fact the pressure of a 6 months foetus. In an access of sudden hope I said: 'Does that mean I shall die quite soon?' 'No.

It means you shall live absolutely for ever in deeper & deeper melancholy.' " To Nancy Mitford in 1953: "I am quite deaf now. Such a comfort." Why are there no good professional proofreaders left in England? "Because," he explains to Tom Driberg, "clergymen are no longer unfrocked for sodomy." Even Waugh's famous wartime joke of pretending to believe that Tito was a woman ("Her face is pretty, but her legs are very thick") registers his moral disillusion with the unlovely allies forced upon the West by impure military and political circumstances.

When Waugh died in 1966, it was said that he died "of snobbery." He really died of boredom, loneliness, loss of interest. And, as Graham Greene has said, of something like a broken heart. The Church he had bravely embraced as the only half-stable institution in the contemporary world let him down with its new prole liturgy, a flagrant offense against language and history and the principle of distinction. As he observed, "catholicism is the enemy of Catholicism." He had been, he thought, betrayed, just as the Army had let him down on Crete. "The Vatican Council has knocked the guts out of me." Near the end he had a further disappointment. He had grown too satiric and drunken and offensive to receive high honors, and he had to watch Greene designated a Companion of Honor, while he, having contemptuously refused a C.B.E. years before, got nothing at all.

Amory's edition of his letters, running from Waugh's eleventh to his sixty-third year, brings him entirely alive, even more than the admirable *Diaries*. There are interesting differences between the account of some events in the *Letters* and the versions in the *Diaries,* and the reason is perhaps not far to seek. Collecting the letters for this edition, Mr. Amory was reminded that Waugh wrote his letters in the morning, "when he was sober." He wrote his diary at night.

Commenting on Waugh's *Letters,* Reyner Heppenstall has concluded that "Waugh clearly never had anything to teach us, except that a man may act like a fool and yet remain a master of English prose narrative, perhaps the finest in this century." But Waugh has a lot to teach us, especially if we aspire to write. In these letters one serious recurring theme is the writer's obligation to write well by revising—that is, self-criticizing. "Revision," he tells Mitford in 1951, "is just as important as any other part of writing and must be done con amore." In addition to reminding writers of the hell that awaits them if they send out slovenly work, Waugh has another valuable thing to teach us, something we greatly need now: namely, the usefulness of the objective comic vision in transforming anger and violence into verbal art and verbal play.

V
VERSIONS OF THE
SECOND WORLD WAR

Some Truth about the War

I think critics and literary historians of the next century are going to patronize us no end. I think they will stigmatize us as canting phonies. For they are bound to perceive that regardless of the class prestige we publicly assign poetry and fiction, our hearts are elsewhere. They will see that our most dearly loved literary forms are really memoir, biography, and popular historiography. These we manage best, with the result that most readers curious about the contours of contemporary experience go not to fiction but to works like memoirs, biographies, topographical books, books trying to explain Hitler and the bunker crowd, popular historical works synthesized from other popular historical works, books conveying truths—or at least *frissons*—about Auschwitz and Vietnam and the prison system and the black predicament, books by Mailer and Tom Wolfe and Anne Frank and Joan Didion and Philip Caputo and Gloria Emerson and Malcolm X.

Two conspicuous recent fictions, Thomas Pynchon's *Gravity's Rainbow* and Anthony Powell's *A Dance to the Music of Time,* different as they are in ambition, range, and style, seem characteristic of our time because both persuade readers that they are being given something like the "real history" of the middle and late twentieth century, a history that would drift off toward mere metaphor or abstraction if it weren't anchored to actuality by frequent contact with a pub like the actual Wheatsheaf, a congeries of houses like the actual Chelsea, a place like the actual Salzkammergut, an event like the actual Blitz. Which is to say that our fictions are now really popular historiography shrewdly disguised. Thus the popularity of Doctorow's *Ragtime* and *Loon Lake,* and of D. M. Thomas's *The White Hotel.*

Re-attaching "Dunkirk" to the facts is what A. J. Barker has in mind in his absorbing illustrated book *Dunkirk: The Great*

Escape, with a text exploiting ships' logs and survivors' testimonies. The truth is that the mythic little boats did less than yachtsmen like to imagine. A more sobering truth is that while the long patient queues of soldiers waiting to embark are typical of Dunkirk, so are appalling scenes of hysteria and madness. "There is no braver epic in all our annals," Anthony Eden announced, but Barker reminds us that to be brave you have to have something terrible to be brave about. The bloody mess which bombing and strafing made of the beaches shamed even the German fliers, one of whom testifies: "I hated Dunkirk. It was just unadulterated killing. The beaches were jammed full of soldiers. I went up and down at three-hundred feet hose-piping." Men torn apart were buried in the sand, but too shallowly, and as Barker observes, "Packs of terrified dogs ran the beaches from La Panne to the Dunkirk mole—hungry and already vicious, seeking out the corpses." Boats standing offshore drifted as corpses fouled their propellers. The dock area swarmed with "sinister groups of deserters and miscellaneous rogues," most of them armed, looting and assaulting.

Barker is copious and clear-eyed about the military events inducing these horrors, and if he is a bit hard on the French and Belgians for pessimism, he is equally hard on the British for unreadiness and deficiency of imagination. While the Germans pressed on the perimeter with up-to-date Michelin maps, the British reposed their faith on maps of the 1924 ordnance survey.

Barker's book would make a fine gift—Christmas, birthday, or graduation—for the offspring of the British or American middle class. Not only would they discover from it the cost to others, strangers now, of their not being enrolled in the Hitlerjugend. They might also perceive a model of energy enlisted in the common good in the image of the man who rowed across the Channel three times, bringing back soldiers each time. Barker concludes: "The BEF did not save France. In trying to do so it lost thirty thousand men, all its transport and all its illusions." It's a ghastly story, and anyone not moved to tears of anger, frustration, and pity by Barker's book should go have his humanity examined.

The beginning of the snail-like comeback is Roger Parkinson's subject in *Dawn on Our Darkness: The Summer of 1940,* which focuses on the period from the dismal return of the Dunkirk escapees in June to the stand-off of the Luftwaffe in September. Despite claims that the book is based on fresh documents—War Cabinet and Chief of Staff papers, Air Ministry and Fighter Command files—there is little new here, and the conclusion, that after a summer of air war "Fighter Command had more machines and more men than three months before," will not surprise many. But the sentimental-nostalgic reader will get a full ration: the Anderson shelters, the silencing of the church bells and the uprooting of signposts, the Local Defense Volunteers (later christened the Home Guard) waiting with their shotguns for the code-word "Cromwell" ("England has been invaded"), and the quaint improvisation everywhere. The pilot of a flagrantly obsolete Whitley bomber noted that because of the plane's ineffective heating and oxygen systems, "the navigator and Commanding Officer were butting their heads on the floor and navigation table in an endeavour to experience some other form of pain as a relief from the awful feeling of frost-bite and the lack of oxygen." As Hitler waffled over Sea Lion (his uncertainly motivated plan to invade England), his bombers jettisoned a load over London accidentally, motivated doubtless by the usual fear and ambiguity and helplessness. The British retaliated on Berlin, setting in train the out-of-control sequence that finally sought justification in "Bomber" Harris's theory that the enemy could be demoralized into defeat by civilian area bombing. That principle understood, Hiroshima was all but inevitable. Just the opposite of Harris's expectations proved true, at least in Germany; and although Parkinson shows no signs of understanding it, he depicts his principals enmeshed already in the absurd world of *Gravity's Rainbow*, where the technology must be used, no matter how nonsensically or self-destructively, because it is available.

Parkinson's narration is tedious, the fault largely of his inhumane communiqué diction. Very little feeling for the actualities can attach to language like *protected at all costs, enemy breakthrough*, and *enemy formations crossed the coast in strength*. Nor does Parkinson's serial narration of daily air battles do anything to make the center of his book more than an exercise in comparative numeration. He seems not to sense the crucial difference between a list and an outline. We feel we know what Samuel Johnson meant when he said of a luckless narrator's performance that it would be impossible to imagine the story told so as to make less impression on the mind.

Because he lacks an instinct for those devices of structure like suspense and irony which set popular historiography above mere annals, Parkinson leaves us as remote from anything real and moral as Peter Cochrane, in *Charlie Company,* makes us intimate with it. This is a civilized, modest memoir of C Company, the 2nd Queen's Own Cameron Highlanders, from 1940 to 1944. Cochrane is a man of winning dispassion, the characteristic that helped him survive (a virtual miracle) nearly four and a half years as platoon leader, second-in-command, and C.O. of an infantry company in North Africa and Italy, and to survive wounds and capture and rescue as well.

Except perhaps for Anthony Eden's *Another World,* I've not read a war memoir more generous to the enemy. A world grown used to calumniating its enemies as Gooks and Squareheads can learn something here. Cochrane will astonish armchair warriors by finding the Italians "very well led," and by concluding that "the Italians . . . must be the finest road engineers in the world." Throughout he never lets us forget that Germans and Italians "were our fellows, though in an unfamiliar uniform."

Like most books of moral use, Cochrane's contains a virtual mini-anthology of maxims and general truths and useful observations. Speaking of the British sense of "the Battalion," he notes that the British in general "seem unable to attach themselves to or find an identity in a group larger than, say, eight hundred or so." Hence, we can note, such indigenous institutions as the Oxbridge colleges, or the London clubs.

As a literary genre, the British war-reminiscence is undoubtedly, as Powell's character Odo Stevens calls it, "a dicey art-form." One must get its conventions right or fail. Instinctively, Cochrane has got the conventions right, even to supplying a period of "pastoral oasis" in the middle—an idyllic two-month propaganda visit to American universities in 1942—so that the ultimate return to the line seems all the more egregious by contrast. After sleeping in the White House and admiring the Roosevelts and after finding New York (Cochrane is generous) "the most beautiful city in the world, as well as the friendliest," Cochrane ultimately finds himself back at the horrible Hill 593 at Cassino, and back to renewed evidence that "war was not merely idiotic, it was wicked and cruel." That point he implies as well by means of other conventional "pastoral" elements like birdsong mingling with artillery crumps and fireflies aping flashes and flares and airplane formations. On the Gothic Line, "The countryside was superbly lovely, although it required a conscious effort to look at it as landscape and not as an actual or potential battlefield. The nightingales sang even through a mortar bombardment and the fireflies were out in glittering squadrons." Such quiet but effective little juxtapositions and ironies are frequent in Cochrane's nice book, and they demonstrate tellingly if modestly the way sensitive literary structure and technique can make personal testimony, as well as popular historiography, as compelling as "fiction."

The Regrettable Decision
of Herman Wouk

The curious mystique of "the novel" has not often been so dramatically demonstrated as by a recent important decision by Herman Wouk. He is obsessed by the Second World War and the Holocaust and anxious to probe into both in search of their fullest intellectual, political, and moral meaning. Attracted thus to "history," he has decided not to write it but to commit a novel instead, a work whose clichés and sentimentalities will pay off handsomely in film rights and the sort of glib celebrity denied the historian but accorded in full measure to novelists who create characters with no complex inner life and who can limit the plausible human motives to about four. The result of Wouk's decision is *War and Remembrance,* a 1042-page continuation of Wouk's 885-page *The Winds of War.* The whole two-volume work constitutes a very good popular history of the war in the guise of a very bad novel. Actually, Wouk is only dubiously a novelist, presumably enticed to that genre by the emoluments and residuals now attaching to it if it become sufficiently crude. His bent has always been toward contemporary historiography, and when he allows himself to function there his work is often interesting and occasionally admirable.

But when he is merely novelizing, merely spinning it out for the silver screen, he is embarrassing. The characters and plot of *War and Remembrance* are pure early 1950's Metro-Goldwyn-Mayer. Victor ("Pug") Henry (to be played by Spencer Tracy) is a mature naval officer married to martini-quaffing Rhoda (Tallulah Bankhead). One of their sons, Byron (Anthony Perkins) is a brave and successful submarine officer. Another, Warren (Van Johnson), is a brave and successful naval aviator, killed at Midway. Their daughter Madeline (Ava Gardner) cohabits for a while with the

U.S.O. entertainer Hugh Cleveland (Jack Carson), but finally comes to her senses and dumps him in favor of a chap working on the Bomb at Los Alamos. Byron is married to Natalie (Claire Bloom), the niece of Aaron Jastrow (Sam Jaffe), said to be an impressive Jewish philosopher. Commander (later Captain and finally Rear Admiral) Victor Henry is away a lot, commanding the heavy cruiser *Northampton* until it's sunk near Guadalcanal, and then running high-powered errands all over the world for Roosevelt—expediting Lend-Lease operations in Persia, clearing up bottlenecks in landing-craft production in England and the States. While he's away, Rhoda falls for the atomic scientist Palmer Kirby (Robert Young). At the same time Pug finds himself beloved by Pamela Tudsbury (Vivien Leigh), the toothsome daughter of famed British broadcaster Alistair ("Talky") Tudsbury (Robert Morley). Aaron Jastrow and Natalie and her infant Louis are trapped in Siena, where they are beguiled by the plausible but cunning German diplomat Dr. Werner Beck (Hume Cronyn). After Aaron bravely resists Beck's pressures to deliver treasonous broadcasts, he and Natalie and her child find themselves delivered to the detention and transportation mechanisms of the Final Solution, and Aaron ends in the gas chamber at Auschwitz. When the war is over, Natalie and Louis are found to have survived and are reunited with Byron. Admiral Henry's marriage with Rhoda having come apart, he finds happiness with Pamela and is appointed naval aide to President Truman. Choral music. House lights up.

The character of Victor Henry, the Lanny Budd of these proceedings, abundantly indicates what's wrong with *War and Remembrance* as fiction. He is not to be believed. As Madeline tells her brother Byron, "You and I have an incredible father." Too true. With his "awkward smile" and habit of being always right, he charms the leaders of the world, who never tire of complimenting him. "You have insight, Pug," Roosevelt tells him, "and a knack for putting things clearly." He is a master of every subject—not just naval and military strategy and engineering, but wine and food, atomic fission, the history of philosophy, international politics, art history, and the history of Europe since 1870. He speaks languages and reads "Shakespeare" and "the

Bible." He drinks but doesn't get drunk. His bravery is legendary. His personal mail is likely to include chatty letters on "creamy" White House stationery. He is gifted at literary composition, and he translates and edits like a scholar. He is one of those rare creatures whose obtuse superiority makes him "popular" instead of hated. "Popular fella, aren't you?" Harry Hopkins says to him once. Powerful fantasy seems to be at work in Wouk's creation of Pug, and unkind readers will suspect autobiographical projection. Although Pug is actually a prig for all seasons, Wouk imagines that the reader will admire him without reservation. Pug's world is as unreal as he is: the telephones always work, people keep appointments and return calls, binoculars and toilet paper are always at hand, soldiers and sailors obey orders, and eyewitness accounts can be relied on.

One stylistic symptom of Wouk's primitive conception of character and his rationalist view of the world is Elegant Variation. Thus Pug is "the naval officer," W. Somerset Maugham (who makes a brief guest appearance) "the British novelist," Stalin "the Communist dictator," Hitler "the Austrian adventurer," and FDR "the masterful old cripple" residing in "the executive mansion." Without typecasting everybody and everything, Wouk would be lost in a world more complicated than he and his readers can tolerate. Unable to conceive an original character or to equip anyone with feelings above the commonplace, he must resort to wholly external classifications, depriving his people of any inner life. Their professional identity is their whole reality and they are entirely what they seem—stick-figures whose only function is to take their places in Wouk's retrograde middle-class allegory of Success.

Although Wouk imputes sadism and unreason to the Nazis, he has eliminated the irrational from the behavior of the Allies, with the result that the war fought by the Henrys, unlike Joseph Heller's war, or Kurt Vonnegut's, or Thomas Pynchon's, lacks the necessary dimension of the lunatic, the cruel, and the self-destructive. As an antidote to Wouk's simple, patriotic dramatization of the justness of the war it is useful to remember Dwight Macdonald on General Patton: "Far from the justness of the war excusing Patton's barbarism, Patton's barbarism calls into question the justness of the war. There is something suspect about an end which calls for such means." (A memorable Pattonism: "There's no such thing as shell shock. It's an invention of the Jews.") The standard by which Wouk's war can be gauged is Evelyn Waugh's war as rendered in the *Sword of Honour* trilogy. "How right he was," says John St. John, "to avoid treating 1939–45 as an epic; instead he unmasked it as an ironic series of muddled, sordid, often cruel and pointless episodes that released men's most unattractive and ridiculous qualities. . . . Waugh's novels are a splendid antidote to the glamorized, lying versions of the war that are now the mode." A mere twenty years after the splendid, willing, cheerful sacrifices Wouk celebrates, infantrymen in Vietnam were fragging their officers. From *War and Remembrance* it would be impossible to guess why. It is depressing finally to discover that a novel whose size, scope, and method remind one of *War and Peace* and whose theme is bound to evoke that of Mann's *Doctor Faustus* has for its real hero the United States Navy.

Thus the soap-opera part of *War and Remembrance*. But there's another part, never satisfactorily joined to the M.G.M. strip-cartoon, written by a much more impressive Wouk, the learned descriptive and analytic essayist, and this part is surprisingly fine. Much of it consists of powerfully imagined strategic theory and military history from the pen of the fictive German general Armin von Roon, whose book *Land, Sea, and Air Operations of World War II*, written while its author is imprisoned for war crimes, is translated by Victor Henry. He annotates the text, setting the author straight (of course) on numerous points. The quality of the military reasoning in this document—the whole comprises 122 pages—is astonishing, and so is Wouk's scholarship (that really is the correct word) in contemporary history. Impressive too is the strategic and tactical understanding in Wouk's accounts of naval battles like Midway and Leyte Gulf. Indeed, in his narration of Leyte Gulf he seems to recognize how much more interested he is in the history of naval operations than in the unbelievable behavior of One Man's Family: he forgets them for pages while he goes on, admirably, in the role of naval historian. As a historian of naval warfare Wouk is as good as Samuel Eliot Morison, while as an analytic narrator of land battles, particularly

Soviet here, he invites comparison with the great B. H. Liddell Hart himself. If the idea of "the novel" had not been his fatal Cleopatra, he could have distinguished himself as a contemporary historian. As it is, his failure ever to write a masterpiece can be seen as a sad generic miscarriage, a tragedy of vanity and publicity.

When he turns from people to significant public environments and "things," Wouk is also wonderful. A modern image hard to forget is the immense floating bottom of a destroyer capsized during the typhoon in *The Caine Mutiny*. Seen from the *Caine,* it is a bizarre shiny red island devoid of life. "Waves were breaking over it in showers of foam," and the observers are properly awestruck by the sight and the silence. Wouk is as good presenting what we would see at a farcical Second Front Now rally at the Hollywood Bowl or what Himmler sees when he inspects the extermination and cremation facilities at Auschwitz. Perhaps Wouk's triumph in this line is his depiction of Theresienstadt, the "Paradise Ghetto" in Czechoslovakia, while it is being prettied up late in the war to hoodwink a delegation from the Danish Red Cross. Aaron and Natalie are confined there together with thousands of "specials" and *prominente,* and the Great Beautification goes on all around them to their astonishment and anxiety. Flowers are set out, bandstands erected and painted, cafés established (with Jews rehearsed to play happy boulevardiers), a soccer field is laid out and "teams" drilled to play on it, fake shops are opened and "shoppers" rehearsed. The Danish delegation believes it all, and a few days later the residents of Theresienstadt are all shipped East. Wouk does even the inside of the cattle cars superbly. Give him an environment of any kind—the Kremlin, Hitler's Wolfsschanze in the East Prussian forest, the President's private quarters in the White House, a gas chamber posing as a mass shower-bath, the flag-plot room on a battleship, an atomic pile, the interior of a submarine or a bomber—and he renders it persuasively. There's hardly a contemporary writer so good at depicting locales authentically, places as varied as Honolulu, Bern, Lisbon, Leningrad, Columbia University, London. They are perfect. I find it also to Wouk's credit that he is serious about the Second World War and conceives that interpreting it is the most pressing modern intellectual and moral problem. I respect the elegiac impulse that prompts him to interrupt his narrative of the Battle of Midway to display on three pages the names of the actual dead naval aviators from *Yorktown, Enterprise,* and *Hornet.* It is only with living people that he fails.

In *War and Remembrance* he has wanted to register the facts of the Holocaust so that they will never be forgotten. It is sad that the vulgarity of his romance of the Henrys compromises this admirable end, and by proximity demeans his skillful historiography.

The Romantic War,
and the Other One

If you are a male over fifty-five and were sound of wind and limb
in 1944 and in those days were not quite at the apex of the class
hierarchy and were neither terribly brave nor terribly cowardly,
you were probably in the Army of the United States. (If you were
at the apex and also at Yale, you were likely to be in the OSS; if
terribly brave, in the Marine Corps; if terribly cowardly, in the
Coast Guard: or so the feeling was at the time.) If you were in the
army in Europe, chances are you're familiar already with the
settings and contexts of William P. McGivern's *Soldiers of '44*
and Norman Lewis's *Naples '44*. McGivern's novel takes place in
the frozen fields and woods of Belgium when the Germans counter-
attacked in December and mangled the American 106th Division,
peopled largely by embittered transfers from the comfy, scholarly
Army Specialized Training Program at home. Lewis's memoir, in
the form of a diary, begins with the Allied landings at Salerno in
September, 1943, and goes on to scrutinize half-satirically, half-
sympathetically the infinite human riches of the Neapolitan scene
during 1944, when under official American auspices the Mafioso
Vito Genovese was virtually in charge.

Despite their common return to the public events of 1944, these
two books are very different, and it is certainly unfair, even if
critically instructive, to juxtapose McGivern's creaky, leaden
American melodrama with Lewis's sensitive, ironic, and intelligent British memoir. But the juxtaposition does suggest a point
worth making. When an American has something personal and
pressing to write about—McGivern was in the army in Belgium
in 1944—his first thought is to write a novel about it, choosing
not to notice that the talent for contriving significant credible
human actions is extremely rare. When an Englishman wants to
register personal experience, he is more likely to do so in a memoir,

a much more compassable form of autobiographical fiction for those who are not, by God's gifts, Joyces or Lawrences. The effects of these two national dispositions are visible in *The Naked and the Dead* and *The Young Lions,* on the one hand, fictions immensely ambitious geographically, politically, and even metaphysically, and, on the other, neat, understated British memoirs like Keith Douglas's *Alamein to Zem Zem* or John Guest's *Broken Images* or W. Stanley Moss's *Ill Met by Moonlight,* works which, modestly declining to attempt The Big Picture, succeed finely in conveying their small one.

McGivern's book and Lewis's are aimed at different audiences, and probably no more than five people are going to require both. The audience McGivern assumes needs elementary instruction about the war and expects diagrammatic simplification of all emotions and motives. From his book you learn (1) that line soldiers are profane and obscene and don't bathe or shave for weeks on end; (2) that if you touch a picture of Hitler in a house just vacated by German troops a booby trap is very likely to go off and kill three men; (3) that armies are like prisons in this respect as in others: lads with long eyelashes and nice smiles are going to capture the hearts of their comrades, sometimes to the detriment of decency and good order; (4) that if you think the war's going to be over by Christmas, you're wrong; (5) that in the combat units of the Second World War the standards of endurance and phlegm were higher for Jews than for others; (6) that although practical ethics has its "grey areas," concepts like cowardice and courage still betoken something like opposites.

This last lesson emerges from the climax of the novel, an implausible judicial inquiry by a panel of field-grade officers who have no more pressing business on hand than to ascertain the facts about the desertion and subsequent heroic redemption of Private Jackson Baird, who (like hundreds of others, actually) has thrown away his rifle and fled in panic from the 106th Division. He has attached himself to the fifteen-man anti-aircraft artillery section of Sergeant Buell Docker, said by the jacket blurb to be "perhaps the most memorable hero in all World War II fiction." If your conception of a hero is Superman, you'll buy that. Otherwise you will find Yossarian, Billy Pilgrim, and Tyrone Slothrop more memorable. Docker is simply Burt Lancaster about twenty years ago, but simplified ("There was a precision in his movements that masked the power and size of his body").

The presence of Private Baird in a rifle company of an undistinguished new division when his West Point father is a moneyed major-general on MacArthur's staff is as hard to credit as the operatic action constituting his apotheosis. Docker's gun section, emplaced on a hilltop, has shot down one of the new German jet fighters, and the Germans conclude that they must destroy the nearby wreckage to protects its "secrets." (Unbelievable: many such planes flew during the Bulge and many were shot down.) This mission is undertaken by the civilized, decent Waffen-SS officer Karl Jaeger, who comes after Docker's section with a King Tiger Tank Mark II, "the most dangerous ground weapon," McGivern pontificates, "in the German arsenal." From here on the thrills and the yards of unreal dialogue and dying speeches are from one of those adolescent war films made for TV. Private Baird, who has read widely in technical military literature, recalls that the belly armor on this model of tank is very thin. He saves the situation by advising Docker to plant a shot there as the tank crests the hill. The shot succeeds, but Baird is killed. The board of inquiry decides that although he was once a coward (a "letter" confessing as much has come to light), he has ended as a hero. His reward is a posthumous Silver Star.

Because it is so false, so corny, and so shallow, and because it misrepresents so pleasingly the emotional conditions of the war, *Soldiers of '44* was mighty popular, chosen as the lead item, for example, by the Literary Guild, and hustled by Waldenbooks, B. Dalton Bookseller, and other purveyors of good cheer to the high- and mid-prole classes. It carried on quite efficiently the work of rationalizing and romanticizing the war begun by Wouk.

McGivern's style as well as his outlook is bound to attract readers, for he cants of "parameters" and "guidelines" and calls houses "homes" and doesn't know what "literal" means, just like his audience. On the other hand, Norman Lewis is an educated person and a master of his medium. His view of events is so unconstrained by the received imagery of the respectable that he can record honestly what he has seen. Set ashore at Salerno with a unit of the British Field Security Service—the equivalent of the American Counter-Intelligence Corps—Lewis observes the Ameri-

can 36th ("Texas") Division in its first action. Where McGivern
turns the actual into the incredible, Lewis turns the unexpected
into the real:

> A line of American tanks went by, making for the battle, and
> hardly any time passed before they were back, but now there
> were fewer of them, and the wild and erratic manner in
> which they were driven suggested panic. One stopped nearby,
> and the crew clambered out and fell into one another's arms,
> weeping. Shortly afterwards there were cries of "gas," and we
> saw frantic figures wearing gasmasks running in all directions.

Where McGivern's coolheaded gunners hit an enemy plane just
as they're supposed to, Lewis watches some "distraught" American
anti-aircraft gunners bring down their third British plane, and
"at about 300 feet." Where McGivern's officers mount solemn
inquiries into their men's cowardice, those Lewis sees pull out
quietly and abandon their troops, or, in Lewis's terms, their
"armed hillbillies."

> Official history will in due time set to work to dress up this
> part of the action at Salerno with what dignity it can. What
> we saw was ineptitude and cowardice spreading down from
> the command, and this resulted in chaos. . . . In the belief
> that our position had been infiltrated by German infantry,
> [the Americans] began to shoot each other, and there were
> blood-chilling screams from men hit by the bullets.

To Lewis's civilized eye the war is a murderous farce, and this
view encompasses British behavior as well as American. At British
Security Headquarters, he reports,

> I saw an ugly sight: a British officer interrogating an Italian
> civilian, and repeatedly hitting him about the head with a
> chair; treatment which the Italian, his face a mask of blood,
> suffered with stoicism. At the end of the interrogation, which
> had not been considered successful, the officer called in a
> private of the Hampshires and asked him in a pleasant,
> conversational sort of manner, "Would you like to take this
> man away, and shoot him?" The private's reply was to spit on
> his hands, and say, "I don't mind if I do, sir." The most
> revolting episode I have seen since joining the forces.

In McGivern's novel rumors prove to be true, and people know
accurately news which assumed its present status as cliché only

after the war, like the bombing of Dresden, the execution of Private Slovik, the drowning of too many sailors on the *Lexington* because so many portholes were welded shut. In Lewis's memoir, as in real life, rumors are false, reports erroneous, evidence dubious, accurate perception virtually impossible. "Suspiciously flashing lights" are reported in a village near Naples, and Lewis's section surrounds the town. When the light winks, they move in, "only to capture a man with a [flashlight] on his way to the single outside latrine, used by the entire village."

Lewis's intelligence section is soon installed in Naples, where it goes to work receiving and investigating reams of local denunciations of collaborators and spies. One man is described by his enemy as "having the face of a hypocrite." There are frequent visitors with special requests, like a prince and his sister:

> Both are remarkably alike in appearance: thin, with extremely pale skin and cold, patrician faces bordering on severity. The purpose of the visit was to enquire if we could arrange for the sister to enter an army brothel. We explained that there was no such institution in the British Army. "A pity," the Prince said. Both of them speak excellent English, learned from an English governess.
>   "Ah well, Luisa, I suppose if it can't be it can't be." They thanked us with polite calm, and departed.

"Naples is extraordinary in every way," says Lewis. It has always been a theater, and in 1944 it combined Grand Guignol with Fellini (we hear of "the famous midget gynaecologist Professore Dottore Salerno"). Its thieves and black-marketeers exhibited an audacity perhaps unequaled until Vietnam. The British Army's telephone wires were cut down and sold openly for the copper, and "at the opening of the San Carlo opera *every* middle- and upper-class woman arrived in a coat made from a stolen army blanket." Later in the season, the orchestra, clad also in garments made from stolen blankets, took a brief recess. When it returned to the pit, it found its instruments stolen. Thieves scaled thirty-foot walls to remove in five minutes all the wheels from the trucks of Lewis's unit, and Lewis registers his amazement at the spectacle of a damaged tank, "which, although no one ever saw a finger laid on it, shrank away day by day, as if its armor-plating had been made of ice, until nothing whatever remained."

But it's not all funny. Lewis dwells also on the starvation, the quasi-medieval religious credulity, the epidemics, the madness and deformities, the fraud and bribery and flagrant injustice, the syphilis and child prostitution, the open banditry, the wholesale rape, and the cruelty. A boys' pastime was to ignite gasoline-soaked rags tied to bats and release them prettily into the night sky; a grave adult Neapolitan "was full of praise for the ingenuity with which they made their own small pleasures."

And yet: "A year among the Italians had converted me to such an admiration for their humanity and culture that I realize that were I given the chance to be born again and to choose the place of my birth, Italy would be the country of my choice." Lewis speaks as the heir of a complex tradition, the tradition of Browning and Ruskin and Lawrence and Norman Douglas and Forster. Compared with Lewis's kind of complicated awareness, McGivern can come up with nothing but cowboys and Indians.

McGivern is not the only American to think that because the war can be conceived as necessary and even "just," it was therefore rational, and even good. Lewis understands that although necessary it was absurd and cruel, reasonable in intent but botched in particulars, a task for professionals bungled by amateurs. His account is credible, funny, ghastly, contemptuous, compassionate, and fully human. As a version of 1944 it will never be popular, but it will always be true.

"Where Are the War Poets?"

At the outbreak of the war, when the British press began to fret over the absence of "war poets" to do for the start of this war what Rupert Brooke and Thomas Hardy had done for the old— that is, generate enthusiasm and commitment—C. Day Lewis responded curtly, observing that conditions were now different. It was not now a case of defending a pastoral paradise against barbarism but of defending something pretty crappy and corrupt against something even worse. The war was a job to be done, but it was a nasty job, and one not attended by artistic joy. As Day Lewis put it in "Where Are the War Poets?",

> They who in folly or mere greed
> Enslaved religion, markets, laws,
> Borrow our language now and bid
> Us to speak up in freedom's cause.
>
> It is the logic of our times,
> No subject for immortal verse—
> That we who lived by honest dreams
> Defend the bad against the worse.

Most people, recalling Wilfred Owen and Edward Thomas and Siegfried Sassoon and Robert Graves and Edmund Blunden, assume that because of this lack of either enthusiasm or very deep outrage the poetry emanating from the Second War is inferior to that of the First. Vernon Scannell, the British pugilist, poet, critic, broadcaster, and wounded veteran, thinks otherwise, and in *Not Without Glory: Poets of the Second World War* argues the excellence of both British and American war poetry from the years 1939–1945, concluding that it at least equals in quality the better-known work from the First World War.

It has never been as popular, probably because most of it is more difficult: its authors and readers alike have had to come to grips with Rilke and Pound, with Hopkins and Auden and Eliot and Stevens, whereas the poets of the Great War addressed an audience whose idea of poetry was comprehended by Kipling, William Watson, Bridges, and Noyes. Brooke and Owen wrote at a moment when, as Scannell says, "Sir Henry Newbolt was regarded as a major poet and a collection of huffing patriotic verses published by him at the outbreak of the war sold 70,000 copies within a few months."

No one has ever puzzled over the meanings of poems like Owen's "Dulce et Decorum Est" or Sassoon's "Base Details." But when we engage the greater indirection of tone and the more subtle irony in the poetry of the Second World War, difficulties enter and interesting disagreements arise. Consider Gavin Ewart's "When a Beau Goes In":

> When a Beau goes in,
> Into the drink,
> It makes you think,
> Because, you see, they always sink
> But nobody says, "Poor lad"
> Or goes about looking sad
> Because, you see, it's war,
> It's the unalterable law.
>
> Although it's perfectly certain
> The pilot's gone for a Burton
> And the observer too
> It's nothing to do with you
> And if they both should go
> To a land where falls no rain nor hail nor driven snow—
> Here, there or anywhere,
> Do you suppose *they* care?
>
> You shouldn't cry
> Or say a prayer or sigh.
> In the cold sea, in the dark,
> It isn't a lark,
> But it isn't Original Sin—
> It's just a Beau going in.

Is Ewart committed to the sardonic findings of that poem, or is it, as Scannell maintains, "an attack on the heartlessness that lay behind the facile attitudes and jargon of journalists and Blimps"? In F. T. Prince's "Soldiers Bathing" does no irony attend the implication of "ownership" in the words "a band/Of soldiers who belong to me"? Scannell finds so little wry and self-guying here that he grows class-peevish, saying, "I take it that no irony is intended . . . and I can imagine what the reaction of those soldiers would be if they had been told that they were the property of the poet and officer." Again, does Keith Douglas's "Cairo Jag" offer a contrast between the squalors of Cairo and the desert front many miles away, as Scannell suggests, or is the point, as A. Banerjee has held, the similarity of leave-town and battlefield, equally squalid, equally "modern"? On the desert battlefield is Douglas's "man with no head" who "has a packet of chocolate and a souvenir of Tripoli" different from "the somnambulists and legless beggars" of Cairo, or so similar as to be virtually the same? One can hardly imagine asking questions like these of any First War poems except, perhaps, Isaac Rosenberg's.

It is not just in being more problematic in tone and emphasis that most of the poetry of the Second War is harder than that of the First. It also presupposes readers interested in idiom almost as a self-sufficient subject, as a significant social and political emblem in itself. Thus Richard Eberhart's classic "The Fury of Aerial Bombardment." If a Great War poet had written a poem so titled, he would have spent his energy deploring the fact of aerial bombardment. But Eberhart is equally interested in testing the adequacy of various languages for registering a suitable emotion. The limitations of abstract words and phrases in doing the job are as much his focus as the scandal of explosions and cruelty. Thus for three exhausting stanzas he exercises himself in the wrong, ambitious idiom ("You would feel that after so many centuries/ God would give man to repent") only to arrive finally at an idiom appropriate in its disinclination to stretch after grandiosity. (It's almost as if he begins the poem as an American and ends it as an Englishman.) The final stanza finds its language in a quiet, positivistic recall of the speaker's "students" of aerial gunnery:

> Of Van Wettering I speak, and Averill,
> Names on a list, whose faces I do not recall;
> But they are gone to early death, who late in school
> Distinguished the belt feed lever from the belt holding pawl.

In the same way it seems important that one of the most memorable poems from the Second War is Henry Reed's "Naming of Parts," a ventriloquial tour de force on idiom, and a poem which is about clichés and sing-song rhythms as much as it is about the lost norms of love and the pre-war spring.

If the poets of 1914–1918 marched briskly away in innocence, those of 1939–1945 slouched unillusioned toward fatality, adept already at understanding evil and expecting nothing. As Scannell shrewdly observes, Rupert Brooke began one of his famous sonnets "with the conditional clause, 'If I should die,' " whereas Keith Douglas begins one of his best poems with the line, "Remember me when I am dead." "The removal of any question of survival," Scannell says of Douglas, "places him squarely before the bone-hard reality of his subject." In the Great War one could produce an acceptable poem by registering shock at discovering that a man who loves also kills. But in *Vergissmeinnicht* Douglas, accustomed by mid-twentieth-century writing to accepting the egregious paradoxes from which the human psyche is constructed, perceives quite unshocked—like Ewart on the Beau going in—that "the lover and killer are mingled" in the dead German anti-tank gunner, "who has one body and one heart." For most poets of the Second World War "battle" is understood as a condition of the human heart, "warfare" a continuation of everyday psychological dynamics by other means.

Scannell, a good poet, is also a good critic, although some will wish him more precise intellectually and analytically. Sometimes he will reprehend a poem by observing, "This is pretty bad writing"; sometimes he will praise one by calling it "wonderfully well-written." But for the most part he is acute and sane, and he brings to bear both a soldier's and a poet's eye for technical detail. His criteria for excellence are intelligence, concreteness, and a poet's willingness to confront honestly "the immediate facts and objects" of military life. One of Karl Shapiro's poems is found wanting because "it does not seem to have taken all the facts of war into account." As a veteran, Scannell wants poems to implicate readers in "the bone-hard reality" of the war. He thus has little patience with poets like Dunstan Thompson who flee toward "beautiful literature" and whose work seems "perversely trivial and narcissistic when the circumstances of its composition are considered."

Accurate registration of the ghastly facts without the sacrifice of a recognizable lyricism is what Scannell demands. "The best poetry of the war, the most truthful and penetrating," he finds, "was written with a respect for that tradition of English verse which is informed by the spirit of Milton's words, 'simple, sensuous, and passionate,' a poetry which is rooted in the ground of physical experience, suspicious of the abstract and conforming to the disciplines of provenly effective forms." With that utterance the British empiricist, the veteran, and the conservative coalesce, and if the critic makes us feel a bit uneasy with a word like *truthful,* at least we sense that our guide is not going to snow us with deconstructionist cant.

Scannell's desiderata are satisfied pre-eminently by Keith Douglas. While still an undergraduate Douglas was discovering his main theme; the war merely offered him an opportunity to behold it lurking in more emergent occasions. His theme was "the paradoxical view of time as thief and donor, the sense of a man carrying his death within him." For Scannell it is Douglas's "hardness of edge, wit, vision, compassion," and, most important, "disciplined intelligence" that establish his work as the equal of Wilfred Owen's. Scannell also like Alun Lewis, who, as "the reluctant, unhappy warrior" registering the boredom of military life and its "remorseless strangling of individuality," becomes "in some ways the representative poet of the Second World War." Scannell is less fond of Sidney Keyes, mainly because "he was primarily set upon producing literature" and too much affected the metaphysics. But Keyes has occasional successes, and his sympathetic poem on Marshal Timoshenko measures the distance between Second World War vision and that of, say, Sassoon and Graves, who can't contemplate any general without turning purple. Scannell thinks well of Roy Fuller too, but I don't think many readers will be persuaded by his generous advocacy, which cannot redeem Fuller's slack texture, unimpressive perceptions, and simple-minded contrasts.

It is Scannell's long chapter on the Americans (Jarrell, Wilbur, Louis Simpson, and others) that most needed doing and that best displays the acute critic. The glory here is his analysis and celebration of Lincoln Kirstein's brilliant *Rhymes and More Rhymes of a PFC,* a book insufficiently known on either side of the Atlantic. Emphasizing Kirstein's prodigous originality, Scannell nicely specifies the way these sardonic verse narratives, character sketches, and ironic vignettes pulse with life. They sound like "popular poetry," and yet, as Scannell finds, Kirstein's work "not only stands up to examination on the page, it discloses subtleties which demand the most serious critical appraisal." Out of such "curiously unfashionable and—one would have thought—unserviceable influences" as Hardy, Kipling, W. S. Gilbert, Housman, Betjeman, and even Hopkins, Kirstein has devised "a style which, despite the echoes, is strangely and completely his own, and—paradoxically in view of the Englishness of his exemplars—speaks with an unequivocally American voice." That voice resembles Berryman's late "Henry" voice, but it seems to avoid Berryman's occasional archness and embarrassing self-consciousness. Here is Kirstein on "Dick Hales," a sissy childhood friend who "Never won games or a girl," yet

> Slid his flakked plane sidewise low over Sussex to spare a girls'
> school;
> No trick for coward or fool.
> He had the presence of heart or head to make his enormous
> bet.
> Now is he hero, haloed and holy. His mummy can get
> Used to life's being cruel.

In "Rank" one Captain Stearnes, drinking in a French café with two enlisted men, fires at the stove to demonstrate his marksmanship and hits instead the proprietor Jean-Pierre's wife. Court-martialled, he is convicted not of manslaughter but

> something worse, and this they brought out time and again;
> Clearly criminal and caddishly vicious
> Was his Drinking with Enlisted Men.
>
> I'm serious. It's what the Judge Advocate said:
> Strict maintenance of rank or our system is sunk.
> Stearnes saluted. Jean-Pierre wept his dead.
> Jack and I got see-double drunk.

As will be apparent, Kirstein has no visible "artistic" pretensions, and certainly no metaphysical ones. It would be funny and splendid is he should ultimately be recognized as "the greatest poet of

the Second World War." It would be nice if the poet finally promoted to that eminence should be one manifesting Kirstein's love
of details, his irrepressible levity and optimism, his social sense, his
cheerfully browned-off vision, his sexiness, his irony, and his humanity. Like Keyes, Kirstein can discriminate among generals,
and the admiring things he has to say about even Patton indicate
his distance from the doctrinaire. Here he is on Eisenhower:

> Painter of sorts in pleasant times, our
> Daddy-O in the unpleasing times,
> Whose decent manner, common sense, justice, stump weak
>   rhymes;
> Who endured stupendous waiting,
> Winning worst wars with the least hating.
>   Praise him.

Scannell's amiable study of these poets is as unpretentious as
Kirstein's poems, equally honest and pleasant to encounter. Its
effect is to suggest that those who wonder where the war poets
are may not have found them because they have not lowered their
gaze sufficiently to take in the popular tradition in which Kirstein
is working. But there is one error in Scannell's book, either the
author's or the printer's, that is bound to strike Americans of a
certain age as bizarre. The attack on Pearl Harbor is said to have
taken place on December 4, 1941. Those of us who late in school
were enjoined most solemnly to Remember Pearl Harbor can
never forget that Sunday, December 7, is the date which will live
in infamy.

Time-Life Goes to War

If the first item in history to be mass-produced was the brick, the second was doubtless the book. So Hugh Kenner suggests. Once printing began to displace hand-copying in the fifteenth century, he says, "It grew evident almost at once that mankind's existing stock of verbal treasures was too small to feed the new technology. Hence instant treasures: books composed solely because entrepreneurs with a press and some type needed something to print." Since then the new technology has grown steadily more voracious, and now Time-Life books are streaming endlessly from the machines in Alexandria, Virginia. This operation is said to constitute one of the most profitable publishing ventures ever. It has certainly changed a great many people's notion of what a book is, as well as changing the general idea of a bookstore from a place with shelves and words to a place full of racks and pictures.

For the consumer of Time-Life books, a book is something that's part of a "series," the way formerly a given issue of *Life* was only a part of the year's accumulation. Considering their merchandising function, some of these series titles are brilliant. One type offers shallow, illogical, or misleading ways of classifying knowledge with a novel vividness: "Great Ages of Man," for example, or "This Fabulous Century," or "The Great Cities," or "The World's Wild Places." Mindful of the dignity still attaching to the term *library* (the Morgan Library, Everyman's Library, even the Modern Library), the devisers of the series titles invoke it wherever possible, as in "The Time-Life Library of Art"—a memorable oxymoron—or "The Time-Life Library of Boating." Sometimes the word *encyclopedia* can confer similar quasi-humanistic cachet, yielding "The Time-Life Encyclopedia of Gardening." And sometimes the series title works by associating "books" (in the new sense) with harmless Saturday afternoon TV programs aimed at the quite young. Thus "The Wild, Wild World of Animals" and "The American Wilderness."

The new "book" is also an artifact with photographs, which means that it must assume the shape of a large quarto, like a college yearbook. And as in a college yearbook, in this sort of book the photographs are always more interesting than the prose attending them. No surprise there, because this new kind of book is a thing produced by a team (rather like a brick, in fact) instead of written by an author. If you go through a catalog of Time-Life books, listing at last count 323 titles, you will discover the names of only nine authors, and these names, as if too shameful for display, are hidden in the paragraphs of ad copy describing some of the new releases. Once a book enters the backlist, the author's name vanishes entirely, and only the title remains. Authors tend to be human, which means idiosyncratic and troublesome. Their publishers very often secretly wish they'd simply disappear, but this catalog is the only one I know which has achieved the Final Solution of the author problem.

On the books themselves the authors' names can't be quite extirpated, although they are banished from the spine and played down even on the title page. When an author must be revealed, he is not allowed to appear unless demeaned by an accompanying train of from two to five consultants and advisers and keepers, as if knowledge, understanding, and eloquence were a function of the committee system, or as if no single intelligence is to be trusted to perform a task unspied on. The idea of a single bright, responsible person writing a single bright, responsible book without the intervention of a platoon of editors, "staff writers," researchers, quality controllers, traffic supervisors, and similar parasites and busybodies is unthinkable.

I base these remarks on the experience of reading for many weeks twelve volumes of the Time-Life series "World War II." Time-Life books range from the god-awful to the quite good, and I must report that the books in this series, in relation to some others, are quite good. But even the best can't overcome the limitations of the picture-magazine mind and format, which determines that contemporary history be diminished to moments of vivid "human interest" and that what resists melodramatic form simply vanish. That is, these books are obliged to pretend that life is like *Life*.

This pursuit of the Higher Disneyfication is more the fault of the genre "picture book" than of the writers, all of them able and some excellent, like the British Barrie Pitt *(The Battle of the Atlantic)* or former *Life* staffer Don Moser *(China-Burma-India)* or Rafael Steinberg of *Time (Return to the Philippines* and *Island Fighting)*. Each author contributes a popular historical narrative of about forty thousand words, digested and paraphrased from secondary sources which are accurately listed in a bibliography. These sources are well-known works of popular history or the often disingenuous memoirs of military or diplomatic figures, which the Time-Life authors tend to embrace unskeptically. An example of the method is Arthur Zich's performance in *The Rising Sun*, devoted to the pre-war expansion of Japan and the Japanese victories of 1942. He draws much material from John Toland's *The Rising Sun* (1970), itself in part a narrative compiled from prior popular histories and self-serving memoirs and self-dramatizing interviews. Here is Toland's Joseph Grew, American ambassador in Tokyo before the war:

> Grew was a tall, courtly man with bushy black eyebrows, mustache and gray-white hair. Born in Boston's Back Bay, as was his great-grandfather, he had attended Groton and Harvard with Franklin D. Roosevelt. . . . He was particularly qualified to serve in Tokyo, since he had a rare understanding and affection for Japan and all things Japanese, as well as a wife who had previously lived in the country, spoke the language and was a descendant of Commodore Perry.

Zich, of *Time, Life,* and *Sports Illustrated,* paraphrases that passage and simplifies it, replacing the arcane reference to the Back Bay with a cliché and explaining to the proles what Groton is:

> Grew was a tall and dignified man, with gray hair and startlingly black and luxuriant eyebrows. Like the proper Bostonian he was, he had gone to Groton preparatory school and Harvard College. At both institutions he had known Franklin D. Roosevelt. . . . He understood Japan remarkably well, thanks in large measure to his wife, who had grown up in Japan and knew the language perfectly.

For any author in the series, the format is the same. His pop-historical narrative is broken up into six chapters with jazzy titles like "Yamashita's Last Stand" or "A Gamble for High Stakes." If his historical narrative should turn out to be a really respectable piece of work, like Robert Wallace's in *The Italian Campaign,* the book can be redeemed for sensationalism and vulgarity by the editors' interposition of numerous "Picture Essays" with titles like "Heading 'Em Off at the Pass." (The Time-Life merchandisers conceive The Wild West and World War II as virtually the same subject, one called "Action Packed Adventure," and the catalog thus encourages the bookseller to "Put Your Windows to Work": series like "World War II and The Old West are such great sellers they could stand in a window all alone. Dressing your window with items such as 10-gallon hats, holsters, medals, and helmets guarantees this display to be a traffic-stopper.")

The picture essays bear all the stigmata of the old 1940's *Life.* There are the same hectoring boldface sans-serif-cap display titles. And there are the picture captions more loyal to space than sense, honoring an ideal of visual neatness by doggedly filling out a given measure to the end. The result is padding and adjectivitis. Here's one below a picture eight inches wide: "Before a sparse audience of curious Poles, German infantrymen led by mounted officers march in a victory parade through Warsaw's Pilsudski Square." The old *Life* style enters the historical narrative too. That's what all those editors and staff writers are for. If the author has neglected to supply sufficient clichés, they put in things like eating his heart out and golden opportunity and fresh as a daisy. They make sure the prose is sufficiently vivid by having the authors' military bands always oom-pah and his boat engines thrum. They make sure his people vie rather than compete. They make sure there's ample sentimental personification, in the tradition of *The Little Engine That Could.* Hence "A Luxury Liner's Masterful End Run." By genteel misrepresentation and coy excision they make sure no author grows too blue for family use. They make him write: "In training camp, the recruit . . . learned a new vocabulary: . . . 'SNAFU' for 'situation normal—all fouled up'; and 'SOS' as the acronym for the chipped-beef-and-gravy abomination that was served to him on toast at six in the morning. (The 'O' and 'S' stood for '. . . on a shingle')." They make sure the author throws in plenty of portentous-sounding but meaningless statistics: "The co-called May Act of 1941 . . . enabled local communities to shut down brothels near military installations. By 1944 some 700 municipalities had closed their red-light districts." Or: "Within a few weeks of the Pearl Harbor attack, six billion dollars in planes and aircraft equipment were on order." They make sure everything gets sufficiently exaggerated: Slim's and Stilwell's retreat through Burma was "a nightmare . . . that had no parallel in military history." They make sure the author uses plenty of peppy illiterate terms like mix for mixture, proportions for size, disinterested for uninterested, and of course escalate. They make sure that no spirit of understanding, tolerance, or forgiveness be allowed to show, for the Allies are still saviors, the Axis brutes. Thus Colonel Tsuji's brilliant pamphlet issued to Japanese troops before their extraordinary march down the Maylayan Peninsula, a work which is virtually the first survival manual for jungle fighting, and still one of the best, is misrepresented as "A Brutal Manual for the Invaders," when actually the bulk of it is about conserving water on the march and not eating tempting but poisonous flora.

It will not surprise us that the World War II volumes have earned their popularity by delivering a version of the war falsely dramatized and falsely cheerfulized. With A. J. Barker's Dunkirk we can compare the sanitized Dunkirk offered here, which does nothing if not bring credit to human nature: "On one pier, men fell in three abreast under fire; as their officer snapped, 'Front rank, one pace forward. Jump!' they leaped with parade precision onto the deck of a barge 15 feet below. With the beach exploding around them, Yorkshire infantrymen bellowed such songs as 'Oh, I *do* like to be by [actually *beside,* but let that pass] the seaside.' In the same mood, a sailor guiding troops aboard his boat mimicked a peacetime excursion tout: 'Any more,' he bawled, 'for the *Brighton Queen?*'" If people are as nice as that, why should we worry about who's got his hands on the atomic bomb?

These books don't just falsify the war. They falsify the conditions of real life in all times and places. But that's what they're supposed to do, for as we know humankind cannot bear very much reality, nor is it the business of a flourishing brickyard to deliver any.

Yank When We Needed It

Some bright World War II veterans in Omaha (once a beach, now merely a city in Nebraska) are reissuing *Yank* ("By the men, for the men in the service") in perfect facsimiles of the original weekly numbers, and even civilians can subscribe.* Which means that every seven days as you wonder how you're going to avoid being shot in the streets, you can raise your morale with *Yank*'s cartoons and jokes and poemlets and pinups and cool, resolute, optimistic human-interest features. Did our morale once need raising as badly as *Yank* implies? Yes, it did.

Especially in November, 1942, when this edition of *Yank* (there were twenty-one worldwide) began appearing in London. The war for Americans was not yet a year old, and the only victories yet visible were those of production and transportation. The Marines hadn't yet won at Guadalcanal, and Americans were just landing in North Africa. There, if the general occupation was going to turn out a success, Kasserine Pass was going to be another disaster—for the army what Pearl Harbor was for the navy. In those days not everyone was sure we were going to win the war. Anyone listening to Rome Radio in June, 1942, would have had his morale shaken by hearing "Dr. Ezra Pound" assert, "You are not going to win this war. None of our best minds ever thought you could win it. You have never had a chance in this war." *Yank*, admittedly not under the conduct of our best minds, argued in its various ways that we were going to win, and it survived until September, 1945, when we had. Its peak circulation was 2,600,000.

A typical issue would include a number of perfectly veracious but inevitably encouraging news roundups like "From Russia to New Guinea the Situation Looks Better" (January 17, 1943). In

* Reprint, Inc., P.O. Box 27386, Omaha, NE 68127.

addition to conveying good news, *Yank* also tried to smooth over inter-service feuds. One problem in 1942 and 1943 was persuading the army that the marines were not the fraudulent glory-hunters they seemed. The unity of "the Armed Forces" is insisted upon. Thus we have a "Navy Issue" and an "Air Force Issue." "The war effort" is projected subtly as an apotheosis of the New Deal. We are all in this together, not just various arms and services, but allies and races as well. We are assured that the Canadians, for all their tiny eleven million population, are really "the fighting Canadians," proud that every bit of their equipment is manufactured at home. We hear of the integrity and courage of various American "Negro" units: a full page in February, 1943, celebrates the first fourteen Negro officers trained in the European Theater of Operations, and one double-spread exhibits "Hooper's Troopers," a black anti-aircraft unit operating in Hawaii.

One odd thing is *Yank*'s relative neglect of stateside sports. The magazine gave sports much less space and emphasis than, say, the current *New York Times*. One infers that in the last forty years sports, by allying itself with big- as well as show-business, has promoted itself to "news." Another sign of the period in *Yank* is the sheer photo interest, the fascination with the very fact of photography as a news and feature medium. One senses the lingering excitement of a fairly recent discovery. Generically, *Yank* seems a conflation of *Life* (wide red strip at top and bottom of the cover, with the title in white sans-serif boldface) and the *New York Daily News* (lots of hustle in the prose, lots of small departments, brief so as not to tax the mind). Each issue the center spread offered a large display of miscellaneous and unrelated photographs, "*Yank*'s Camera Report" or "Variety Show," paying tribute to the convention of *Life*'s "Miscellany" page that photographs "say more" than prose.

In the early 1940's, while American boys were preparing to bomb women and children, their moral purity was still under the guardianship of the Postmaster General. Thus the astonishing chastity of the full-page pinups in *Yank*. With the bikini as unthought-of as the event from which it was named and with toplessness literally unthinkable outside burlesque houses, the girls, all well known like Jinx Falkenberg, Betty Grable, Betty Hutton, and Jane Russell, are depicted either in costly evening gowns, to make them glamorous, or one-piece bathing- or sun-suits, to make them cute. Occasions of snobbery they may be, but triggers of lust they are not, as one "Ground Crew Private" complained in "Mail Call": "I know you want to keep it clean, but after all the boys are interested in sex, and *Esquire* and a few other magazines give us sex and still get by the mail, so why can't *Yank?*" But *Yank* couldn't because its function was to soothe, not to excite. Besides, it displayed its girls on the no-touch principle. Unlike the current high-school chicks and playmates, mighty accessible girls next door, *Yank*'s pinup girls are café society, socially out of reach. They please not because they're terribly erotic but because they're terribly famous.

But when all is said and when all *Yank*'s features are rescrutinized, it's Sad Sack who remains its permanent glory. With Sad Sack one goes all to water. Only a transversion of Samuel Johnson's rhapsodies on the character of Falstaff seems appropriate: "But [Sad Sack], unimitated, unimitable [Sad Sack], how shall I describe thee?" He was devised by Sergeant George Baker, before the war an animator at Walt Disney Studios. Baker died in 1975, and in my view his memory should be honored like Hašek's for inventing Schweik, Joyce's for Bloom, Chaplin's for the Tramp. Private Sack (he never makes PFC) is the army's version of the twentieth-century anti-hero, the man things are done to. His world is populated by marvelous grotesques, all of them "true." There are supply sergeants who go to any lengths to avoid issuing the slightest bit of equipment. When finally they must put out, they cry over their counters like babies. All sergeants have great garrison bellies hypertrophying in direct proportion to their rank, and first-sergeants look like pigs, precisely, fat with bristles on their necks. Two kinds of people have very wide mouths with fangs instead of teeth: tall, vulpine Second Johns, shoulders glittering coarsely; and men in white coats giving injections. All are torturers and madmen. And they and Sack inhabit a world of bizarre ugliness. Everyone's trousers bag at the seat, the buildings are hideous inside and out, the floor is always dirty, cigarette butts are everywhere, the women wear too much makeup. The airplane Sack labors to scrub clean returns from its mission as filthy as before. He can make the latrine sparkle only because the troops are away for the day. When they return, he watches it instantly turn dirty again.

But Sad Sack always springs back, and that seems part of the point. Actually, he's more than a butt: in one way he's a model soldier, and well behind the comedy of his predicaments a quasi-serious point is being made. The point is that no one gives up. Sack endures, although he expects to be shafted for doing so. He captures a spy by error and finds himself decorated and fêted with a ticker-tape parade. When he returns beaming in triumph to his home orderly room, his first-sergeant looks at him with contempt and instantly puts him on KP. Sad Sack fights bravely to reach Paris, dodging shot and shell but animated by dreams of women and champagne glasses. When he arrives on the outskirts, exhausted and tattered but slavering with desire and thirst, he finds an MP guarding a sign: "Off Limits to American Troops."

The implicit point is that the saddest sack does not despair, nor will he ever surrender. The soldier smiling over Sad Sack is absorbing something he needs to learn if that war is going to be won. No more running away from Kasserine Passes. No more self-pity. Do you want to live forever? Do you expect somebody to *thank you* for what you're doing?

George Baker, "Latrine Orderly" (*Yank*, January 31, 1943)

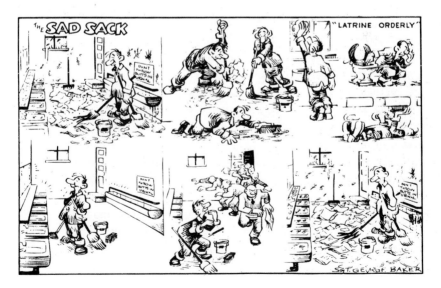

The War in
Black and White

It's hard to realize that the war began over forty years ago. I mean the war that matters, the one that divided Europe down the middle, shrank Germany, transformed China, begot the Third World, conferred Southeast Asia on the luckless Americans for a generation, and reduced Britain to the status of the Netherlands. The one that killed fifty-five million people and spawned the acronym habit (CINCPAC, ETOUSA, AMGOT), and, as Belsen and Maidenek were uncovered, jolted the progressive modern sensibility into an understanding, dormant since the Renaissance, of the reality of evil. The one that extinguished European Jewry but redeemed the New York intellectual tone and made America a culturally serious place for the first time in its existence. The one that created thirteen million veterans and then established the contemporary middle-class conception of the desirable by sending them to universities, installing them in professions, and lending them money to start businesses and buy the proclaimed ideal one-family suburban American house, with lawn, garage, and barbecue patio. The war matters too because it brought forth the jet engine and the rocket with a warhead and penicillin and the atomic pile and the proximity fuse and the Pentagon and the paperback.

Those who had direct adult access to the war and who experienced firsthand its forms and textures are now (not to put too fine a point on it) elderly. Others curious about it must depend upon volumes of history and memoir, and upon paintings and drawings and photographs. Paintings like those in James Jones's *WWII* are of little use: their news is less about the war than about the state of representational painting and illustration and hack portraiture during the early forties. We could use a *Guernica* about Oradour-sur-Glane or Manila or Aachen. In its absence we can read, or re-read, some photographs from the war, photographs so familiar they risk growing dull. Now is a good time to interpret them, before they begin to look as if Mathew Brady took them and before those who can never forget the look and feel of what they depict are gone.

Our historical instinct about the war, our "myth," if you will, is that it constituted a notably moral common cause, one moment at least in our history when the well-known American greed, centrifugalism, and jealous individualism briefly subdued themselves in the interests of virtue. Because the concentration camps and the Japanese treatment of prisoners were so much more loathsome than anything the Americans did—with the possible exception of dropping the second atomic bomb—the war, as Paul Addison has said, "served a generation of . . . Americans as a myth which enshrined their essential purity, a parable of good and evil." And it would be a mistake to imagine that *myth* betokens some sort of fraud or self-deception. Myths assume solidity and staying power only when they are essentially true. If we locked away and humiliated the Nisei, we gassed no Jews, Gypsies, or homosexuals, and we hanged no partisans. If we bombed Dresden, it was someone else who exterminated the Polish officer corps in the Katyn Forest. We did not starve or work our prisoners to death in Siberia or Manchuria, nor hack off the heads of enemy airmen brought down. We did, to be sure, our share of soldierly looting and raping, but in context these are peccadilloes. For purposes of American self-definition, the war was, in the words of Geoffrey Perrett, "the perfect war, . . . a war against palpable evil," a war that confirmed the purposes of the Republic. The solidity of this myth can be measured by the energy and originality Joseph Heller and Thomas Pynchon have had to deploy to make a dent in it.

For the myth-making memory, the principle of anonymity is one way of sanctifying the war. The myth requires that "servicemen" be depicted, at least in photographs, as virtually anonymous. Because the war was a common cause, no ordinary person in it has a right to appear as anything but anonymous. Thus we feel that American photographs of the war are the more significant, useful, and "authentic" the less they render identifiable individual human faces. "Stars" are not wanted. A case in point is the fa-

miliarity of the one classic photograph of the war, Joe Rosenthal's
flag-raising marines at Iwo Jima. Six men are at work, but the
face of only one is visible, dimly and in profile—and in repro-
ductions his face is often blacked into unidentifiable silhouette.
The photograph is not about facial expressions but about body
expressions, suggesting, in a way bourgeois faces can never do,
powerful and simple communal purpose. Change the flag to red
and you have "Soviet Art." Strip the men and you have Italian
fascist sculpture. The visible right legs of the six are all "in step,"

Flag-raising at Iwo Jima (Joe Rosenthal; Wide World Photos, © 1945 The
Associated Press)

bent the same way, and those parts of faces not obscured by helmets are concealed by the arms reaching up in common. The
image is that of a committee, soiled and exhausted, to be sure, but
nevertheless acting "as one man" in a rare, and thus precious, moment of unanimity. Indeed, the man at the back wants to keep
touching the pole as it's raised—he wants not to return to his selfhood but to continue being part of what's going on in common.
The picture seems "right" because it is so successful an emblem
of the common will triumphant. It seems right because it finally
brings the myth of the New Deal to a satisfying climax. It closes
out an era. After this picture, there's no place to go but "postwar,"
which will mean a return to the old individualism, personality,
and competitiveness.

Because it became famous, research has ascertained the names
of the men in Rosenthal's photograph, and we know their subsequent, often touching history. But that's because the picture's
special. Mostly we don't know the names, and there's a simple
professional and technical reason why soldiers in most photographs
come out anonymous. For a combat photographer, taking down
names for captions after making a photograph is intolerably irrelevant and tedious. You can avoid this painful duty and get on
quickly with the next shot if you arrange your pictures so that no
individual is identifiable, or just hurry off without getting the
data. The opposite convention, which asserts the identity and
uniqueness of individuals, belongs to the journalistic prose of the
war rather than to its photographs. Correspondents like Richard
Tregaskis and Ernie Pyle work by getting in as many hometown
names as possible. Thus Tregaskis in *Guadalcanal Diary* (1943):
"Our guide was a sturdy young man in high boots, a Capt.
Stallings (Capt. George R. Stallings of Augusta, Ga.)." In *Brave
Men* (1944) Pyle grows even more circumstantial: "When I went
up the trail my guide was Pfc. Fred Ford, of 3037 North Park
Drive, East St. Louis." In language, even the dead can be designated. Pyke's much-loved Captain Waskow, whose body is brought
down an Italian mountain by muleback and revered in the moonlight by his men ("I sure am sorry, sir"), is identified as Capt.
Henry T. Waskow, of Belton, Texas. One reason the reportorial
prose of the war seems so dated is this constant locating of everyone within a presumably static American scene with significantly

different "areas." The post-war mobility and national uniformity make the habit quaint, a last twitch of the local-color impulse.

But photographs possess *mana*, while prose does not. The dead in the photographs must not be identifiable. Henry Waskow's next of kin are pleased to see his name in print, but they must not see his body, nor ever his face. The first published picture of American war dead, which appeared in January, 1943, thirteen months after the United States declared war, ostentatiously shows them face down on Buna Beach, mercifully half-covered with drifts of wet sand. Processors of the Malmédy massacre photographs painted snow over the faces of the dead to prevent recognition, and in a well-known set of Robert Capa photographs showing one of the last Americans to be killed in Europe dying on a Leipzig balcony, the face is commonly blacked out by "the censor."

Faces of combat infantry in action are rare, too, in photographs, because the photographer is seldom in front of the attacking troops: what we see are expressive but anonymous backs, packs with entrenching tools, helmets from the rear. The picture of the troops landing on Omaha Beach is characteristic. If you were

Debarkation at Omaha Beach (U.S. Coast Guard)

carrying a camera instead of a rifle who could blame you for being the last man off the boat and sheltering within it as long as possible?

Anonymity is such a powerful convention in World War II American photography that the picture of the Russian boy partisan about to be hanged near Minsk in October, 1941, strikes one as completely "European," and thus as a useful contrast. Regardless of the common cause, this boy is flaunting his identity, the very extremity of his situation focusing his selfhood. The normality, even the respectability of the Germans in the picture is worth noticing. They are *Wehrmacht,* regular German army, not *SS,* and the one at the lower right, with the glasses, looks positively elderly and thus harmless. As a further photograph will indicate, when they have finished this job they will hang on the girl a sign reading, WE ARE PARTISANS AND HAVE SHOT AT GERMAN SOLDIERS. The sign will be in both Russian and German: this is so that, in addition to conveying its intended warning to the local populace, it will cheer up scared German troops marching past, persuading them that "something is being done."

Partisans Hanged near Minsk (Novosti Press Agency)

The girl has been hanging a few minutes. She is only a foot lower than the boy whose turn is next, indicating that she has been standing on a low chair or box, since kicked away. She has been slowly strangled in the wartime German way, and the boy does not want to look at her. Is he really smiling? If it is a real smile and not a fleeting grimace, is the cause self-consciousness, bitterness, or despair? or—a remote possibility—ironic triumph? His wearing his light-colored cap to the end is a beau geste. The two-colored decorative rope, suggestive of a bathrobe cord or a gift-tie, is an almost frivolous touch harmonizing with the boy's ambiguous expression, making the whole image almost too terrible to be borne. We recognize that if we contemplate it too long and intensely, associating the girl and boy with, say, our own children, it will do us harm. Our only defense against it must be an attitude of ironic dispassion, like Ewart's toward the drowned pilot and observer:

> It's nothing to do with you
> And if they both should go
> To a land where falls no rain nor hail nor driven snow—
> Here, there, or anywhere,
> Do you suppose *they* care?

If that picture memorably registers "personality," anonymity and a vision of the common cause in jeopardy dominate the photograph of the Naval Air Station on Ford Island in Pearl Harbor, taken just after eight o'clock in the morning, Sunday, December 7, 1941. Japanese planes have just made several bombing and strafing passes while most of the sailors have been sleeping late, showering, breakfasting, or going about their business in their solid and comfortable permanent barracks. A few of the people who have poured onto the field are running, but most are so shocked they are just looking, taking in the unbelievable, the mangled inert floatplanes and Catalinas on the ground and the spectacular hot fireball whooshing up in the background, where the battleship *Arizona* has just exploded. Fifteen hundred men are dying over there, but these watchers don't know that yet. The shirtless man on the ground looks less wounded than simply appalled, as if his legs have given away and he's had to sit down. Why

Ford Island, December 7, 1941 (U.S. Navy)

is the standing man who has been talking to him half-dressed in white, his wallet (he's left-handed) in his back pocket? He has been planning to go into Honolulu on a day-pass and has been getting dressed for town. The man a bit farther away, walking, not running, has been caught in the latrine in his shorts, and he wears a towel or skivvy shirt around his neck. Decency and normality at all costs. He's so shocked he's decided not to pay attention to the fireball. The emotions here are less terror or horror, even, than disbelief, a dogged, near-psychotic determination to insist that what's happening is not taking place. That's what the wind-sock on the hangar at the left seems to be doing, too. The photograph can be taken at all only because the war is so new: no one knows, as everyone will in a few months, that he should be down in a slit trench, not standing around.

Because, as Susan Sontag has said, "photography inexorably beautifies," there is complicated irony in the relation of personal disaster to sharp technique in the photograph of the dead sailor

Dead Sailor on Gun
Mount (Arthur Green;
U.S. Coast Guard)

hanging over his gun mount. An ugly picture, to be sure, in the
Weegee auto crash or suicide-jump tradition of tough American
spot-news frontal-flash photography of the late thirties. And yet,
ironically, beautifully composed—a little body, a lot of metal.
Here it looks as if some immense projectile has smashed across the
gun mount, carrying away most of the sailor's 40-mm anti-aircraft
gun and his helmet. (Actually his Destroyer Escort has just been
torpedoed in the Mediterranean, losing sixty feet of its stern. The
photographer is Arthur Green, Photographer's Mate 1st Class,
United States Coast Guard.) In some versions of this print the
dark, ragged top of the ammunition box blown off the gun mount
is airbrushed white to simplify the lower half of the picture. The
sailor's spine and left arm are broken, and the shock has undone
his left cuff button. In photographs dead sailors are often more
shocking than dead soldiers if their feet show, because they wear

quasi-civilian shoes and nice thin "dress" socks. We don't expect them to be treated so badly.

A man's face can sometimes be shown and the picture still project anonymity, as in the one of the small overcoated soldier eating his first hot meal after fifteen days of fighting in the Hürtgen Forest. The artistic tradition here is that of thirties documentary, the tradition of Walker Evans's *American Photographs* (1938) or Evans and James Agee's *Let Us Now Praise Famous Men* (1941). To cite Sontag again, documentary aspires to rack the conscience by ferreting out losers like Okies, sharecroppers, and residents of the Tennessee Valley, "the poor and the dispossessed, the nation's forgotten citizens." Or, in the terms James Jones invokes to interpret Sad Sack, "the army's and the war's 'pore dumb fuck' of an eternal victim." The soldier in this photograph is pre-eminently one of the nation's forgotten citizens, and although the camera singles him out, he is depicted as the prototypal invisible man, representative of the millions of forgotten citizens—who remembers even General Hodges and Patch and Devers?—consigned to the line in France during the winter of 1944–1945.

The paradigm of this soldier's manner as he eats is the victim-tramp Chaplin asserting his unshakable dignity by dainty gestures involving toothpicks, napkins, saltcellars. This soldier's management of his bread and fork registers a determination to recover his humanity after two weeks of animal existence. Every gesture, even the dancerly position of the feet, seems to say, "I am not an animal. I am not." In aid of this point, his tongue is delicately shifting a food particle from a tooth. His hands are shockingly filthy. He's wielding the white bread both to insulate the food from his dirty fingers and to help him pretend he's sitting in a restaurant or at his own dinner table and that the canteen cup is made of porcelain. It is very cold, but he has taken off his gloves while eating to promote this illusion.

Past the need for such rationalizations is the rifleman killed by German mortar-shell fragments when he has almost got safely across a pontoon footbridge on the Roer in 1945. The shell has hit the east bank a few feet away. Hence the bits of dirt on the body. The two men running up are engineers "in charge of" the

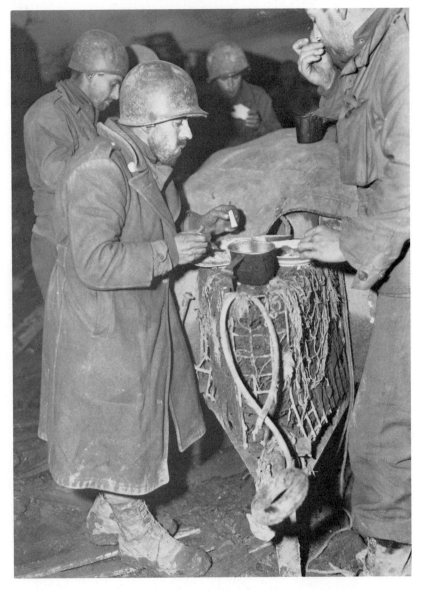

Soldier from the Hürtgen Forest (U.S. Army)

bridge. They are going to remove the body so that other infantry-men waiting on the far bank to cross will not be demoralized by it. The dead soldier wears a field jacket and a bandolier of rifle ammunition, and his raincoat is properly folded in his cartridge belt behind. He is a neat and obedient man, and all his articles are arranged the way they're supposed to be. The fingers of his right hand are "extended and joined" as they are when he's at attention or saluting. A good soldier, this man has followed all instructions, and when he has been ordered to run across the bridge even though the mortar shells are dropping, he has run across. He has been wearing a life preserver in case he falls into the river. His rifle will be salvaged, repaired, and reissued.

As these photographs suggest, you can do things with black and white that you can't do with color, just as you can do things with radio and print that you can't do with television. In photographs blood is black, but truce flags and nurses' caps and hospital sheets

Soldier on a Footbridge Over the Roer (George Silk; *Life* Magazine, © 1945 Time Inc.)

are white. White is safety and peace and innocence and clean oblivion, the tone of the imagination's final silent snow, secret snow. Hence in these photographs the eloquence of the partisan's cap, the Ford Island sailor's innocent pass-whites, the white of the broken sailor's gun mount, the white hand of the good soldier on the Roer pontoon bridge. And there's some pregnant white in the Omaha Beach picture, too. The last man off the boat appears to be wearing on his left shoulder a crude bandage, hastily applied, and the remains of bandages and dressings lie at the right front of the boat, where someone has also decided to abandon a heavy roll of sound-power telephone wire he's supposed to carry ashore. Most likely it belonged to the wounded man, who now feels satisfactorily out of it and licensed to drop everything, honoring the convention that, once wounded, a soldier turns instantly into a noncombatant and sheds helmet, arms, grenades, and ammunition as fast as possible. One has done one's bit, and there's no need to do it twice.

Reading photographs of the war is a way of experiencing its very different looks in different places. Topography and flora determine different contexts, with the result that the war takes on multiple visual meanings. In the South Pacific, the setting usually includes palm trees, coconut logs, and sand, lending the proceedings something of the look of a sexy beach-party travesty, especially when sleeves are rolled up or shirts off. The Pacific war takes place in settings romanticized for a generation by South Seas films (and before that by Robert Louis Stevenson and Rupert Brooke), and to be shot at or blown apart in a venue associated with the ecstasies of Jon Hall and Dorothy Lamour is much more disillusioning than to be so treated in, say, mountainous country appropriate for hunting. That kind of country, if you add mules and mud and occasional barren fruit and olive trees, is the theater of the Italian campaign, and of North Africa and Sicily before it. The look of those soldiers is entirely different from the look of the South Pacific soldiers and marines. In Italy, no loose fatigues but olive drab woollens, and plain helmets instead of helmet covers, the Marine fixture affected in the South Pacific. Leggings at first, then leather combat boots with the two straps and buckles. But the real sign of the Italian campaign soldier is the "armored unit" field jacket with knitted neck, cuffs, and waist, an unwitting allusion to the treasured high-school letterman's athletic jacket. If the troops in Italy resemble a lot of bulky, dispirited, dirty, and scared high-school athletes, those in France and Germany, as the war proceeds, resemble padded automatons programmed less to prosecute hostilities than to defend themselves against freezing. Long, curiously formal overcoats together with gloves and wool scarves and knitted wool caps are the stigmata; even the helmets, with their shrimp nets, look padded and overdressed. At first, combat boots. Then, for the winter of 1944–1945, clumsy black shoe-pacs, of the type made by L. L. Bean. Fir trees. Fog and snow. Barely holding on when the war was supposed to be over by Christmas. Instead of malaria, trench foot.

Like a sick and swollen organic thing, the war altered its appearance as it aged. At first soldiers looked like thirties strikebreakers, with canvas leggings, flat World War I helmets, long bayonets, Springfield rifles, gas masks worn in the oddly chic triangular carrier under the arm: they looked pert and devoted and spry and successful. Every man a Prewitt. Officers wore ostentatious insignia on shoulders. Bataan and Kasserine Pass ended that look; thereafter wariness and lack of sleep begin to dominate every gesture. The student of World War II photographs can spot that change from behind, in the hunch of shoulders (make yourself small), the helmet worn well down, the bend in the knees, scarves and mufflers hiding gold and silver collar insignia. Things get progressively thicker and less delicately defined. Faces vanish within helmets as eyes learn to look down, alert for the three little prongs of anti-personnel mines sprouting from the earth. The elegant, slender Springfield thickens to the M-1, waists bulk out with more and more equipment: compasses, wire-cutters, first-aid packets (sometimes two, to be safe). "Heavy duty" is the industrial concept that begins to dominate as the war itself, rather than its presumed purposes, takes over. It becomes for those engaged in it a non-ideological, self-running enterprise, and increasingly it is about equipment and matériel.

Some things, however, never changed. Always the insufficiently armored tanks protected with rows of ad hoc sandbags stacked against the armor: this from the greatest steel-producing country in the world. The second-rate anti-tank mines, unstable in cold weather, which went off when you moved them or when truckloads of them went over bumps. The showy gray-white cloud of smoke from American smokeless powder, which always gave your position away and made the men terrified to fire their rifles. The technologically pretentious little Handy-Talkie radios, optimistic in conception but quite hopeless in practice. The archaic Browning automatic rifle from World War I, heavy and inept and slow, with its insufficient magazine. All the result of failures in imagination or never-to-be-punished corruptions in procurement. The world's greatest industrial power left it to the Germans to devise the 88-mm gun, the most effective single weapon of the war, while as usual it disguised its defects of mind and invention and discipline with advertising: "The American soldier is the best-equipped in history." Actually, pathetic makeshift was the rule, from the hedgerow scoops welded onto tanks in Normandy to the white snow capes hastily run up by seamstresses in Nancy during the winter of 1945. Maybe the Air Corps was better served, with radar and "window." It was the "pore dumb fucks" of the ground forces who were expected to shift for themselves while contemplating the operations of the American class system. As James Jones says, "You might find a Princeton or Harvard graduate leading a forward infantry platoon, but it was rare. And you almost never found a Princeton or Harvard grad serving as a private in such a platoon."

It's the black and white of the photographs that brings it all back—better, it would sometimes seem, than the language of reporting or fiction. Perhaps this is because "news" photographs are the perfect medium for registering events of the twentieth century, events that have so often proved calamitous. Sontag is not writing about war photographs, but what she says is especially true of them: "Photographs state the innocence, the vulnerability of lives heading toward their own destruction, and this link between photography and death haunts all photographs of people."

The survivors of that war are now old men. I hope the anonymous wearer of the shoulder bandage at Omaha is alive and well and that the man sitting on the ground at Ford Island has recovered his composure and that the little soldier eating off the back of the trailer in the cold has found a nice warm restaurant that he likes.

Battle Trauma
and the NATO Problem

Here's an officer's report on a search-and-destroy mission:

> In contrast to previous days, the 24 assault search parties, which were again dispatched today, did not start their sweep . . . from one flank only but proceeded simultaneously from all sides. Since the operation did not start until 1000 hours, the remaining Vietcong apparently believed that the matter had ended yesterday. Today's search operation was therefore especially successful. But our success is also due to the fact that the noncommissioned officers and men have become accustomed to the underhanded fighting and tricks of the VC, and have acquired great skill in tracking down the innumerable bunkers.

Actually, the mission described there took place not in Vietnam in 1963 but in Poland in 1943. (In two places I have substituted "Vietcong" and "VC" for the original "Jews" and "Jews and bandits.") The author of the report is not some brisk, close-cropped thirty-year-old captain from Dallas; he is a forty-eight-year-old SS major general from Detmold. But the problems facing each are similar, and their respective solutions are scarcely to be distinguished by ethical criteria.

I have quoted from *The Stroop Report,* a translation of the after-action report submitted to Himmler by Jürgen Stroop, the SS Brigadeführer assigned the unhappy task of reducing the Warsaw ghetto in April and May, 1943. Stroop was hanged in 1951. His report, captured after the war, was first published in West Germany in 1960. It consists of Stroop's introductory summary of the whole month-long operation, thirty-two daily teletype reports of progress, and an album of forty-eight photographs. The object was to persuade Himmler that the job had been done effectively, that Stroop had in no way shirked his duty. The American edition, published in 1979, is translated by Sybil Milton, and it contains notes on the text and an introduction by the Polish scholar Andrzej Wirth. He is, predictably, more angry than precise. When he speaks of "mass-criminality," we know what he's getting at. But we should also understand that restricting a term like that to the behavior of the SS in Warsaw is to misapprehend the nature of modern soldiering. It is all mass-criminality, even if interested parties insist on significant degrees of difference. Generaloberst Alfred Jodl, about to be hanged at Nuremberg and anxious to assure himself that his wartime performance was different in kind from Stroop's, considered the Stroop report unique and designated its author a "dirty arrogant SS swine." "Imagine," he said, "writing a 75-page boastful report on a little murder expedition, when a major campaign fought by soldiers against a well-armed enemy takes only a few pages." But Jodl's complaint deals less with substance than with literary and narrative emphasis. Those who without self-interest study what soldiers are obliged to do will find it not at all easy to distinguish a "murder expedition" from a "major campaign." Actually, Stroop's men were soldiers, and their enemy was shrewdly emplaced and well armed, as the SS casualties suggest. Stroop admits to 16 dead and 85 wounded. Polish sources claim between 400 and 700 German killed and wounded. The "cleansing" (Stroop's word) of the Warsaw ghetto was a vile business. So is any infantry attack.

In his self-righteous introduction Wirth makes much of Stroop's euphemisms—fortified apartments become "residential bunkers," the shipment of captured Jews to Treblinka becomes "transfer" or "resettlement"—without perceiving sufficiently that euphemism is indispensable to the military enterprise, whether conducted by the SS or anyone else. No officer of any country or any military tradition has ever found himself able to submit an accurate, uneuphemized report like this:

> Two adolescent boys dressed in "enemy" uniform tried to sneak up on our position. We machine-gunned them both. The brains of one came out his nose and he lived for a half-hour, making a terrible snoring sound and looking at us with bright blue eyes. The other died soon too: his leg was severed and folded back beneath his body. He cried for his

mother for some time. I don't think I can stand any more of this.

The only way to make the work bearable is to think of the men opposite as targets. To speak of destroying these targets (the proclaimed mission of the infantry, as is well known, being "to close with the enemy and destroy him") is to achieve an indispensable insulation from the business. Thus "pacification centers" for the concentration camps in Vietnam and "protective reaction strikes" for bombing raids.

The work soldiers must do is so loathsome that they ease their task likewise by a constant verbal demeaning of the enemy. Thus Stroop's "Jews, bandits, and criminals" (sometimes "Jews, bandits, and sub-humans"), the equivalent of our own "Krauts" and "little yellow bastards." Stroop and his men performed their stomach-turning mission by conceiving of it as a necessary *purging* of an area of Warsaw described thus by Baedeker in 1914: "Whole quarters of the town . . . are occupied by Jews, whose inattention to personal cleanliness has become proverbial." That is the context of Stroop's final relieved, self-gratulatory cry: "The Jewish Quarter of Warsaw is no more!" He has come though by fancying himself a scourge of filth, a chaser of dirt like the Dutch girl on the household cleanser.

Because he is submitting a formal report to a superior, fear, like the trauma of wounds an inseparable attendant of wartime soldiering, receives no treatment from Stroop. The subject is nicely dealt with by the French novelist and journalist Jean Lartéguy in *The Face of War: Reflections on Men and Combat,* a translation by Beth de Bilio of *La Guerre Nue.* "Weren't you ever afraid?" Larféguy once asked his father, who now and then reluctantly spoke about World War I. "All the time," answered his father. That's from Larféguy's first section, "War I Was Told About," where he recounts the *frisson* engendered by discovering in his family's house a locked room containing memorabilia of the Great War, including stereoscopic depictions of the trench scene. "On those plates of sepia-colored glass were inscribed all the horrors of the world"—the images that by now have familiarized themselves to unthreatening cliché: trenches oozing with mud, stumps of trees, bodies "sprawled everywhere in every position, bundles

of mangled, trampled flesh," "a cadaver halfway out of his hole of
clay, arm stiffened, a wedding ring on his finger." For Lartéguy
those images, imprinted on his boy's mind, were the beginning
of his lifelong obsession with war, as a combatant and a writer.
They were the starting point of his refusal ever "to allow myself
that kind of selective memory which makes certain old soldiers
incense-bearers for war, however unconsciously." Mobilized into
the French infantry in 1940, he studied his beaten fellows, smelling
of "fear, of vomit, of red wine," and came to appreciate Céline's
witticism,

> "Little soldier, what have you done with your rifle?"
> "I left it on the field of honor."

After the Armistice he fled to Spain and arrived finally in Casa-
blanca, where he joined a French commando group destined for
the invasion of southern France. This was Lartéguy's "War I
Fought In": through the Vosges and into Alsace, men dropping
all the time. Here, he says, he came to know "real fear, the kind
that can turn you into a wet rag, unable to do anything." Here
he came to know "the long nights when the least noise starts a man
to shaking with fear. And dawn—that terrible hour of dawn, the
cursed hour—when everything is discord, when the exhausted
sentries give in to sleep, and when the enemy attacks." All this in
an atmosphere of absurd command quarrels between General de
Lattre de Tassigny ("the great prima donna") and General Le-
clerc. In World War II Lartéguy learns the truth of what Roger
Caillois once wrote (and what Brigadier Pudding, in Pynchon's
Gravity's Rainbow, understands as he muses fitfully on his experiences in the Great War): "War possesses the essential characteristics of sacred things. She forbids an objective consideration of
what she really is. She paralyzes the spirit of investigation."

-   Lartéguy's final section, "War I Wrote About," deals first with
his life as a lieutenant of infantry in Korea, where, witnessing the
Americans coming down from Heartbreak Ridge, he observed that
"many, many soldiers had gone mad." Then as a correspondent
he covers the French and later the American war in Indochina.
What he learns there would seem to apply both to Henry Kissinger's Cambodians and Jürgen Stroop's Jews: "War likes to simplify things. . . . All those who are different, who are colorful, who

give savor to the world, the minorities with their customs and their folklore, all must be destroyed in [war's] big bloody tracks. . . . She knows nothing of nuances." She has thus forwarded that current state of things which Lévi-Strauss has called "monoculture," where the Hilton in Istanbul is indistinguishable from the Hilton in Tokyo, and where even the terrorism grows uniform. The computer, which worked so inefficiently in Vietnam, can be seen not just as war's current toy but as one of her inevitable gifts to the world at large.

But war's biggst trap, Lartéguy concludes, is seducing her beholders into imagining they can distinguish between "just" and "unjust" examples of her work. Wars are one, just as Stroop and Patton are finally one. Does Lartéguy propose a remedy? Only this: "I see only one acceptable remedy: that we do not any longer deceive ourselves about war, that we tell as much as we have come to know of her as eye-witnesses, without glossing anything over." The soldier's memory has its own tricks of euphemism he must guard against:

> You only remember the moments of friendship, of great pub crawls, of drinking sprees, of cities taken, and of willing girls. But you sweep under the carpet the wounded who howl their lives away with gaping belly wounds, the fatigue, the exhausting marches, the idiotic orders, the even more stupid counterorders, the disorder, the mess, the lost time, the wasted energy. And the despair you carry with you everywhere as you contemplate the immense stupidity. . . .

> The best way to retain a grip on the essence is to remember your fear, your panic. Have you forgotten them? . . . You know that in three hours you have to attack. . . . Your stomach is knotted, you're sweating, you feel like pissing forever. . . . It's the hour at which they awaken those men in their cells who are condemned to death. And you are one of them.

I don't expect Lartéguy's book to be widely distributed by the U.S. Army as required reading for the NATO troops, rehearsing for the event which John Keegan, in *The Face of Battle*, terms "the land battle in Central Europe." One such rehearsal is the subject of Frederick Wiseman's instructive documentary film *Manoeuvre*. Like his earlier military film *Basic Training* (1971), which laconically suggested the military's usefulness as an arm of the wider welfare system (boys being taught to brush their teeth, etc.), *Manoeuvre* is sensitive and sympathetic, alert to the stubborn differences between individuals despite the uniforms and the jargon and the official prohibition of subtlety. Wiseman follows an armored infantry company from Fort Polk, Louisiana (a dope-sniffing dog goes over everyone's equipment before departure), as it is airlifted to Germany and takes up positions 30 km this side of the border during the annual fall NATO exercises. If in *Basic Training* the focus was largely on NCO's and recruits, here it is on the young officers selecting tank positions and the young umpires computing fictional damage (all, of course, euphemized) from their little portable actuarial tables. As the archaic spelling of Wiseman's title implies, it is all as unreal as only "war games" can be: people do get realistically tired, but no one is terrified, and the tone is that of a professional social event based on male bonding—rather like a convention held outdoors. It's here that we can perceive the effect of phenomena like Wouk and McGivern and Time-Life on the current understanding of war, even among professionals. It can all be rather jolly and wholesome, "Action Packed Adventure," as Time-Life says. And even if things get really bad one can redeem the situation by consciousness of membership in an exclusive male sodality. Jargon is a good way to register this consciousness. After President Reagan had been shot, Al Haig, the Secretary of State, said, Yes, it was true; the President had "taken three rounds." In imagining oneself licensed to talk that way, there's the comfort of warm clubmanship. The mere ordinary non-club person would have to say, in his ordinary way, that the President had been shot three times. (It's worth inquiring in passing why the Secretary of State of this country so often strikes the intelligent and sensitive as a horse's ass: consider John Foster Dulles, the Princeton Presbyterian who seems never to have met a poor person; Henry Kissinger, the war criminal who managed never to hear a shot fired in anger; and Alexander Haig, the Brown Shirt presidential aspirant who imagines that none of his auditors has had any experience wider than that of the NCOs' mess.)

Wiseman as usual makes no comment, but his film as a whole makes one: the maneuver is charming and absurd, it says, utterly unrelated to war. No one's eye is found lying on the path to the mess tent. No one's intestines are perceived to be hanging from the fir tree.

It is an assumption of the whole NATO enterprise that in the 1980's soldiers asked to immolate themselves in an armored European land battle of the time-honored kind will do so. I wonder. Without a Pearl Harbor to remember, how do you motivate soldiers to prosecute immense traditional land battles, especially when they conceive that the deployment of some atom bombs will make their bodily sacrifice unnecessary? Vietnam, with its main-lining of heroin, showed that soldiering may be changing drastically. In *Manoeuvre* I felt certain that only two people would stick it at the critical moment: one was a nutty lieutenant colonel commanding a tank battalion, wild-eyed and adept at chewing out subordinates rhetorically, like an accomplished actor. I think he would hold his position, shouting foul-mouthed imprecations, to the death. The other was the captain commanding the armored company. I think he'd probably not run because he was deadly serious about setting an example. About the others I had my doubts. Their talk was largely of pensions and boondoggles, cushy ripoffs in the States or abroad.

John Keegan, who brilliantly perceives that "tanks . . . should be thought of not so much as weapons as theatrical devices," is persuaded that people will not consent to soldier anymore in the old way. "We are faced now with a prospect of battle," he writes, "which through the physical and nervous strain, the 'multiple stress pattern' it will impose on the combatants, threatens to break them down whether or not they come into direct contact with the enemy." And draft or no draft, "the young have already made their decision. They are increasingly unwilling to serve as conscripts in armies they see as ornamental. . . ." (A straw in the wind: the question repeatedly asked me by my university students baffled by the docility of British troops in the Great War. Why did they go over the top? Why, when the whistle blew, did they all not sit down? Why did they allow themselves to be victimized so? Why, indeed, did they behave like ur-Jews in an ur-Holocaust, lining up and marching to their own destruction? I try to answer by talking about the former class-system and the once obligatory public avowal of precepts of religion and duty and the kind of

·patriotism and national pride necessary to hold an empire together. But I know they do not understand and that they are not satisfied. They will not accept, and I doubt if they'll willingly participate in, a world where an infantry assault is thinkable.) Thus Keegan may be right when he says:

> It remains for armies to admit that the battles of the future will be fought in never-never land. While the great armored hosts face each other across the boundary between east and west, no soldier on either side will concede that he does not believe in the function for which he plans and trains. As long as states put weapons in their hands, they will show each other the iron face of war. But the suspicion grows that battle has already abolished itself.

Whether we believe that or not, there's one consolation: having experienced trauma once, a generation will not readily consent to encounter it again.

My War

I recognize that in the foregoing pages I have given the Second World War a bad press, rejecting all attempts to depict it as a sensible proceeding or to mitigate its cruelty and swinishness. I have rubbed the reader's nose in some very noisome materials—corpses, maddened dogs, deserters and looters, pain, Auschwitz, weeping, scandal, cowardice, mistakes and defeats, sadism, hangings, horrible wounds, fear and panic. Whenever I deliver this unhappy view of the war, especially when I try to pass it through a protective screen of irony, I hear from outraged readers. Speaking of my observations on the photograph of the ruined sailor on his ruined gunmount, for example, a woman from Brooklyn finds me "callous," and focusing on my remarks about the photograph of the German soldiers engaged in hanging the partisan boy and girl, she says,

> As the daughter of survivors of the Holocaust, it is beyond my comprehension how Mr. Fussell can ramble on about the "respectability" and "normality" of the Germans . . . while a young girl hangs from a rope and a young boy, his hands bound behind his back, waits to be hanged. While this photograph should elicit pathos and anger at seeing young lives being so cruelly blotted out, Mr. Fussell is concerned about the "almost frivolous touch" of the "two colored decorative rope, suggestive of a bathrobe cord or gift tie."

In short, my approach has been "insensitive": I have demonstrated an "overwhelming deficiency in human compassion." Another reader, who I suspect has had as little empirical contact with the actualities of war face-to-face as the correspondent from Brooklyn, found the same essay "black and monstrous" and concluded that the magazine publishing it "disgraced itself." It seems like the old story of punishing the messenger for bringing bad news. But one has always known that irony has a hard time of it in this country, especially irony reflecting some skepticism about the human instincts for reason and virtue.

How did I pick up this dark, ironical, flip view of the war? Why do I enjoy exhibiting it? The answer is that I contracted it in the infantry, and I suspect I embraced it with special vigor once I found how it annoyed people who had not fought at close quarters in terrible weather and shot people to death and been hit by a shell from a German gun. My view of the war is a form of revenge. Indeed, the careful reader will have discerned in all the essays in this book a speaker who is really a pissed-off infantryman, disguised as a literary and cultural commentator. He is embittered that the Air Corps had beds to sleep in, that Patton's Third Army got all the credit, that non-combatants of the Medical Administrative and Quartermaster Corps wore the same battle-stars as he, that soon after the war the "enemy" he had labored to destroy had been re-armed by his own government and positioned to oppose one of his old Allies. "We broke our ass for nothin'," says Sergeant Croft in *The Naked and The Dead*. These are this speaker's residual complaints while he is affecting to be annoyed primarily by someone's bad writing or slipshod logic or lazy editing or pretentious ideas. As Louis Simpson says, "The war made me a footsoldier for the rest of my life," and after any war foot-soldiers are touchy.

My war is virtually synonymous with my life. I entered the war when I was nineteen, and I have been in it ever since. Melville's Ishmael says that a whale-ship was his Yale College and his Harvard. An infantry division was mine, the 103rd, whose dispirited personnel wore a colorful green and yellow cactus on their left shoulders. These hillbillies and Okies, drop-outs and used-car salesmen and petty criminals were my teachers and friends.

How did an upper-middle-class young gentleman find himself in so unseemly a place? Why wasn't he in the Navy, at least, or in the OSS or Air Corps administration or editing the *Stars and Stripes* or being a general's aide? The answer is comic: at the age of twenty I found myself leading forty riflemen over the Vosges Mountains and watching them torn apart by German artillery and machine-guns because when I was sixteen, in junior college, I was fat and flabby, with feminine tits and a big behind. For years the thing I'd hated most about school was gym, for there I was obliged to strip and shower communally. Thus I chose to join the R.O.T.C. (infantry, as it happened) because that was a way to get out of gym, which meant you never had to take off your clothes and invite—indeed, compel—ridicule. You rationalized by noting that this was 1939 and that a little "military training" might not, in the long run, be wasted. Besides, if you worked up to be a cadet officer, you got to wear a Sam Browne belt, from which depended a nifty saber.

When I went on to college, it was natural to continue my technique for not exposing my naked person, and luckily my college had an infantry R.O.T.C. unit, where I was welcomed as something of an experienced hand. This was in 1941. When the war began for the United States, college students were solicited by various "programs" of the navy and marine corps and coast guard with plans for transforming them into officers. But people enrolled in the R.O.T.C. unit were felt to have committed themselves already. They had opted for the infantry, most of them all unaware, and that's where they were going to stay. Thus while shrewder friends were enrolling in Navy V-1 or signing up for the pacific exercises of the Naval Japanese Language Program or the Air Corps Meteorological Program, I signed up for the Infantry Enlisted Reserve Corps, an act guaranteeing me one extra semester in college before I was called. After basic training, advancement to officer training was promised, and that seemed a desirable thing, even if the crossed rifles on the collar did seem to betoken some hard physical exertion and discomfort—marching, sleeping outdoors, that sort of thing. But it would help "build you up," and besides officers, even in the Infantry, got to wear those wonderful pink trousers and receive constant salutes.

It was such imagery of future grandeur that in spring, 1943, sustained me through eighteen weeks of basic training in 100-degree heat at dreary Camp Roberts, California, where to toughen us, it was said, water was forbidden from 8:00 a.m. to 5:00 p.m. ("water discipline," this was called). Within a few weeks I'd lost all my flab and with it the whole ironic "reason" I found myself there at all. It was abundantly clear already that "infantry" had been a big mistake: it was not just stupid and boring and bloody, it was athletic, and thus not at all for me. But supported by vanity and pride I somehow managed to march thirty-five miles and tumble through the obstacle course, and a few months later I found myself at the Infantry School, Fort Benning, Georgia, where, training to become an officer, I went through virtually the same thing over again. As a Second Lieutenant of Infantry I "graduated" in the spring of 1944 and was assigned to the 103rd Division at Camp Howze, Texas, the local equivalent of Camp Roberts, only worse: Roberts had white-painted two-storey clapboard barracks, Howze one-storey tar-paper shacks. But the heat was the same, and the boredom, and the local whore-culture, and the hillbilly songs:

> Who's that gal with the red dress on?
> Some folks call her Dinah.
> She stole my heart away,
> Down in Carolina.

The 103rd Division had never been overseas, and all the time I was putting my rifle platoon through its futile exercises we were being prepared for the invasion of southern France, which followed the landings in Normandy. Of course we didn't know this, and assumed from the training ("water discipline" again) that we were destined for the South Pacific. There were some exercises involving towed gliders that seemed to portend nothing at all but self-immolation, we were so inept with these devices. In October, 1944, we were all conveyed by troop transports to Marseilles.

It was my first experience of abroad, and my life-long affair with France dates from the moment I first experienced such un-American phenomena as: formal manners and a respect for the language; a well-founded skepticism; the pollarded plane trees on the Av. R. Schuman; the red wine and real bread; the *pissoirs* in the streets; the international traffic signs and the visual public language hinting a special French understanding of things: *Hôtel de Ville, Defense d'afficher;* the smell of Turkish tobacco when one has been brought up on Virginia and Burley. An intimation of what we might be opposing was supplied by the aluminum Vichy coinage. On one side, a fasces and *Etat Français.* No more Republic. On the other, *Liberté, Egalité, Fraternité* replaced by *Travail* (as in *Arbeit Macht Frei*), *Famille,* and *Patrie* (as in *Vaterland*). But before we had time to contemplate all this, we were moving rapidly northeast. After a truck ride up the Rhone Valley, still pleasant with girls and flowers and wine, our civilized period came to an abrupt end. On the night of November 11 (nice irony there) we were introduced into the line at St. Dié, in Alsace.

We were in "combat." I find the word embarrassing, carrying as it does false chivalric overtones (as in "single combat"). But synonyms are worse: *fighting* is not accurate, because much of the time you are being shelled, which is not fighting but suffering; *battle* is too high and remote; *in action* is a euphemism suited more to dire telegrams than description. "Combat" will have to do, and my first hours of it I recall daily, even now. They fueled, and they still fuel, my view of things.

Everyone knows that a night relief is among the most difficult of infantry maneuvers. But we didn't know it, and in our innocence we expected it to go according to plan. We and the company we were replacing were cleverly and severely shelled: it was as if the Germans a few hundred feet away could see us in the dark and through the thick pine growth. When the shelling finally stopped, at about midnight, we realized that, although near the place we were supposed to be, until daylight we would remain hopelessly lost. The order came down to stop where we were, lie down among the trees, and get some sleep. We would finish the relief at first light. Scattered over several hundred yards, the two hundred and fifty of us in F Company lay down in a darkness so thick we could see nothing at all. Despite the terror of our first shelling (and several people had been hit), we slept as soundly as babes. At dawn I awoke, and what I saw all around were numerous objects I'd miraculously not tripped over in the dark. These objects were dozens of dead German boys in greenish-gray uniforms, killed a day or two before by the company we were relieving. If darkness had hidden them from us, dawn disclosed them with open eyes and greenish-white faces like marble, still clutching their rifles and machine-pistols in their seventeen-year-old hands, fixed where they had fallen. (For the first time I understood the German phrase for the war-dead: *die Gefallenen*.) Michelangelo could have made something beautiful out of these forms, in the *Dying Gaul* tradition, and I was startled to find that in a way I couldn't understand, at first they struck me as beautiful. But after a moment, no feeling but shock and horror. My adolescent illusions, largely intact

to that moment, fell away all at once, and I suddenly knew I was
not and never would be in a world that was reasonable or just.
The scene was less apocalyptic than shabbily ironic: it sorted so
ill with modern popular assumptions about the idea of progress
and attendant improvements in public health, social welfare, and
social justice. To transform guiltless boys into cold marble after
passing them through unbearable fear and humiliation and pain
and contempt seemed to do them an interesting injustice. I decided to ponder these things. In 1917, shocked by the Battle of
the Somme and recovering from neurasthenia, Wilfred Owen was
reading a life of Tennyson. He wrote his mother: "Tennyson, it
seems, was always a great child. So should I have been but for
Beaumont Hamel." So should I have been but for St. Dié.

After that, one day was much like another: attack at dawn, run
and fall and crawl and sweat and worry and shoot and be shot at
and cower from mortar shells, always keeping up a jaunty carriage
in front of one's platoon; and at night, "consolidate" the objective, usually another hill, sometimes a small town, and plan the
attack for the next morning. Before we knew it we'd lost half the
company, and we all realized then that for us there would be no
way out until the war ended but sickness, wounds, or oblivion.
And the war would end only as we pressed our painful daily ad-
vance. Getting it over was our sole motive. Yes, we knew about
the Jews. But our skins seemed to us more valuable at the time.

The word for the German defense all along was clever, a word
that never could have been applied to our procedures. It was my
first experience, to be repeated many times in later years, of the
cunning ways of Europe versus the blunter ways of the New World.
Although manned largely by tired thirty-year-old veterans (but
sharp enough to have got out of Normandy alive), old men, and
crazy youths, the German infantry was officered superbly, and their
defense, which we experienced for many months, was disciplined
and orderly. My people would have run, or at least "snaked off."
But the Germans didn't, until the very end. Their uniforms were
a scandal—rags and beat-up boots and unauthorized articles—but
somehow they held together. Nazis or not, they did themselves
credit. Lacking our lavish means, they compensated by patience
and shrewdness. Not until well after the war did I discover that

many times when they unaccountably located us hidden in deep woods and shelled us accurately, they had done so by inferring electronically the precise positions of the radios over which we innocently conversed.

As the war went on, the destruction of people became its sole means. I felt sorry for the Germans I saw killed in quantity everywhere—along the roads, in cellars, on roof-tops—for many reasons. They were losing, for one thing, and their deaths meant nothing, though they had been persuaded that resistance might "win the war." And they were so pitifully dressed and accoutered: that was touching. Boys with raggedy ad hoc uniforms and *Panzerfausts* and too few comrades. What were they doing? They were killing themselves; and for me, who couldn't imagine being killed, for people my age voluntarily to get themselves killed caused my mouth to drop open.

Irony describes the emotion, whatever it is, occasioned by perceiving some great gulf, half-comic, half-tragic, between what one expects and what one finds. It's not quite "disillusion," but it's adjacent to it. My experience in the war was ironic because my innocence before had prepared me to encounter in it something like the same reasonableness that governed prewar life. This, after all, was the tone dominating the American relation to the war: talk of "the future," allotments and bond purchases carefully sent home, hopeful fantasies of "the postwar world." I assumed, in short, that everyone would behave according to the clear advantages offered by reason. I had assumed that in war, like chess, when you were beaten you "resigned"; that when outnumbered and outgunned you retreated; that when you were surrounded you surrendered. I found out differently, and with a vengeance. What I found was people obeying fatuous and murderous "orders" for no reason I could understand, killing themselves because someone "told them to," prolonging the war when it was hopelessly lost because—because it was unreasonable to do so. It was my introduction to the shakiness of civilization. It was my first experience of the profoundly irrational element, and it made ridiculous all talk of plans and preparations for the future and goodwill and intelligent arrangements. Why did the red-haired young German machine-gunner firing at us in the woods not go on living—marrying, going to university, going to the beach, laughing, smiling—but keep firing long after he had made his point, and require us to kill him with a grenade?

Before we knew it it was winter, and the winter in 1944–1945 was the coldest in Europe for twenty-five years. For the ground troops conditions were unspeakable, and even the official history admits the disaster, imputing the failure to provide adequate winter clothing—analogous to the similar German oversight when the Russian winter of 1941–1942 surprised the planners—to optimism, innocence, and "confidence":

> Confidence born of the rapid sweep across Europe in the summer of 1944 and the conviction on the part of many that the successes of Allied arms would be rewarded by victory before the onset of winter contributed to the unpreparedness for winter combat.

The result of thus ignoring the injunction "Be Prepared" was 64,008 casualties from "cold injury"—not wounds but pneumonia and trench-foot. The official history sums up: "This constitutes more than four 15,000-man divisions. Approximately 90 percent of cold casualties involved riflemen and there were about 4,000 riflemen per infantry division. Thus closer to 13 divisions were critically disabled for combat." We can appreciate those figures by recalling that the invasion of Normany was initially accomplished by only six divisions (nine if we add the airborne). Thus crucial were little things like decent mittens and gloves, fur-lined parkas, thermal underwear—all of which any normal peacetime hiker or skier would demand as protection against prolonged exposure. But "the winter campaign in Europe was fought by most combat personnel in a uniform that did not give proper protection": we wore silly long overcoats, right out of the nineteenth century; thin field jackets, designed to convey an image of manliness at Fort Bragg; and dress wool trousers. We wore the same shirts and huddled under the same blankets as Pershing's troops in the expedition against Pancho Villa in 1916. Of the 64,008 who suffered "cold injury" I was one. During February, 1945, I was back in various hospitals for a month with pneumonia. I told my parents it was flu.

That month away from the line helped me survive for four weeks more but it broke the rhythm and, never badly scared before, when I returned to the line early in March I found for the first time that I was terrified, unwilling to take the chances which before had seemed rather sporting. My month of safety had renewed my interest in survival, and I was psychologically and morally ill-prepared to lead my platoon in the great Seventh Army attack of March 15, 1945. But lead it I did, or rather push it, staying as far in the rear as was barely decent. And before the day was over I had been severely rebuked by a sharp-eyed lieutenant-colonel who threatened court martial if I didn't pull myself together. Before that day was over I was sprayed with the contents of a soldier's torso when I was lying behind him and he knelt to fire at a machine-gun holding us up: he was struck in the heart, and out of the holes in the back of his field jacket flew little clouds of tissue, blood, and powdered cloth. Near him another man raised himself to fire, but the machine-gun caught him in the mouth, and as he fell he looked back at me with surprise, blood and teeth dribbling out onto the leaves. He was one to whom early on I had given the Silver Star for heroism, and he didn't want to let me down.

As if in retribution for my cowardice, in the late afternoon, near Engwiller, Alsace, clearing a woods full of Germans cleverly dug in, my platoon was raked by shells from an 88, and I was hit in the back and leg by shell fragments. They felt like red-hot knives going in, but I was as interested in the few quiet moans, like those of a hurt child drifting off to sleep, of my thirty-seven-year-old platoon sergeant—we'd been together since Camp Howze—killed instantly by the same shell. We were lying together, and his immediate neighbor on the other side, a lieutenant in charge of a section of heavy machine-guns, was killed instantly too. And my platoon was virtually wiped away. I was in disgrace, I was hurt, I was clearly expendable—while I lay there the supply sergeant removed my issue wristwatch to pass on to my replacement—and I was twenty years old.

I bore up all right while being removed from "the field" and passed back through the first-aid stations where I was known. I was deeply on morphine, and managed brave smiles as called for.

But when I got to the evacuation hospital thirty miles behind the lines and was coming out from the anesthetic of my first operation, all my affectations of control collapsed, and I did what I'd wanted to do for months. I cried, noisily and publicly, and for hours. I was the scandal of the ward. There were lots of tears back there: in the operating room I saw a nurse dissolve in shoulder-shaking sobs when a boy died with great stertorous gasps on the operating table she was attending. That was the first time I'd seen anyone cry in the whole European Theater of Operations, and I must have cried because I felt that there, out of "combat," tears were licensed. I was crying because I was ashamed and because I'd let my men be killed and because my sergeant had been killed and because I recognized as never before that he might have been me and that statistically if in no other way he was me, and that I had been killed too. But ironically I had saved my life by almost losing it, for my leg wound providentially became infected, and by the time it was healed and I was ready for duty again, the European war was over, and I journeyed back up through a silent Germany to re-join my reconstituted platoon "occupying" a lovely Tyrolean valley near Innsbruck. For the infantry there was still the Japanese war to sweat out, and I was destined for it, despite the dramatic gash in my leg. But thank God the Bomb was dropped while I was on my way there, with the result that I can write this.

That day in mid-March that ended me was the worst of all for F Company. We knew it was going to be bad when it began at dawn, just like an episode from the First World War, with an hour-long artillery preparation and a smoke-screen for us to attack through. What got us going and carried us through was the conviction that, suffer as we might, we were at least "making history." But we didn't even do that. Liddell Hart's 766-page *History of the Second World War* never heard of us. It mentions neither March 15th nor the 103rd Infantry Division. The only satisfaction history has offered is the evidence that we caused Josef Goebbels some extra anxiety. The day after our attack he entered in his log under "Military Situation":

> In the West the enemy has now gone over to the attack in the sector between Saarbrücken and Hagenau in addition to the previous flashpoints. . . . His objective is undoubtedly to drive

in our front on the Saar and capture the entire region south
of the Moselle and west of the Rhine.

And he goes on satisfyingly: "Mail received testifies to a deep-
seated lethargy throughout the German people degenerating
almost into hopelessness. There is very sharp criticism of the . . .
entire national leadership." One reason: "The Moselle front is
giving way." But a person my age I met thirty years later couldn't
believe that there was still any infantry fighting in France in the
spring of 1945, and puzzled by my dedicating a book of mine to
my dead platoon sergeant with the date March 15, 1945, confessed
that he couldn't figure out what had happened to him.

To become disillusioned you must earlier have been illusioned.
Evidence of the illusions suffered by the youth I was is sadly
available in the letters he sent, in unbelievable profusion, to his
parents. They radiate a terrible naïveté, together with a pathetic
disposition to be pleased in the face of boredom and, finally,
horror. The young man had heard a lot about the importance of
"morale" and ceaselessly labored to sustain his own by sustaining
his addressees'. Thus: "We spent all of Saturday on motor mainte-
nance," he writes from Fort Benning; "a very interesting subject."
At Benning he believes all he's told and fails to perceive that he's
being prepared for one thing only, and that a nasty, hazardous
job, whose performers on the line have a life expectancy of six
weeks. He assures his parents: "I can get all sorts of assignments
from here: . . . Battalion staff officer, mess officer, rifle platoon
leader, weapons platoon leader, company executive officer, com-
munications officer, motor officer, etc." (Was it an instinct for
protecting himself from a truth half-sensed that made him bury
rifle platoon leader in the middle of this list?) Like a bright
schoolboy, he is pleased when grown-ups tell him he's done well.
"I got a compliment on my clean rifle tonight. The lieutenant
said, 'Very good.' I said, 'Thank you, sir.'" His satisfaction in
making Expert Rifleman is touching; it is "the highest possible
rating," he announces. And although he is constantly jokey, always
on the lookout for what he terms "laffs," he seems to have no
sense of humor:

> We're having a very interesting week . . . , taking up the
> carbine, automatic rifle, rifle grenade, and the famous

The Author in 1944
(Noel Studio)

"bazooka." We had the bazooka today, and it was very enjoyable, although we could not fire it because of lack of ammunition.

He has the most impossible standards of military excellence, and he enlists his critical impulse in the service of optimistic self-deception. Appalled by the ineptitude of the 103rd Division in training, he writes home: "As I told you last time, this is a very messed up division. It will never go overseas as a unit, and is now serving mainly as a replacement training center, disguised as a combat division."

Because the image of himself actually leading troops through bullets and shellfire is secretly unthinkable, fatuous hope easily comes to his assistance. In August, 1944, with his division preparing to ship abroad, he asserts that the Germans seem to be "on their last legs." Indeed, he reports, "bets are being made . . . that the European war will be over in six weeks." But October finds him on the transport heading for the incredible, and now he "expects," he says, that "this war will end some time in November or December," adding, "I feel very confident and safe." After the epiphanies of the line in November and December, he still entertains hopes for an early end, for the Germans are rational people, and what rational people would persist in immolating themselves once it's clear that they've lost the war? "This *can't* last much longer," he finds.

The letters written during combat are full of requests for food packages from home, and interpretation of this obsession is not quite as simple as it seems. The C and K rations were tedious, to be sure, and as readers of *All Quiet on the Western Front* and *The Middle Parts of Fortune* know, soldiers of all times and places are fixated on food. But how explain this young man's requests for "fantastic items" like gherkins, olives, candy-coated peanuts (the kind "we used to get out of slot-machines at the beach"), cans of chili and tamales, cashew nuts, devilled ham, and fig pudding? The lust for a little swank is the explanation, I think, the need for some exotic counterweight to the uniformity, the dullness, the lack of point and distinction he sensed everywhere. These items also asserted an unbroken contact with home, and a home defined as the sort of place fertile not in corned-beef hash and meat-and-vegetable stew but gum drops and canned chicken. In short, an upper-middle-class venue.

Upper-middle-class too, I suspect, is the unimaginative cruelty of some of these letters, clear evidence of arrested emotional development. "Period" anti-Semitic remarks are not infrequent, and they remain unrebuked by any of his addressees. His understanding of the American South (he's writing from Georgia) can be gauged from his remark, "Everybody down here is illiterate." In combat some of his bravado is a device necessary to his emotional survival, but some bespeaks a genuine insensitivity:

Feb. 1, 1945

Dear Mother and Dad:

Today is the division's 84th consecutive day on line. The average is 90–100 days, although one division went 136 without being relieved. . . .

This house we're staying in used to be the headquarters of a local German Motor Corps unit, and it's full of printed matter, uniforms, propaganda, and pictures of Der Führer. I am not collecting any souveniers [sic], although I have had ample opportunity to pick up helmets, flags, weapons, etc. The only thing I have kept is a Belgian pistol, which one German was carrying who was unfortunate enough to walk right into my platoon. That is the first one I had the job of shooting. I have kept the pistol as a souvenier of my first Kraut.

It is odd how hard one becomes after a little bit of this stuff, but it gets to be more like killing mad dogs than people. . . .

Love to all,
Paul.

The only comfort I can take today in contemplating these letters is the ease with which their author can be rationalized as a stranger. Even the handwriting is not now my own. There are constant shows of dutifulness to parents, and even grandparents, and mentions of churchgoing, surely anomalous in a leader of assault troops. Parental approval is indispensable: "This week I was 'Class A Agent Officer' for Co. F, paying a $6000 payroll without losing a cent! I felt very proud of myself!" And the complacency! The twittiness! From hospital, where for a time he's been in an enlisted men's ward: "Sometimes I enjoy being with the men just as much as associating with the officers." (*Associating* is good.) The letter-writer is more pretentious than literate ("Alright," "thank's," "curiousity"), and his taste is terrible. He is thrilled to read Bruce Barton's *The Man Nobody Knows* ("It presents Christ in a very human light"), Maugham's *The Summing Up,* and the short stories of Erskine Caldwell. Even his often-sketched fantasies of the postwar heaven are grimly conventional: he will get married (to whom?); he will buy a thirty-five-foot sloop and live on it; he will take a year of non-serious literary graduate study at Columbia; he will edit a magazine for yachtsmen. He seems unable to perceive what is happening, constantly telling his addressee what will please rather than what he feels. He was never more mistaken than when he assured his parents while recovering from his wounds, "Please try not to worry, as no permanent damage has been done."

But the shock of these wounds and the long period recovering from them seem to have matured him a tiny bit, and some of his last letters from the hospital suggest that one or two scales are beginning to fall from his eyes:

> One of the most amazing things about this war is the way the bizarre and unnatural become the normal after a short time. Take this hospital and its atmosphere: after a long talk with him, an eighteen-year-old boy without legs seems like the *normal* eighteen-year-old. You might even be surprised if a boy of the same age should walk in on both his legs. He would seem the freak and the object of pity. It is easy to imagine, after seeing some of these men, that *all* young men are arriving on this planet with stumps instead of limbs.
>
> The same holds true with life at the front. The same horrible unrealness that is so hard to describe. . . . I think I'll have to write a book about all this some time.

But even here, he can't conclude without reverting to cliché and twirpy optimism:

> Enough for this morning. I'm feeling well and I'm very comfortable, and the food is improving. We had chicken and ice cream yesterday!

He has not read Swift yet, but in the vision of the young men with their stumps there's perhaps a hint that he's going to. And indeed, when he enrolled in graduate school later, the first course he was attracted to was "Swift and Pope." And ever since he's been trying to understand satire, and even to experiment with it himself.

It was in the army that I discovered my calling. I hadn't known that I was a teacher, but I found I could explain things: the operation of flamethrowers, map-reading, small-arms firing, "field sanitation." I found I could "lecture" and organize and make things clear. I could start at the beginning of a topic and lead an audience to the end. When the war was over, being trained for nothing useful, I naturally fell into the course which would require largely a mere continuation of this act. In becoming a college teacher of literature I was aware of lots of company: thousands of veterans swarmed to graduate schools to study literature, persuaded that poetry and prose could save the world, or at least help wash away some of the intellectual shame of the years we'd been through. From this generation came John Berryman and Randall Jarrell and Delmore Schwartz and Saul Bellow and Louis Simpson and Richard Wilbur and John Ciardi and William Meredith and all the others who, afire with the precepts of the New Criticism, embraced literature, and the teaching of it, as a quasi-religious obligation.

To this day I tend to think of all hierarchies, especially the academic one, as military. The undergraduate students, at the "bottom," are the recruits and draftees, privates all. Teaching assistants and graduate students are the non-coms, with grades (only officers have "ranks") varying according to seniority: a G-4 is more important than a G-1, etc. Instructors, where they still exist, are the Second and First Lieutenants, and together with the Assistant Professors (Captains) comprise the company-grade officers. When we move up to the tenured ranks, Associate Professors answer to field-grade officers, Majors and Colonels. Professors are Generals, beginning with Brigadier—that's a newly promoted one. Most are Major Generals, and upon retirement they will be advanced to Lieutenant-General ("Professor Emeritus"). The main academic administration is less like a higher authority in the same structure than an adjacent echelon, like a group of powerful congressmen, for example, or people from the Judge Advocate's or Inspector General's departments. The Board of Trustees, empowered to make professorial appointments and thus confer academic ranks and privileges, is the equivalent of the President of the United States, who signs commissions very like Letters of Academic Appointment: "Reposing special trust and confidence in the . . . abilities of ———, I do appoint him," etc. It is not hard to see also that the military principle crudely registered in the axiom Rank Has Its Privileges operates in academic life, where there are plums to be plucked like frequent leaves of absence, single-occupant offices, light teaching loads, and convenient, all-weather parking spaces.

I think this generally unconscious way of conceiving of the academic hierarchy is common among people who went to graduate school immediately after the war, and who went on the G.I. Bill. Perhaps many were attracted to university teaching as a post-war profession because in part they felt they understood its mechanisms already. Thus their ambitiousness, their sense that if to be a First Lieutenant is fine, to work up to Lieutenant-General is wonderful. And I suspect that their conception of instruction is still, like mine, tinged with Army. I think all of us of that vintage feel uneasy with forms of teaching which don't recognize a clear hierarchy—team-teaching, for example, or even the seminar, which assumes the fiction that leader and participants possess roughly equal knowledge and authority. For students (that is, enlisted men) to prosecute a rebellion, as in the 1960's and early 70's, is tantamount to mutiny, an offense, as the Articles of War indicate, "to be punished by death, or such other punishment as a court-martial shall direct." I have never been an enthusiast for The Movement.

In addition to remaining rank-conscious, I persist in the army habit of exact personnel classification. For me, everyone still has an invisible "spec number" indicating what his job is or what he's supposed to be doing. Thus a certain impatience with people of ambiguous identity, or worse, people who don't seem to do anything, like self-proclaimed novelists and poets who generate no apprehensible product. These seem to me the T-5's of the postwar world, mere Technicians Fifth Grade, parasites, drones, non-combatants.

Twenty years after the First World War Siegfried Sassoon reports that he was still having dreams about it, dreams less of terror than of obligation. He dreams that

> the War is still going on and I have got to return to the Front. I complain bitterly to myself because it hasn't stopped yet. I am worried because I can't find my active-service kit. I am worried because I have forgotten how to be an officer. I feel that I can't face it again, and sometimes I burst into tears and say, "It's no good, I can't do it." But I know that I can't escape going back, and search frantically for my lost equipment.

That's uniquely the dream of a junior officer. I had such dreams too, and mine persisted until about 1960, when I was thirty-six, past re-call age.

Those who actually fought on the line in the war, especially if they were wounded, constitute an in-group forever separate from those who did not. Praise or blame does not attach: rather, there is the accidental possession of a special empirical knowledge, a feeling of a mysterious shared ironic awareness manifesting itself in an instinctive skepticism about pretension, publicly enunciated truths, the vanities of learning, and the pomp of authority. Those who fought know a secret about themselves, and it's not very nice. As Frederic Manning said in 1929, remembering 1914–1918: "War is waged by men; not by beasts, or by gods. It is a peculiarly human activity. To call it a crime against mankind is to miss at least half its significance; it is also the punishment of a crime."

And now that those who fought have grown much older, we must wonder at the frantic avidity with which we struggled then to avoid death, digging our foxholes like madmen, running from danger with burning lungs and pounding hearts. What, really, were we so frightened of? Sometimes now the feeling comes over us that Housman's lines which in our boyhood we thought attractively cynical are really just:

> Life, to be sure, is nothing much to lose;
> But young men think it is, and we were young.

Note

The pieces in this book originally appeared in the places indicated. All have been reconsidered and rewritten.

"The Boy Scout Handbook": *The New Republic,* May 19, 1979

"The Persistent Itchings of Poe and Whitman": *The Southern Review,* 3 (Winter, 1967)

"Earnestness Abroad": *Los Angeles Times Book Review,* June 25, 1978

"The Life of Art": *New York Times Book Review,* August 22, 1976

"William Carlos Williams and His Problems": *Virginia Quarterly Review,* 52 (Spring, 1976)

"What We Look Like": *The New Republic,* November 24, 1979

"Notes on Class": *The New Republic,* July 19, 1980

"The Purging of *Penrod*": *Encounter,* April, 1970

"Smut-Hunting in Pretoria": *The New Republic,* February 23, 1980

"Literary Biography and Its Pitfalls": *Los Angeles Times Book Review,* November 29, 1970; *The New Republic,* August 25, 1979

"Nabokov as 'Comparatist' ": *Encounter,* April, 1966

"Can Graham Greene Write English?": *The New Republic,* December 27, 1980

"Being Reviewed: The A.B.M. and Its Theory": *Harper's,* February, 1982

"Terrors and Delights of the Traveler Abroad": *New York Times,* August 13, 1977

"Footwork as Scholarship": *American Scholar,* Winter, 1977–1978

"An Impediment to Pilgrimage": *The New Republic,* April 7, 1979

"Latin America Defeats Intelligent Travel Writer": *New York Times Book Review,* August 26, 1979

"A Place To Recuperate": *Harper's,* November, 1981

"Boswell and His Memorable Scenes": *Encounter,* May, 1967

"Kingy and Some Coevals": *Saturday Review,* May 1, 1976; *New York Times Book Review,* April 20, 1980

"Baron Corvo, Sturdy Beggar": *Spectator,* January 15, 1977

"Poor Ivor Gurney": *New Statesman,* October 20, 1978

"Rider Haggard, The Public Man": *London Review of Books,* September 18–October 1, 1980

"The Hearst of Literature": *The New Republic,* March 8, 1980

"Waugh in His Letters": *New York Times Book Review,* November 2, 1980

"Some Truth about the War": *Spectator,* October 29, 1977

"The Regrettable Decision of Herman Wouk": *The New Republic,* October 14, 1978

"The Romantic War and the Other One": *The New Republic,* March 3, 1979

" 'Where Are the War Poets?' ": *Times Literary Supplement,* June 25, 1976

"Time-Life Goes to War": *The New Republic,* August 18, 1979

"*Yank* When We Needed It": *The New Republic,* March 14, 1981

"The War in Black and White": *Harper's,* September, 1979

"Battle Trauma and the NATO Problem": *The New Republic,* January 19, 1980

"My War": *Harper's,* January, 1982

Index